Argentina in the
Twentieth Century

Edited by David Rock

University of Pittsburgh Press

First published in 1975 by
Gerald Duckworth & Co. Ltd.
43 Gloucester Crescent, London NW1.

Published 1975 in the U.S.A. by
the University of Pittsburgh Press

Library of Congress Catalog Card Number 74-17705
ISBN 0-8229-1116-7

Typeset by Specialised Offset Services Limited, Liverpool
Printed by Compton Printing Limited, Aylesbury.

Argentina in the Twentieth Century

Contents

Notes on Contributors

JORGE FODOR was born in Buenos Aires in 1944. He studied Economics in the universities of Buenos Aires and Cambridge, and in 1969 began as a Research Student at Cambridge. In 1970 he was awarded a visiting research post for studies in Turin by the Fondazione Luigi Einaudi. His research studies at present are principally concerned with the economic policies of the Peronist governments.

A.G. FORD was born in Leicester in 1926. His undergraduate and postgraduate studies were spent at Oxford. Between 1953 and 1965 he was Lecturer and Senior Lecturer in Economics at Leicester University and in 1965 he became Reader in Economics at the University of Warwick. Since 1970 he has been Professor of Economics at Warwick. For some years he has worked on aspects of Anglo-Argentine economic relations in the years before 1914.

ROGER GRAVIL was born in Yorkshire in 1940. He studied Economics and Economic History at Nottingham and London universities and from 1966 to 1970 he was Research Fellow at the London Institute of Latin American Studies. At present he is Lecturer in Latin American Economics at Portsmouth Polytechnic and is preparing a study on Anglo-Argentine commercial relations between 1900 and 1939.

COLIN LEWIS was born in Wales in 1944. He read Economic History at Exeter University and since 1970 he has been Lecturer in Economic History, a post held jointly at the Institute of Latin American Studies in the University of London and the London School of Economics and Political Science. He is at present preparing an extensive study of British-owned Argentine railways.

WALTER LITTLE was born in Newcastle-upon-Tyne in 1945. He

read History at Nottingham University and between 1966 and 1967 he completed a Master's degree in International Relations at the Johns Hopkins University, Baltimore. Between 1967 and 1971 he prepared a doctoral dissertation at Cambridge University on the subject of Peronism. At present he is Lecturer in Politics in Liverpool University.

DAVID ROCK was born in Lancashire in 1945. He read History at St. John's College, Cambridge and continued in Cambridge during his doctoral research period between 1967 and 1970. Since 1970 he has been Research Officer at the Cambridge Centre of Latin American Studies and is currently working on aspects of middle- and working-class political development in Argentina.

IAN RUTLEDGE was born in Bradford in 1946. He read Economics at Jesus College, Cambridge, beginning his initial research in Cambridge in 1968. In 1971 he was appointed to a joint research and lecturing post in Rural Sociology at the London Institute of Latin American Studies and at Wye College, London. For some time he has concentrated his academic interests upon peasant society in north-west Argentina.

Preface

This book is the outcome of a symposium organised by the Centre for Latin American Studies at the University of Cambridge. Its completion has only been possible through the active and constant collaboration of many friends, who as contributors, critics and advisers have given me necessary and indispensable assistance. I must first thank Professor D.C.M. Platt, formerly Director of the Centre, who was directly involved with the project from its earliest stages. I am also indebted to John Wells who gave much time to reading and criticising draft manuscripts.

My debt to the contributors goes far beyond the obvious one. Different contributors have read and criticised each other's work with enthusiasm — of the constructive sort — and this has significantly reduced the more painful tasks of editorial organisation. All the contributors willingly subjected themselves to my overall control in the final preparation of the manuscripts. I must emphasise that I did have this overall control, so that any inadequacies in the work as a whole must be my responsibility alone.

I also wish to thank Ana Gray for her work at the symposium and for her patience in typing and re-typing different draft manuscripts. Invaluable assistance with correspondence was given to me by Denise Pierce and by Gillian Cooke-Priest.

D.P.R. September 1974

Introduction

DAVID ROCK

Argentina is today to many outside observers a pale shadow of what she was in the past. Until at least the First World War she was generally regarded as being capable of repeating in Latin America the phenomenal expansion of the United States. Now she is more frequently seen as just another bankrupt and stagnant, weak and exploited corner of 'South America', compelled to exist in the future, as she now has done for so long in the past, in a maelstrom of disorganisation and decay. Her future as a growth pole in the capitalist world seems uncertain. The more her links with advanced society are established, the more chronically unstable she becomes. All the signs are at present that these internal conflicts will increase rather than diminish with the passing of time.

This book attempts to trace the origin of many of these conflicts over the twentieth century. Its perspectives and subjects for discussion range widely over a series of different problems, all of which have contributed directly to the situation as it stands at the present day. However, another of the aims of the book has been to show different sides of each argument in different areas of economic and political development. Thus each of the essays reflects different approaches and conclusions.

In one respect there is a broad parallel between Argentina's development in the twentieth century and Great Britain's — the influence of both countries in the world at large reacl_ed an apogee in the years around 1914 and thereafter underwent a fitful decline. Such parallelism is no coincidence since it reflects the intimate character of the economic linkage between the two countries up to around a generation ago. Argentina flourished with such vitality in the early years of the twentieth century largely because her development and exploitation coincided with the interests of the world's dominant industrial, commercial and imperial power. Britain, it may be argued, was largely responsible for making Argentina what she was, and for this reason the development of the relationship between the two countries provides an interesting and revealing perspective upon the major stages of Argentina's overall development.

British capital investment, especially in the years between 1880 and 1914 was one of two basic factors, the other being immigration from southern Europe, which led to Argentina's swift transformation from an unknown primitive appendage to the world's periphery into one of its foremost producers and exporters of agricultural and pastoral products. In spite of every subsequent change the country has undergone, the broad effects of this transformation remain indelible. Even today the great bulk of Argentina's foreign earnings still stem from the traditional primary sector, in spite of considerable industrial diversification. However, the first essay in this volume is concerned with the analysis of the investment mechanisms governing the inflow of British capital in the years up to 1914, and with the definition of the salient patterns of financial linkage between the two countries. The aim is to provide an interpretative scheme of the manner in which investments in Argentina yielded their return, and the effects this had upon the cyclical nature of further investments. It leads to the conclusion that conventional cyclical models, valid in terms of the internal development of industrialised societies, are not applicable on the international level in terms of foreign investment. If foreign investment patterns during this period share with the conventional industrial cycle a fluctuating and unstable character, the cycle itself is much longer in duration. This reflects on the manner in which loans of an infrastructural or developmental nature yield their returns. It suggests that the various financial crises undergone by Argentina during these years were not exclusively a consequence of credit conditions in Great Britain, but partly reflected the character of the development process in Argentina itself. Nevertheless a point of this sort, which emerges from close empirical analysis, must not disguise the degree of Argentina's economic subordination to Britain at this time. Argentina depended upon the British market to a quite extraordinary degree. At the same time she was merely one among a whole series of peripheral economies competing for a share of Britain's capital surplus. This meant that Argentina faced serious problems when changes began to take place in Britain. She was liable to lose both her source of capital investment and her export markets. The British connection was also vital in creating the basic outlines of the country's structure — her concentration on cereal and pastoral products, the concentration of her population in the Atlantic coastal regions and the emergence of an internal communications system narrowly geared to international trade

Compared with her situation fifty years previously, in 1914 Argentina was flourishing, thanks largely to her intimate economic links with Britain. But the shaky foundations of her prosperity, and the weaknesses implicit in her situation of acute dependence, were soon to be revealed. This was to accompany, and in part result from, the disruption of her links with Britain and the major readaptation of her relationship with other countries. Even before the onset of world economic depression in 1929, Britain's hold on Argentina, and on Latin America generally, was gradually loosening. With the First World War, and its tremendous drain upon her accumulated resources, Britain lost the capacity to export capital on the same massive scale as before, and through this the power to foment the reciprocal commercial activities upon which her close relations with Argentina rested. If the British market remained important until after 1945 for Argentine exports, Britain lost her position as Argentina's leading importer. From 1914 onwards in Argentina Britain faced an intensifying challenge from the United States. By the end of the Second World War British influence in Argentina was little more than symbolic. Control and economic domination had passed to the Americans, who retain them up to the present day. For the United States, however, Argentina has never been necessary as a bilateral trading partner, only as a target for investments and a market for imports. This was to accentuate the negative effects of dependence, since the real, if sometimes unequal, bonds of mutual interest linking Britain and Argentina were now replaced by ties of a more openly and comprehensively exploitative character.

The replacement of British by American influence in Argentina appears now an inevitable historical process conditioned by the changing world position of both countries. At the time, however, the British put up a strong fight in the defence of their position, and it is to the analysis of an important phase of this struggle that the second essay is dedicated. The first point which this study makes clear is the extent and intensity of the American challenge in the years after the First World War. The Americans intended not so much to compete with the British within a free market situation, but to drive them out by acquiring their major assets. As the conflict developed, it was evident that the Argentine government knew exactly what was at stake and that if close connections with the major commercial powers were seen as necessary and unavoidable, then the weaker British were preferable to the aggressive, expansive Americans. Even so, in spite of every attempt by the Argentines to encourage the

British and ward off the Americans, the latter's greater financial and economic power eventually triumphed. At this point the consummation of an American victory was only delayed by the impact of the World Depression in 1930. For a short time during the 1930s, when Argentina was struggling desperately to maintain her overseas trade markets, the connection with Britain underwent a shortlived revival, only to disappear a decade later. From henceforth the Americans reigned supreme.

Argentina's status before the Second World War as a dependent primary producer linked to overseas trade was the most vital factor impinging upon her social and political development. Her narrow specialisation upon the great beef and cereal staples created a peculiar form of social development which concentrated and maintained land and power in the hands of a rural-based oligarchy to the exclusion of the rapidly forming urban sectors in the eastern coastal regions. While, however, the oligarchy held this power, its control did not go undisputed. In parallel with such countries as Chile, Mexico and Uruguay at this time, the procedures and institutions whereby political power was exercised underwent a series of important, if eventually unsustained, changes. As early as the 1890s it was proving extremely difficult for the landowning oligarchy to maintain control by the system of open coercion which had evolved in the nineteenth century. Argentina's primary exporting economy had generated a complex pluralist society in the urban centres with interests, aspirations and class affiliations which conflicted, on occasion fundamentally, with those of the ruling groups. Nevertheless in Argentina these tensions did not lead to the classical European-like bourgeois revolution. Instead the conflict remained in an unresolved state. As a result of this, and in an effort to minimise political tensions, the oligarchy began to search for a compromise which would satisfy the middle classes but not lead to a loss of power by the landed interests.

In 1912 a democratic suffrage was introduced. Four years later presidential authority passed to a political party with close and expanding links among the middle classes. At this moment it seemed that the country had embarked on a new course which would soon establish her among the great popular republics of the western world. Yet eighteen years after 1912 'democracy' had collapsed and the oligarchy was once more in the saddle. The third essay in this book examines the course of the first abortive experiment with liberal representative government, and attempts to draw broad conclusions to explain its fall. It suggests that traditional notions of the revolutionary character of the 1912 reforms are almost completely without foundation. The change which occurred was on a narrow institutional level alone, which, if it generated a wider government sensitivity to the urban sectors in general, including the workers, failed to affect the underlying political power structure, and establish effective political change. Ultimate power remained a monopoly prerogative of the landed sectors, which, when the occasion to do so emerged, were able to overthrow the elected government without difficulty.

On a broader level, the period between 1912 and 1930 clearly delineates the political corollaries of the type of economic and social development Argentina had undergone during this period. The 'bourgeois revolution' in Argentina ultimately failed because the middle and working classes were not linked to an economic base separate from and in conflict with the traditional structure. Because of the continuing economic importance of the land, and the dependence of a great part of urban society upon it, the middle classes lacked the means to push forward towards a radical confrontation with the traditional landed elite groups. Given these conditions, the buttresses of the economic and political dominance of landed society remained inviolate.

Yet the conservative-military coup d'etat of 1930 did not eclipse the political challenge of the middle classes, nor that of the nascent urban working class. When industrialisation began to occur on a large scale in the 1930s, the challenge of these groups intensified.

If any general perspective upon Argentina must begin with the attempt to analyse the most central political and economic issues which directly impinge upon the interests of the great majority of her population, it must also take account of the wide differentiation of conditions in the country as a whole. While Argentina has been for the greater part of the twentieth century politically and economically dominated by the landed sectors, the specific conditions under which such dominance has been exercised have varied according to time, region, and economic activity. In the coastal regions, the power of the oligarchy, though real enough, has frequently operated in a discretional or in an indirect manner. By contrast, in areas like the far Interior, in the northern regions bordering Bolivia, it has generally been present in a quite undisguised and crude form. In these areas, where there is a large concentration of the sugar industry, plantation conditions apply, with the same social and political corollaries as elsewhere in Latin America. Here, in contrast to the complex, pluralistic society of the eastern coast, the traditional dichotomy of wealthy *latifundista* and poverty-stricken peasant still survives largely intact.

An analysis of the major social and political consequences of a plantation structure of production in Argentina is presented in the fourth essay. It points to the tremendous concentration of land-ownership over the region embraced by the provinces of Jujuy and Salta, and to the manner in which the traditional landlord elite has been able to develop the instruments of coercion to assure a pliant and flexible labour force in the sugar industry. In this way there have evolved social conditions and political instruments which closely correspond to the major economic interests of the local dominant groups. The essay also makes a number of important theoretical observations on the precise character of the social system which has evolved in the region. On the one side it rejects any approach to the problem of backwardness and underdevelopment based on the dichtomy of 'traditional' and 'modern', a conceptual focus which owes its origin to the Parsonian 'pattern variables'. On the other it criticises aspects of the neo-Marxist analyses of Gunder Frank on the grounds that techniques of labour recruitment and exploitation in the region do not conform to the 'capitalist' conditions Frank specifies. This whole question is, of course, fundamental to any understanding of plantation, *latifundio* production in this and the many areas like it in Latin America and beyond.

While Argentina still remains in many ways the creature of her past history, this should not obscure the fact that many of the problems she faces at present are traceable to events over the past thirty years. During this period the underlying contradictions in her economy, her society and politics have produced the state of overt and endemic internal conflict which overlies her existence as a national community. Two great issues have faced the country since 1945, industrial development and the political role of the working class. The great difficulty with industrial development has been the replacement of structures geared to primary production for export by a dynamic and self-sufficient national economy capable of overcoming the debilitating consequences of external dependence. The obstacles to this have assumed a two-fold aspect, the one revolving around the mechanics of abstract planning and develop-ment strategies, and the other socio-political, the drives and counter-drives stemming from class and sectional interests.

In fact the distinction between strategy and socio-political conditions is merely analytical, since the great feature of planning strategies in Argentina, as elsewhere, has been the close manner in which they have corresponded to perceived class interests. Thus opinions over development strategies have been both multiple and contradictory, oscillating between the rejection of the goal of industrialisation by some sectors of the traditional landed groups to the advocacy of a crash programme of industrialisation on the lines of Russian experience in the 1930s. But generally views are more moderate than this. One common constellation of views has tended to emphasise policies encouraging the inflow of foreign investment on a scale large enough to develop a national industrial infrastructure. This, in creating the necessary conditions of supply, would simultaneously trigger employment, demand, and finally industrial growth. Another view has stressed the continuing importance of the primary sector as a means to maintain export levels, and through this the inflow of foreign exchange necessary for the purchase of basic capital equipment. In contrast with these programmes, still further groups have operated from the basic premise of the need for 'national' capitalist development as a means to overcome foreign dependence. At different times this view has advocated either a programme of industrial import substitution by means of tariff protection and active state support, or, alternatively, it has emphasised the factors of demand in the industrialisation process. The argument here has been that an increase in real wages among the working class would stimulate the domestic consumer sectors and thus help to develop the capital goods sector, upon which effective industrialisation depends.

Aspects of these different, and still inconclusive, arguments can be seen in the fifth and sixth essays in this book. In the former an attempt is made to assess Argentina's experience with industrialisation through the analysis of her commercial links with Great Britain since the Second World War. The paper again points to the extensive traditional dependence of Argentina trade upon the British market; there was no easily available substitute to replace it when it declined. The author argues, moreover, that this decline was the fault of the Argentines themselves, since they failed to take advantage of favourable world conditions in the years after 1945 for the export of their traditional cereal and meat products. The point about this is that in failing to export, the country deprived itself of the opportunity to industrialise. Instead of exploiting opportunities in the traditional trading sphere, and accumulating vital foreign currency reserves which could then be turned to the domestic industrial sector, the post-war Peronist government neglected the primary sector in a vain attempt to accomplish industrialisation at a stroke. Industrial expansion at this point forced the primary sector to compete with industry for the factors of production, and by increasing domestic real wages, it increased domestic demand and thereby reduced the exportable surplus of primary produce. Exports consequently suffered because on the one hand primary producers found it impossible to increase production for cost reasons, and on the other what production there was was increasingly absorbed by the domestic market. Besides, at a moment when investment in the primary sector should have been increasing, it was severely curtailed by the competition of industrial enterprises for investable savings. Such failure to allow for the growth of the primary sector at this point has been responsible for the retardation of industrial development for much of the period in the 1950s and 1960s.

The sixth essay concentrates similarly on the vital period of the late 1940s when it was alleged that the great opportunity to establish a firm basis for industrialisation was thrown away. Here, however, a diametrically opposite view of the situation emerges. The author criticises the doctrine of 'failed opportunities' on the grounds that it is unhistorical — that it fails to take account of the economic conditions of the time and of the real options open to Argentine policy-makers. On the one side the most informed and objective observers of Argentina's opportunities after the Second World War were highly pessimistic over the commercial prospects of the traditional agricultural staples: Europe was in chaos and lingering protectionism in the United States eliminated her as a possible alternative market. Moreover, even if the problem of markets could be successfully resolved, it was thought that Argentina was unlikely to be able to expand her production of agrarian commodities far enough to take advantage of rising international demand. These predictions, it is contended, were accurate in the sense that if there was strong European demand for Argentine cereal products immediately after the War, the Europeans' complete inability to pay effectively reduced the size of the market.

A further generally accepted criticism of Argentine economic policy immediately after the War was that it failed not only in maintaining agricultural production but that it also permitted the agricultural sector to decline to such an extent that the rural areas underwent massive depopulation. This view is also opposed in this paper on the grounds that while cereal production did undergo a decline during these years, meat production did not suffer to anything like the same extent. Thus areas which had formerly been cereal producers now became meat producers, a type of activity which is much less labour intensive. The result of this was rural unemployment and finally a reinforcement of the trends making for depopulation. Finally the essay rejects the accusation that State pricing policies were responsible for the decline of the agricultural sector. It asserts that Argentina obtained the best conditions she could hope for at this juncture given her international bargaining position.

The importance of the period immediately after the Second World War lies not only in the realm of Argentina's economic development.

Of equal and parallel significance have been the political questions which have emerged since the remote days of 1943 when Juan Domingo Perón first became a figure of national importance. For more than thirty years Peronism, in some form or other, has remained the country's most important mass political movement, and its endurance testifies to the intensifying character of the country's internal conflicts. Or at least this seemed to be the case until 1973, when Perón reappeared as President eighteen years after his overthrow in an apparent alliance with his lower opponents in the army and big business. The great dispute about Peronism revolves round the degree to which it represents a revolutionary political force or whether, on the contrary, it can merely be treated as a transitional but essentially conservative populist movement which will disappear with the death of its leader. At one time the latter interpretation was the more current since Perón's success was attributed to the great migrations which had taken place in the country from the mid-1930s onwards. According to this view Peronism emerged as a response to the political demands of a newly formed working class engaged in recently established industrial activities; it was a populist but essentially reformist phenomenon, an intensification of past demands for 'political participation', and the communication of this demand to new groups.

The seventh essay takes up important aspects of this last argument. A popular view of Peronism in the past had been that it reflects a state of dualism within the working class, where the workers have been divided into members of the 'old' proletariat linked to the primary exporting economy and the 'new' proletariat emerging during the period of industrial growth in the 1930s and 1940s. Peronism has been seen frequently as the political vehicle for the 'new' working class formed mainly of migrants who made their way to the cities after being displaced from the land during the Great Depression. The author disagrees with this view, he suggests that the migration phenomenon is more complex than this and may well have involved a series of stages where former agricultural workers first moved into small local towns and then gradually moved towards the major industrial centres. There is no evidence, he contends, for many of the other major suppositions implied by the dualist model. There is no proven relationship between migration and the formation of the industrial working class, nor that migrants played any significant role in industrial unions. More likely they were incorporated haphazardly into any type of activity where there was a demand for unskilled labour. Turning to Peronism itself the author has similar doubts that the migrants were responsible for the authoritarian characteristics of the Peronist governments, as advocates of the dualist approach have frequently argued. Finally, in his relations with the unions, Perón was not impelled by any desire to favour the industrial working class. His benefits were framed according to explicit political calculations, which meant towards those sections of the working class where the power of numbers and organisation was most marked. This yields a view of Peronism where the working class occupied a more subordinate role than has often been recognised. At its core the movement was dominated by sections of the bourgeoisie, which exploited a number of limited benefits to the working class in order to establish its own political supremacy. This would explain many of the contradictions apparent in Peronism in the past and at present. It explains why the movement often seems more inclined to the Right than to the Left. It suggests that rather than working-class revolution, Peronism is the advocate of 'class harmony' whose ultimate objective is the consolidation of capitalism in Argentina.

The final essay tends on the whole to support this view. Its aim is to develop a schematic framework explaining the varied fortunes of Peronism during the last thirty years. It suggests that the most important basic variable for this is economic performance. It is no accident that Peronism should have emerged during a period of economic readaption based on industrial growth during a major upswing period in the Argentine economy. This conjuncture of circumstances enabled Perón in the early post-war period to increase the volume and scope of real benefits to a number of different groups simultaneously, including the working class. The groups injured by this policy either benefited in other ways from it, or did not suffer enough to be pushed by it into rebelling against the government. However, economic stagnation over much of the period from the early 1950s has undermined populism, since it made it impossible to reward different class groups at once. A class alliance cannot subsist unless held together by recognised benefits to each party. Attempts to recreate the class alliance and supplant Peronism have been a major characteristic of Argentine politics since 1955. But all these efforts have foundered against the objective divisions fostered by economic stagnation and its by-products of inflation, violent changes in the size and distribution of income, and the major structural changes in Argentine industry. Finally the author offers an explanation for the remarkable train of events leading to the emergence of new Peronist governments in 1973. A series of major popular protest movements between 1969 and 1972, combined with increasing guerrilla action, raised for the first time in Argentina the possibility of a takeover by the Left. Peronism, the author argues, has been allowed to escape its past ostracism because of its usefulness to combat this danger. Once more, therefore, a view emerges of

Peronism as a preventive rather than a spur to revolution.

The themes traced in this book are not of course peculiar to Argentina alone. Many of them are directly related to the course of historical development which has taken place in other areas of the Third World. Argentina's peculiarity was that she acquired high levels of social and economic development very early. What was for her an historical experience has become part of the reality of the present day for other areas in Latin America, Africa and Asia. There are still many parts of the world which depend, as Argentina once did, on a single overseas market for agricultural exports. The phenomenon of competition among the major imperialist powers for control of a peripheral economy is as much a feature of today as it was in Argentina in the period between the wars. There are many countries too which are engaged in the effort to achieve industrial self-sufficiency, and in the power struggle which underlies the formation of development strategies. Equally there are parallels between the different populist movements which have emerged in Argentina and those which recurrently appear in different parts of the world, and, as in Argentina, these are intimately bound up with the manipulation of political power by different elite groups. For all these kinds of problems Argentina is something of a laboratory for the student of economic and political development.

1

British Investment and Argentine Economic Development, 1880-1914

A.G. FORD

Between 1880 and 1914 the Argentine economy was transformed into one of the world's major exporters of primary produce and the foundations of modern Argentina were laid, while the process gave rise to certain economic legacies which have not all been to her benefit. This transformation had come about as a result of specialisation of production in accordance with comparative advantage and as a result of rapid growth in the limited range of output. In particular, production and) export of cereals, meat, and hides grew rapidly as did import in exchange of manufactures, fuels and chemicals. The main agents of this transformation were the immigration of labour and capital which enabled this labour-scarce, capital-scarce economy to exploit its abundant natural resource — fertile, but hitherto unused, land. Of critical importance here was the creation and development of transport facilities in order that primary production could reach major markets cheaply; it was of no avail to produce wheat, maize, and linseed if there were no low cost transport services to move them to the ports or to Buenos Aires. Without doubt, the single most important factor here was the Railway, and it was in this area above all others that foreign interests were dominant.

When considering this development pattern, we must not only pay regard to domestic elements, but we must see it within the context of contemporary world economic development in terms of growing markets for Argentina's products and in terms of the varying supply of factors of production from abroad by the immigration of capital and labour. Much international economic development of this period took place on the basis of the comparative advantage of particular areas for producing particular products, and this advantage dictated the pattern of investment, especially that from abroad.

Further, it gave rise to a particular pattern of international economic relations in which countries were not equal but were grouped on a solar system basis. At the centre were the (European) lending and industrial economies, while on the periphery were the developing, borrowing primary producers who were forced into a dependent status — almost colonial — by the pressures of economic power. These economies were dependent on Europe for their imports of manufactures, for their export sales of primary produce, and for their supplies of capital. Yet it should not be forgotten that some of the 'centre' countries, Britain in particular, relied on these developing economies to provide outlets for their sales of manufactures. Furthermore, key sectors of their economies were shaped and owned by foreigners (particularly by the British). Argentina was no exception to this, and it has been suggested that what the British failed to achieve by force of arms at the beginning of the nineteenth century they achieved by trade and lending.

This scheme of things led to a large percentage of Argentine output being exported and to the elimination of some domestic (handicraft) manufactures as imported manufactures claimed a growing share of the domestic market. Argentina was thus clearly dependent for its well-being on the terms of trade between manufactured goods and primary produce. Furthermore, Argentina became subject to considerable economic dependence on Europe both for sales and purchases of goods (in the role of junior partner) and for capital formation of particular kinds. Borrowing this capital abroad naturally brought its costs into the reckoning with interest and dividends payable abroad mounting as a charge on production and foreign currency earnings — indeed, on average these foreign debt-service charges amounted to some 35 per cent of merchandise export sales in 1911-14. Foreign capital (mainly British) had flowed over the period especially into transport, utilities, finance and the public sector, while Argentine domestically financed investment was concentrated much more on residential construction and the acquiring and improving of land. This essay, indeed, seeks to examine the influence of British investment in Argentina on her economic development, and to discuss the forces influencing the variable flow of British lending to Argentina.

Argentina's growth performance

In Table 1.1 a comparison is made of the main economic aggregates at the beginning (1881-4 average) and at the end of our period (1910-14) average). Population nearly trebles, corresponding to an annual growth rate of 3.4 per cent, while export values increase by 6½ times (an annual growth rate of 6.4 per cent) and import values

Table 1.1 Argentine growth 1881-1914

	Annual averages		Increase
	(1)	*(2)*	*(3)*
	1881-4	*1910-14*	*(2)÷(1)*
Population (thousands)	2,680	7,200	2.7
Railway length (thousand km)	3	31	10.3
Export values (million gold pesos	62	402	6.5
Export values per head (gold pesos)	23	56	2.4
Import values (million gold pesos)	73	359	4.9
Import values per head (gold pesos)	27	50	1.9
Railway receipts (million gold pesos)	8	123	14.6

For sources of series, see Table 1.2. The figures are rounded.

grow fivefold (an annual growth rate of 5.4 per cent), and little of this growth performance of trading items can be attributed to rising prices. However, Table 1.1 should not be allowed to create the impression that growth was smooth and regular. It was uneven, as reference to Table 1.2 and Figure 1.1 will indicate.

Railway length grows rapidly to the early 1890s and then slackens noticeably but its growth revives in the early 1900s. This unevenness is shown by the series for total railway length, but more strongly by the series for increments in railway length between the five-year periods. Import values, again, stagnate in the 1890s and only surpass the peak of the late 1880s after the turn of the century.

Export values which had grown sharply in the 1880s slackened their growth thereafter until the 1900s when they grew phenomenally at an annual rate in excess of 7 per cent. One factor here was the behaviour of export prices which, it should be noted, were settled on world commodity markets outside the control of the Argentine economy. Their decline in the 1890s offset somewhat the growing volumes of cereal and wool exports, but in the twentieth century their rise enhanced the growth in the volumes of cereals and frozen meat exported and mitigated the decline in wool export volumes.

The changing structure of Argentine exports over the period should be noted. In the 1880s pastoral exports (wool, fleeces, hides) were very important but gradually gave way to cereals, especially in the 1890s. This indeed reflected the process of economic change as

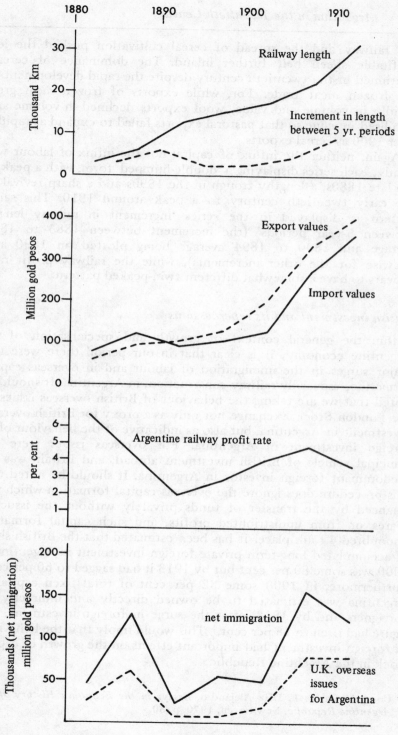

Figure 1.1 Annual averages for five-year periods

the railway and the spread of cereal cultivation pushed the less profitable sheep belt further inland. The dominance of cereals continued in the twentieth century despite the rapid development of the frozen meat trade. For, while exports of frozen meat grew rapidly in volume and value, wool exports declined in volume and stabilised in value so that pastoral exports failed to expand as rapidly after 1900 as cereal exports.

Again, neither the influx of capital nor the influx of labour was steady, each series displaying a 'double-humped' form, with a peak in the late 1880s, a lengthy trough in the 1890s and a sharp revival in the early twentieth century to a peak around 1910. This same pattern is displayed in the series 'increment in railway length between 5-year periods' (the increment between 1885 to 1889 average and 1890 to 1894 average being plotted on 1890 and likewise for the other increments), while the railway profit rate appears to have a somewhat different twin-peaked pattern.

British investment and its repercussions

Within the general context of growth and specialisation of the Argentine economy, it is clear that in our period there were two major surges in the immigration of labour and in overseas capital formation, especially railway construction, in Argentina. It should be stated that we are taking the behaviour of British overseas issues on the London Stock Exchange not only as a proxy for British overseas investment in Argentina, but also as indicative of the behaviour of all foreign investment in Argentina. For overseas issues were the principal vehicle of British investment abroad, and Britain was the predominant foreign investor in Argentina. It should be noted that this procedure does ignore the overseas capital formation which was financed by the transfer of funds privately without the issue of shares or from undistributed profits, and such capital formation undoubtedly took place. It has been estimated that the British share of accumulated long-term private foreign investment in Argentina in 1900 was some 80 per cent but by 1913 it had sagged to 60 per cent. Furthermore, in 1900 some 32 per cent of total fixed capital in Argentina was estimated to be owned directly and indirectly by foreigners and by 1913, after the surge in foreign investment, this figure had risen to 48 per cent.[1] This would imply that the behaviour of foreign investment had important effects on the growth of capital stock in the Argentine Republic.

[1]   Compare Carlos F. Díaz Alejandro, *Essays in the Economic History of the Argentine Republic*, New Haven, 1970, p. 30.

Table 1.2 Argentina 1881-1914 (annual averages for 5-year periods)

	(i) Population (thousands)	(ii) Net immigration (thousands)	(iii) U.K. issues for Argentina (million gold pesos)	(iv) Railway length (thousand km)
1881-4	2,680	46	24 †	3.0
1885-9	3,066	128	60	6.5
1890-4	3,612	21	7	12.7
1895-9	4,219	54	7	15.0
1900-4	4,860	49	19	17.7
1905-9	5,803	155	77	22.2
1910-4	7,203	122	77	31.1

	(v) Railway profit rate per cent	(vi) Export values (million gold pesos)	(vii) Export prices (1900=100)	(viii) Cereal exports (thousand tons)
1881-4	6.13	62	..	131
1885-9	4.31	92	..	389
1890-4	2.02	103	87*	1,038
1895-9	2.85	131	82	1,711
1900-4	4.02	197	101	3,011
1905-9	4.76	335	124	4,825
1910-4	3.87	402	139	5,294

	(ix) Wool exports (thousand tons)	(x) Frozen meat exports (thousand tons)	(xi) Import values (million gold pesos)	(xii) Import prices (1900=100)
1881-4	112	..	73	..
1885-9	129	12	119	91
1890-4	139	27	98	88
1895-9	211	56	106	81
1900-4	178	137	130	90
1905-9	170	239	267	93
1910-4	137	376	359	103°

† 1882-4   * 1892-4   ° 1910-13

Sources:
(i), (vi), (xi)   *Extracto estadístico de la República Argentina correspondiente al año 1915*, Buenos Aires, 1916.
(ii)   E. Tornquist, *The Economic Development of the Argentine Republic in the last 50 years*, Buenos Aires, 1919, p. 15.
(iii)   *The Economist*, 'New Issues' sections.
(iv), (v)   E. Tornquist, *op. cit.*, p. 117.
(vii), (xii)   A.G. Ford, 'Export Price Indices for the Argentine Republic 1881-1914', *Inter-American Economic Affairs*, 1955.
(viii), (ix), (x)   *Extracto estadístico*, pp. 67-73.

It will be noticed that the gap between the two surges of the late 1880s and the early twentieth century is much longer than in the case of the trade cycles which Europe and the United States experienced. The Argentine fluctuations in capital formation are thus far too separated in time to form part of an ordinary trade cycle but are perhaps more reminiscent of 'long swings' or Kuznets cycles of 18 to 20 years duration which have been identified for North America and for British home and overseas investment of this period.[2]

In Figure 1.2 are plotted total British home investment and overseas issues together with new issues on the London Stock Exchange for Argentine ventures, which formed on average some 8 per cent of total British overseas issues on the London Stock Exchange. It will be seen that Argentine new issues display the same long-run pattern as British overseas issues in aggregate but with greater volatility, while they display an opposite pattern to British home investment. The pattern of two major booms or surges separated by about 20 years is clear so that one major source of instability in Argentine capital formation would seem to lie in the general behaviour of British overseas lending. Furthermore, it leads to the proposition that events in Argentine economic development are not explicable in purely endogenous terms, but that international influences were powerful.

How then, did foreign investment in Argentina affect the economy? Before invoking some economic analysis to assist in answering this question, it is important to consider the nature of British investment in Argentina as revealed in the break-down in Table 1.3 of new issues on the London Stock Exchange for Argentine ventures. It will be seen that these issues have a predominantly 'developmental' character and are concentrated on (social) overhead capital projects (especially transport), while it should be pointed out that some of the public loans in the early period were raised for state developmental projects. Comparison with the estimated distribution of capital stock (irrespective of ownership) in Argentina in 1900, as presented in Table 1.4, reveals sharp contrasts, and it comes as no surprise to learn that the bulk of the Argentine railway system was owned by British investors.[3]

---

[2]   See for example, Brinley Thomas, *Migration and Economic Growth*, Cambridge, 1954; M. Abramovitz, 'The Passing of the Kuznets Cycle', *Economica* 35, 1968, 349-67.

[3]   In 1913 the estimated capital of Argentine railways was 1,267 million gold pesos, of which 1,175 million gold pesos worth was in foreign ownership and the British share was 1,075 million gold pesos. See E. Tornquist, *The Economic Development of the Argentine Republic in the Last 50 years*, Buenos Aires, 1919, p. 117, and V.L. Phelps, *The International Economic Position of Argentina*, London, 1938, p. 99.

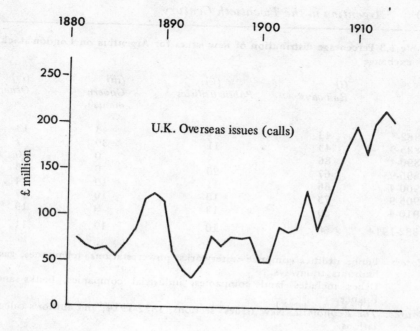

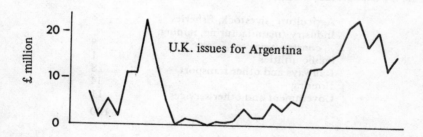

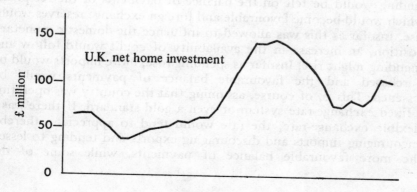

Figure 1.2

Table 1.3 Percentage distribution of new issues for Argentina on London stock exchange

	(i) *Railways*	(ii) *Public utilities*	(iii) *Govern- ments*	(iv) *Other*
1882-4	43	1	43	13
1885-9	43	11	39	7
1890-4	86	4	0	10
1895-9	67	20	0	13
1900-4	66	11	19	4
1905-9	73	10	10	7
1910-4	59	13	9	19
1882-1914	60	10	19	11

Notes: Public utilities comprise waterworks, power stations, telephones, gas, harbours, tramways.
Other includes land companies, industrial companies, banks and finance.
Source: The Economist 'New Issues' sections, 1882-1914, and author's calculations.

Table 1.4 Capital stock in Argentina in 1900 (percentage distribution)

Agriculture, livestock, fisheries	28
Industry (manufacturing, mining, construction	8
Public utilities	1
Railways and other transport	18
Housing	34
Government and other services	11
	100

Source: Díaz Alejandro, *op. cit.*, p. 7.

The impact of a new influx of investment from abroad or foreign lending would be felt on the balance of payments of the recipient, which would become favourable and foreign exchange reserves would rise. Insofar as this was allowed to influence the domestic monetary position, an increase in the availability of credit would follow and spending might rise. Insofar as spending rose, more imports would be purchased and the favourable balance of payments would be lessened. This is, of course, assuming that the country was operating a fixed exchange-rate system or even a gold standard. If there was a flexible exchange-rate, the rate would tend to appreciate, thereby encouraging imports and discouraging exports and tending to lessen the more favourable balance of payments, while some of the expansionary credit effects might still persist and encourage importation further. In both these cases we should note the tendency for imports to rise and the merchandise trade balance to deteriorate.

However, it is very important, especially with loans of a developmental character, when assessing their impact on an economy, to ask how the recipients of the foreign lending employ the proceeds. Do they just bank the proceeds and leave their increased balances untouched? In this case the effects mentioned in the preceding paragraph would operate. But it is highly unlikely that borrowers in a developing economy would act in this way, for they have surely borrowed in order to use the funds for spending purposes, for capital formation. It is more realistic to envisage them using some portion of the proceeds to purchase directly goods from abroad, thereby increasing imports. (If all of the loans were immediately spent thus, the effects of the preceding paragraph would not take place as there would be no rise in reserves and no increase in money supply). The portion which was not employed to buy imports directly, would be available for spending by the enterprise locally. For example, a railway company could use such funds to hire extra navvies and to buy local materials. This would increase spending in the recipient economy and lead to increased purchases of imports. It should also be noted that this use would increase economic activity in the borrowing economy and could lead to a sharp boom. If factor supplies were limited, excess demand inflation could follow and a further switch to imported goods.

Hence, in various ways an influx of new foreign loans will lead quickly to an increase in import purchases, and it may very well lead to an increase in home spending and a (booming) rise in economic activity. By the same reasoning, a decline in foreign loans would bring a fall in import purchases and perhaps a decline in economic activity. In terms of the balance of payments, an improving capital account as loans flow in will be associated with a deteriorating merchandise account, assuming exports are constant; a worsening capital account as loans cease with an improving merchandise account, so that foreign exchange reserves do not rise or fall as sharply as the changes in the influx of capital.

To these effects which can be expected to follow rather briskly from the influx of lending from abroad — or its cessation — we must add the growth in service charges on the foreign borrowing. For capital loaned from abroad has its price, as the foreign lender expects to receive dividends or interest remittances from the borrower. These constitute a charge on the output of the borrower and an increase in payments items in the balance of payments. In the case of borrowing from abroad by means of fixed-interest-bearing bonds, the interest charges payable abroad will need to be made immediately, perhaps long before the project for which these bonds provide finance has been completed and is producing extra output. If the borrowing has been in the form of ordinary shares, then the dividend remittances will only commence when the project has been completed and is yielding profits. Clearly, heavy borrowing by means of fixed-interest-bearing bonds could pose difficulties and impose strain on the borrowing economy.

So much, then, for the more immediate effects of an influx of loans from abroad. The major long-term influence of a capital influx from abroad should be found in its effects on the stock of capital and the capacity to produce of the recipient economy. Funds from abroad, wisely used, may accelerate the growth of the economy; funds squandered on showy low productivity projects and armaments may only create a debt service-charge problem. However, it must be emphasised that very frequently there is a certain lapse of time between the borrowing of funds and the completion of the project, and that this can be considerable in the case of overhead capital projects. For example, it may take four years or more before a railway can be completed and develop traffic so that it becomes profitable. Developmental projects typically take time to construct and come to maturity.

The first surge of British investment

Let us turn to Argentina's developmental experiences and use the above economic analysis to examine the various influences of British investment on the economy. First, let us consider the surge of foreign investment in Argentina in the 1880s, which culminated in the Baring Crisis and collapse in 1890. Although British businessmen had long been interested in the River Plate area, it was not until the 1860s that Argentina had approached the fringe of the European capital market. By 1875 British capital was invested in the main sectors of the economy with the pattern established of railways, public loans, and public utilities, while the Argentine investor concentrated on land and real estate. However, these early developments had only scratched the surface to prepare the way for the dramatic developments in the 1880s.

Various features came together in the early 1880s to enhance the attractiveness of Argentina to the European lenders who were essentially 'profit-seeking' or 'high-fixed-interest-seeking'. Military expeditions of 1878-81 had put down the Indians of the interior and made the Pampas safe for permanent cultivation, while a strong federal government had assumed power and had undertaken monetary reforms, including joining the gold standard. From 1878 wheat was exported: in small quantities, it is true, but this gave evidence of the capabilities of the economy. Furthermore, the railway profit rate was high, averaging over 6 per cent of capital employed in the period 1881-4. All these features, together with the pushing of the Argentine lobby in London and the previous success of certain British ventures (the Buenos Aires and Great Southern Railway and the London and River Plate Bank) served to attract the European lender to Argentine projects at this moment in time, while the Argentine government was prepared to guarantee interest payments on certain railway loans.

Furthermore, the pull of Argentine projects was enhanced by the transport innovations which brought falling ocean freight rates in the late 1870s and increased the profitability of exports for Argentina by cutting freight costs. Interest yields were secularly low in Europe, while British home investment and the building cycle were in their 'long-swing' trough phase, so that finance was more readily available for overseas ventures. Domestic prospects in Britain seemed gloomy, with the fears of articulate contemporaries about the Great Depression and with economic activity in Britain slumping from a cyclical peak in 1882-3 to a trough in 1886. With all the talk of Argentina being the second 'United States' fund-seekers could count on a more favourable reception in the London capital market, while prospective lenders were aware of the growing markets of free-trade Britain for the primary produce which Argentina was capable of producing and which her railways would carry.

Once affairs looked settled in Argentina and finance was available, as was the case in the 1880s, the influx of capital and labour began in earnest, to reach a hectic peak in 1888-9. Some 700 million gold pesos were borrowed abroad between 1885 and 1890, of which almost half was raised by new issues on the London Stock Exchange and additionally perhaps a fifth by the sale of land mortgage bonds (*cédulas*) to British investors.[4] Euthusiasm waxed speedily into mania, but disillusion set in amongst the European investors by 1889 and the flow of loans had all but ceased by 1890. The immediate result of this borrowing which had a large fixed-interest-bearing-bond element was to raise foreign debt-service charges to 60 per cent of export proceeds by 1890.

It should be noted that fixed-interest loans were typical of much British overseas lending. Governmental loans (which formed some 30 per cent of total British lending abroad) are an obvious case, and

[4] Of this borrowing, public loans comprised 35 per cent., railways 32 per cent, and land mortgage bonds 24 per cent.

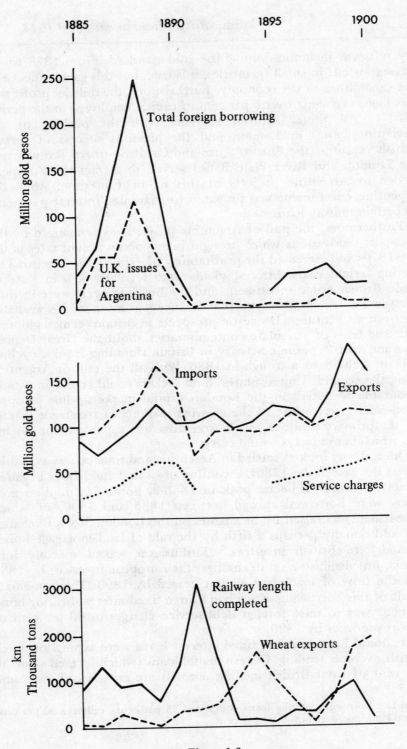

Figure 1.3

Table 1.5

	(1) Total foreign borrowing	(2) British new issues	(3) Net immigration	(4) Service charges	(5) Import values	(6) Export values	(7) Railway length completed	(8) Wheat exports	(9) Maize exports	(10) Wool exports	(11) Gold premium annual average 1884=par
	(million gold pesos)		(thousands)	(million gold pesos)	(million gold pesos)		(Km)	(000 tons)	(000 tons)	(000 tons)	
1884	40	30	63	28	94	68	474	108	114	114	100
1885	39	9	94	23	92	84	864	78	198	128	137
1886	68	56	79	27	95	70	1334	38	232	136	139
1887	154	56	107	37	117	84	853	238	362	109	135
1888	248	117	139	50	128	100	882	179	162	132	148
1889	154	62	220	60	165	123	567	23	433	142	191
1890	45	25	30	60	142	101	1294	328	707	118	251
1891	8	0	-30	32	67	103	3043	396	66	139	387
1892	..	6	29	n.a.	91	113	1207	470	446	155	332
1893	..	3	36	n.a.	96	94	170	1008	85	123	334
1894	..	0	39	n.a.	93	102	178	1608	55	162	357
1895	17	3	44	38	95	120	86	1010	772	201	344
1896	37	1	89	40	112	117	345	532	1571	188	296
1897	38	5	48	44	98	101	294	102	357	206	291
1898	46	18	42	51	107	134	696	645	717	221	258
1899	25	8	49	55	117	185	962	1713	1116	237	225
1900	26	8	50	59	113	155	150	1929	713	101	231

Sources: (1), (3), (11) J.H. Williams, *Argentine International Trade under Inconvertible Paper Money 1885-1900*, pp.45, 101, 152; (2) *The Economist*, 'New Issues' sections; (5), (6), *Extracto estadístico de la República Argentina correspondiente al año 1915*, p.3; (7) E. Tornquist, *op.cit.*, p.117; (8), (9), (10), *Extracto estadístico*, pp.67-73.

there was a high share of debentures in company borrowing by new issues on the London Stock Exchange.[5]

The movements in the main variables are depicted in Figure 1.3 and set out in Table 1.5. The sharp rise and fall in both total foreign investment and in London new issues for Argentina should be noted with the heavy bunching of projects, and the build-up of the service charges on the foreign loans. Import values rose sharply to a peak in 1889, lagging (a year) behind foreign borrowings as our analysis has suggested, and declining from 1889 to 1891 in the wake of the collapse of foreign borrowings, while debt-service payments remained steady until cut by repudiation in 1891.

Argentina had barely joined the gold standard before the fixed exchange-rate was abandoned in 1885 under temporary balance of payments strain and the exchange rate between domestic paper currency and gold remained flexible until 1900. At first the rate showed a modest depreciation and appeared to give no concern to the foreign investors as they poured funds in. However the rate began to fall more rapidly after 1889 when the influx of funds was ceasing, and this rapid depreciation was a further factor producing disillusion and aversion amongst foreign investors who earlier had not worried about the abandonment of the gold standard. The course of the exchange rate is shown in Table 1.5 under the heading of the gold premium, a rise in which is equivalent to a fall in the exchange rate and *vice versa*.

Despite the peak of foreign loans in 1888, the peak in railway length completed did not come until 1891, after which land had to be prepared for the crops, so that it is not surprising to find that the major expansion in wheat production only came in 1893 and afterwards. This lag in the development process between the raising of finance and the eventual expansion in output and exports as the projects matured is of great importance. For it meant that the fixed portion of the foreign debt-service charges fell immediately onto the

[5] For example, in 1904-13 the following pattern emerged: Relative use of ordinary shares, preference shares, debentures by companies making new issues on the London Stock Exchange:

	Amount £ million	O.S. %	P.S. %	D.
Issued in London only for use at home	261	34.5	30.5	35.0
Issued in London only for use abroad	659	32.3	12.3	55.4
Issued in London and some other centre for use abroad	213	31.3	2.7	66.0

From: A.R. Hall, *The London Capital Market and Australia 1870-1914*, Canberra, 1963, p. 202.

Argentine economy in a period where output was relatively unexpanded, and export values had not grown sufficiently to provide foreign exchange to remit thus. So long as the flow of loans continued, these difficulties could be glossed over by paying the interest charges out of fresh borrowings while new loans provided a source of foreign exchange. At the beginning of 1889 disquieting reports begin to reach London about affairs in Argentina for the huge investment boom had been magnified by domestic currency expansion, while allegations of corruption and malpractice were rife, and it was recalled that the gold standard had been abandoned as early as 1885. Furthermore, the railway profit rate had sagged alarmingly, but predictably as capital had to grow in advance of traffic.

The British investor moved as sharply away from Argentina as he had come and thereby thrust acute strain on the economy and its balance of payments. As the proceeds from foreign loans declined, the exchange rate depreciated rapidly, especially in 1890 and 1891 and secondly investment spending and economic activity slackened in 1890. Furthermore, foreign debt-service charges now bore alarmingly on unexpanded exports as the sole source of foreign exchange, and, if met, implied the reduction of imports by two-thirds, to say nothing of output to this value being transferred to the foreign investors. This was the price of foreign capital with a vengeance! Not surprisingly the national and provincial governments repudiated their debt-service payments in 1891 and this act as well as the immediately gloomy economic record put Argentina outside the European capital markets for the next few years.

With hindsight it is not difficult to see that the crisis which turned foreign investors away for nearly a decade had a strong developmental nature and was not merely a matter of malpractice, incompetence and speculation. The time-horizon of foreign investors was shorter than the time taken for the projects to mature so that loans fell off before production of exportables had expanded sufficiently. This was especially important when bonds, on which the fixed-interest charge was payable immediately, had to be offered abroad on such a large scale to acquire funds. The problems would have been less severe if Argentine enterprises had been able to acquire more funds by the issue of ordinary shares on which dividends would only be paid when profits were being earned. There are surely lessons here for countries currently seeking to accelerate their economic development by attracting foreign investment.

Recovery and the second surge

As a result of this hectic surge of foreign investment (particularly
from Britain) Argentina was undoubtedly overprovided with railways
in the 1890s, into which, however, she gradually grew as output
expanded by the later 1890s. For example, wheat production rose
from an annual average of 20 million bushels in 1885-9 to 60 million
bushels in 1894-9 and to 93 million in 1899-1904.[6] Exportable
production, despite always being susceptible to pests, locusts, and
drought, showed an expanding trend which was reflected in export
volumes. Export prices, which had sagged from 1890 to 1895 and
somewhat offset rising volumes in the earning of foreign exchange,
were now rising after 1895 and enhanced the foreign-exchange
earning power of the growing export volumes. The economy was
now recovering from the crisis, and in 1897 the service charges on
governmental foreign debt were resumed — an essential step, if the
London capital market was to be approached again on any substantial scale. Enterprises were showing improving profit records, and the
exchange rate was appreciating until it was stabilised in 1900 and the
gold standard rejoined. Furthermore, the problems which had been
besetting the frozen meat trade were now solved, just as the
American exportable surplus of meat was dwindling.

This process of attraction-revulsion-recovery which has been
outlined for Argentina in the twenty years before 1900 can be traced
out in a different way as is shown in Figure 1.4. Here is plotted the
course of the Argentine railway profit rate which can be used as a
crude indicator of the varying pull of Argentina for the British or
European investor. Alongside this series is drawn the behaviour of
export values per kilometre of railway length. This is included as an
imperfect indicator of the utilisation of capacity of the railway
system, which would be an important influence on the profit rate.[7]
Low capacity utilisation would imply low profits, but as primary
production, exports, and traffic rose, so capital stock would be more
fully utilised and the profit rate would rise. Eventually full capacity
operation would bring a high profit rate, which might attract fresh
investment.

The profit rate and exports per kilometre were high in the early
1880s, clearly an attraction to foreign investors, but both began to
fall in the later 1880s as capital and track grew in advance of a

[6]   P. de Hevesy, *World Wheat Planning*, Oxford, 1940.
[7]   The Argentine railway system was designed to convey primary products to the
      ports and main cities, so that exports would provide a useful measure of
      traffic. Ideally, one would like export volumes at constant prices but this is
      unavailable.

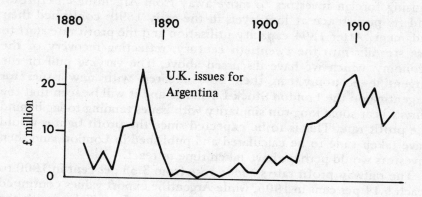

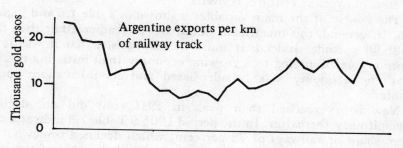

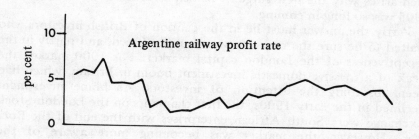

Figure 1.4

corresponding rise in primary production and traffic. The sharp decline in the profit rate after 1888 must have been one element causing foreign investors to move away from Argentine enterprises, and its persistence at low levels in the early 1890s confirmed their judgment. After 1894 capacity utilisation and the profit rate start to rise steadily into the twentieth century, reflecting recovery of the economy which we have discussed above. The varying pull of the Argentine economy can then be compared with new issues for Argentina on the London Stock Exchange and it will be seen that the curves bear some long-run similarity with issues tending to lag behind the profit rate. This is to be expected since the profit figures would have taken time to be calculated and published in London, and then investors would perhaps have taken time to react.

The railway profit rate steadily rose from 3.33 per cent in 1900 to reach 5.14 per cent in 1905, while Argentine export values continued to expand, aided by rising primary product prices. Taken with the other signs of recovery and expansion discussed earlier, the question even arises why the new surge in British investment which started in 1905 was so long in coming.

Partly the answer must lie in the caution of British investors who waited to be sure the recovery was soundly based, and partly in the receptiveness of the London capital market. For 1900 marked the peak of a massive domestic investment boom in Britain, which had been absorbing the attention of investors. As home investment declined in the early 1900s, the first claimants on the London Stock Exchange were South African enterprises with the end of the Boer War. However, the market was becoming more aware of the improving Argentine prospects and Argentine new issues were in the van of the massive rise in overseas issues 1905-14 as British lenders' interest in overseas ventures revived.

The course of the main variables is shown in Table 1.6 and Figure 1.5. In general, this investment boom was a steadier affair than the 1885-90 episode. Indeed, it must be emphasised that it was now more a case of adding to a growing economy than initiating it, and that the economy was broader-based and its institutions more stable.[8]

New issues reached their peak in 1910, but did not decline precipitously thereafter. In the period 1905-9 Table 1.3 indicates the large share of railways of 73 per cent, which declined somewhat in the following five years to 59 per cent. The behaviour of the new issues bears some lagged relation to the course of the railway profit rate which started to decline after 1905, and the behaviour of

---

[8] Foreign loans now bore a lower ratio to exports than in 1885-90.

Table 1.6 Argentina 1900-14

	(1) British new issues (million gold pesos)	(2) Immigration (thousands)	(3) Export values	(4) Import values	(5) Consumption imports	(6) Investment imports	(7) Imports as percentage of exports (three-year moving average)
				(million gold pesos)	(million gold pesos)		
1900	8	50	155	113	76	37	68
1901	25	46	168	114	75	39	66
1902	16	17	179	103	68	35	62
1903	26	38	221	131	77	54	63
1904	21	94	264	187	103	84	65
1905	61	139	323	205	105	100	76
1906	63	198	292	270	123	147	85
1907	72	120	296	286	122	164	88
1908	80	176	366	273	130	143	83
1909	109	141	397	303	147	156	82
1910	115	209	373	352	173	179	95
1911	84	110	325	367	177	190	96
1912	101	206	480	385	184	201	93
1913	60	145	484	421	197	224	82
1914	76	−61	349	272	134	138	—

Sources: (1) *The Economist*, 'New Issues' sections;
(2) E. Tornquist, *op. cit.* p. 15;
(3),(4) *Extracto estadístico*, p. 3; (5),(6) *ibid.* p. 74.

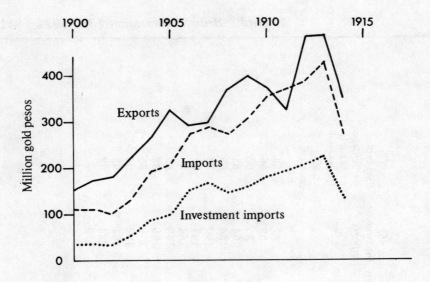

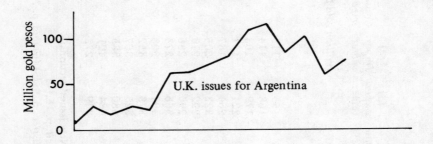

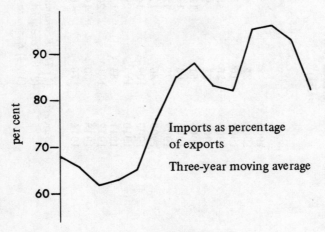

Figure 1.5

exports per kilometre, whose trend started to decline after 1907 (see Figure 1.4). Furthermore, British investors were being attracted by other overseas ventures, while higher interest rates in 1912-13 made certain Argentine ventures postpone new issues. Immigration of labour also displays a very similar pattern to Argentine new issues.

This influx of capital from Britain, which was matched by a growing influx from France and Germany, was a main factor in raising the foreign liabilities of Argentina, estimated at 1,013 million gold pesos in 1900, with a debt-service charge of 57 million (average for 1899-1900),[9] to 3,250 million gold pesos in 1913 with a debt-service charge of 156 million (average for 1911-4).[10] However, it is important to note that despite this trebling of the foreign liabilities the share of service charges as a percentage of exports remained roughly constant at 35 per cent. However, if export prices had remained at 1900 levels, this share would have risen to 48 per cent.[11]

While export values rose threefold between 1900 and 1913 import values quadrupled under the influence of the rising activity generated by rising exports and foreign investment. The influence of the rise in foreign investment can be seen in the disproportionate rise in investment good imports (Table 1.6) and in the behaviour of imports as a percentage of exports (Figure 1.5).

Railway length doubled from 16.6 thousand kilometres in 1900 to 33.5 thousand in 1914 and the railway still retained its key role as an agent of economic growth and development. Besides linking the pampas to ports it had now linked together cities and had widened the domestic market for domestically produced goods such as wine, sugar and tobacco, while flour-milling, breweries, tanneries and a dairy industry were taking root by the twentieth century. Processing plants using rural goods as their main input made an important contribution to manufacturing which however only amounted to 11.5 per cent of gross domestic product in 1910-14.[12] Nevertheless, by 1914 Argentina had not entered the industrial phase as is suggested by Table 1.7 which sets out the production census for 1913 and shows the small-scale nature of industry.

What is perhaps curious about the development process is the almost complete reliance of Argentina on foreign interests for the evolution of this vital railway system. In the earlier stages the lack of

[9]   Williams, *op. cit.*, pp. 103, 150.

[10] Phelps, *op. cit.*, p. 99.

[11] A.G. Ford, *The Gold Standard 1880-1914: Britain and Argentina*, Oxford, 1962, p. 156.

[12] Díaz Alejandro, *op. cit.*, p. 10.

Table 1.7 Argentine industry in 1913

	(1) Number of establishments	(2) Capital	(3) Production	(4) Raw materials	(5) Net output	(6) Net Employment (000)	(7) Employees per establishment
		(million gold pesos)					
Food	18,983	336	436	290	146	135	7.2
Clothing & toilet	7,081	44	71	39	32	58	8.2
Construction	8,582	95	101	43	58	87	10.2
Furniture and vehicular	4,441	28	38	18	20	29	6.5
Arts & crafts	996	6	7	3	4	4	4.3
Metallurgy	3,275	47	41	20	21	29	9.0
Chemical	567	17	25	13	12	10	17.6
Graphic arts	1,439	15	17	6	11	13	9.3
Fibre, thread, cloth	2,458	15	18	10	8	16	6.3
Various	957	184	65	36	29	29	30.0
Total	48,779	787	819	478	341	410	8.4

Source: Tornquist, *op. cit*, p. 37, quoting from the National Census of Production of 1914.
Note: Original data for columns (2)-(5) were in paper pesos and have been converted to gold pesos at the official rate.

interest of Argentines in financing railways is understandable on the grounds of unfamiliarity, but the continued lack of interest could hardly be attributed to conservatism. The answer probably is that real estate and land were more profitable; certainly they were price-flexible real assets in an economy with a history of inflation.

One can only speculate as to what might have happened to the Argentine economy had there been no First World War. British new issues for Argentina had turned down somewhat after 1910, as had immigration. In the second half of 1913 there were growing difficulties confronting the Argentine economy as a result of balance of payments strain and the operation of the gold standard mechanism. Furthermore, the harvest of 1914 was a failure and export values slumped disastrously. Certainly this was no repetition of the Baring Crisis troubles, but it was an undoubted recession. Had peace prevailed, one suspects that this second surge of overseas investment would have ended.

Explanations

An ingredient in the uneven economic development of Argentina and the surges of British new issues for Argentina was the behaviour of the railway profit rate which we have taken as representing the varying pull of the Argentine economy for British investors. Secondly, the scale of issues would be influenced by the general attitude of British investors to overseas ventures and the receptiveness of the London stock market.

In Figure 1.6 are presented the series depicting the suggested main determinants of Argentine new issues on the London stock exchange. Argentine issues exhibit a similar long-term behaviour pattern to British overseas issues in total in that they are high when the latter are high and *vice versa*. However, secondly they do not remain a constant proportion of British overseas issues, but form a higher percentage in long-swing peak periods and a lower percentage in long-swing trough periods than the overall average of 8 per cent. Furthermore, both the absolute series and the proportionate series of Argentine issues show a similar long-run pattern to the Argentine railway profit rate although following it with a time-lag. This is only to be expected for it took time to calculate the profits, and for them to be declared, and for investors to react. It is suggested that this association reflects the pull of the Argentine economy influencing the British investor.[13] Finally, as no account has been taken of other

---

[13] In another paper I have attempted to explain the behaviour of Argentine new issues on the London Stock Exchange with reference to the Argentine railway

competing overseas claims for British funds, a final series is added in
Figure 1.6, which comprises the ratio of the Argentine railway profit
rate to the United States railway profit rate.[14] This series again
exhibits similarity to the absolute and proportionate behaviour of
Argentine issues.

Argentine economic development was clearly linked to the long
swings of the 'North Atlantic' economy via total overseas issues and
the general prospects for primary production. However, the railway
profit rate shows distinct long-run swings which may be explained
with reference to events within the Argentine economy by the
notion of a 'development cycle' whose periodicity exceeds that of a
trade cycle. Essential ingredients in this development cycle are
volatility of expectations amongst leaders and overhead capital
projects which take time to construct and time to mature.

Foreign investors are attracted by prospects of profit in an
underdeveloped economy and a rise in foreign investment takes place
perhaps on an exaggerated scale as the enthusiasm of investors runs
riot and projects are bunched. To the extent that much borrowing is
in the form of fixed-interest-bearing securities, foreign debt-service
payments mount while output and exports remain unexpanded.
Capital stock is growing but output and profits remain steady so that
the profit rate of enterprises falls in this phase. Speculative excesses
overtake any expansion of output to bring a rapid reversal of
opinions, crisis, and cessation of lending as it is realised that earlier
judgments were too optimistic. The decline in funds from abroad
brings immediate balance of payments strain, while the service
charges claim a growing share of export receipts (as yet unexpanded
in the development process). The interest payments may be
repudiated and moratoria sought, while profits and yields may be
low or even negative until sales have built up.

In this succeeding period of low foreign investment and antipathy

---

profit rate (lagged two years) and British total overseas issues (less those for
Argentina) by calculating the following regression equation (see *Journal of
Economic History*, Vol. 31, no. 3, September, 1971, p.654.)

$$A_t = -10.890 + 1.987P_{t-2} + 0.129F_t \qquad R^2 = 0.752$$
$$(2.406) \quad (0.563) \qquad (0.020) \qquad d = 1.482$$

A = British new issues for Argentina (£ million)
P = Argentine railway profit rate (per cent)
F = Total British overseas issues less those for Argentina (£ million)
Standard errors of estimated coefficients are in brackets.

The results seem satisfactory, although the Durbin-Watson statistic is rather
too low for comfort.

[14] For the U.S.A. it is the ratio of net operating income to railroad capital
outstanding. Source: *Historical Statistics of the U.S. from Colonial Times to
1957*, pp. 428, 433-4.

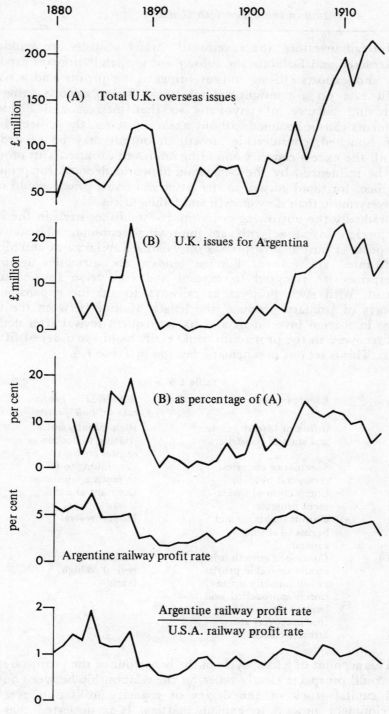

Figure 1.6

of foreign investors, the (overhead) capital projects are gradually constructed and facilitate the subsequent growth in primary production and exports. Rising output brings rising profits and a rising profit rate on a constant capital stock. Rising exports bring an improving balance of payments so that interest and dividend payments can be resumed without strain. Insofar as the projects have been bunched, considerable growth in output may be needed to absorb the excess capacity and bring improved earnings. This process will be influenced by the behaviour of world demand for primary produce, for rapid growth in the latter and rising prices would help recovery more than slow growth and falling prices.

Gradually the borrowing economy re-establishes itself in the eyes of foreign investors with an improving economic climate and prospects as output now presses on existing capital stock and higher profit-rates are earned. Foreign lenders are attracted again as enterprises are tempted to expand and seek fresh finance from abroad. With such projects as railways to aid the expansion of exports of primary produce, the length of time between the first surge in foreign investment and its subsequent revival after decline and recovery in the profit-rate could easily be of the order of fifteen years. This is set out in schematic fashion in Table 1.8.

Table 1.8

Years	Events in cycle	Behaviour of profit-rate or 'pull' factor
1-5	Influx of foreign funds and start of construction	High initially but starting to decline as capital grows
6	Speculative excesses, crisis, end of loans	Continuing to fall to reach a minimum
4-8	Completion of investment projects	Constant at a low level
7-11	Output builds up and begins to absorb capacity	Modest revival
10-14	Continued growth brings steady revival in profits as full capacity operation is approached, and lenders are convinced that prospects are attractive again	Continuing steady revival to high levels

This account of a long cycle in the behaviour of the profit-rate and the 'pull' prospects clearly relies on the relationship between output and capital stock or the degree of capacity utilisation over the development process to explain matters. It is suggested that the course of the railway profit rate in Argentina can be explained to some considerable extent by these sorts of 'cyclical' influences.[15] A rather similar trend-pattern to British overseas investment and North Atlantic long swings has been produced but for reasons mainly endogenous to Argentina.

Conclusions

We can conclude that the uneven flow of British new issues for Argentina and the uneven economic development of Argentina can be explained to a considerable extent with reference to economic features in the development process under private enterprise conditions. On the one hand important features were the state of the British capital market and world prospects together with the exaggerated behaviour of investors; on the other hand, there was the varying pull of Argentine prospects which we sought to explain by invoking a rather *ad hoc* development cycle. Economic factors in Argentina, Britain, and the world contributed to bring unsteady growth in an interlocking and almost inevitable way. However, the economic forces upon which I have concentrated do not explain everything. I would not wish to claim this: in the developmental process there is much scope for political, social, even military, elements and a place for chance elements and random discoveries.

Thus were laid the foundations of the modern Argentine economy after 40 years of rapid but uneven growth. In terms of the then system of international economic relations, Argentina had been a periphery economy with a *potential* comparative advantage in primary production, which was turned into an *actual* pattern of specialisation by immigration and by foreign investment from the centre. The latter served to shape the productive structure of the Argentine economy into a particular specialised form which by the

[15] See Figure 1.4 for a graphical version. The previous mentioned paper examined the degree of relationship between the Argentine railway profit-rate and a crude measure of capacity utilisation (exports per kilometre of railway track) and the results were somewhat reassuring, particularly when it is recalled that the profit-rate could be influenced by many other factors — for example, the pricing policies of railways.

The following regression equation was calculated for Argentina for 1881-1914:

$$P_t = 0.650 + 0.257 \, x_t \qquad R^2 = 0.665$$
$$\quad (0.434) \, (0.032) \qquad\quad d = 1.461$$

P = Argentine railway profit-rate
x = Argentine exports values per kilometre of railway track
Standard errors of the estimated coefficients are in brackets.
See A.G. Ford *op. cit.*, p. 661.

stage of development reached in 1914 had brought high real incomes. Yet it was a vulnerable position, should the terms of trade move against primary producers or should technological change promise a dramatic alteration in the comparative cost position in favour of manufacturing production. However, at the time to contemporaries with the amounts of information available and the prevailing beliefs and aspirations it seemed the natural and understandable way to develop the Argentine economy.

Nevertheless, it did give rise to a pattern of international economic relations for Argentina, which emphasised the dependence of the economy, and which brought considerable foreign control over key economic sectors, besides leading to a heavy foreign debt-service outflow — the price of capital or economic tribute exacted! In this respect it led some contemporaries and later scholars to ask who were the major beneficiaries other than the Argentine landowners and the foreign investors. In some senses we can look with admiration at the pace of development of the economy on this specialised basis and realise the critical role of foreign capital, but in others we can note unsatisfactory aspects of the way it was achieved, and the mixed legacies which it bequeathed to later generations of Argentines.

2

Anglo-U.S. Trade Rivalry in Argentina and the D'Abernon Mission of 1929

ROGER GRAVIL

At the end of the 1920s rumours were increasingly prevalent in South America that the British had decided to abandon the area as a sphere of influence. It was widely believed among businessmen that some kind of agreement had been reached under which British enterprises in South America were to pass into North American hands in exchange for relief from United States pressure within the British Empire. In 1929 alone about £40m worth of British shares, mainly in South American activities, were sold to United States investors and the high prices paid in many cases seemed to testify to confident United States expectations of an untrammelled future in South America free of British competition. The City of London was thought to have written off South America as an area for further British investment.[1] While it seems inconceivable that stories of a formal agreement had any basis in fact the persistence of the rumours is readily explicable by reference to the extreme feebleness of most British responses to the North American advance. That the southward movement of United States expansion should eventually extend to Argentina is not surprising since by the mid-1920s this republic transacted 50 per cent of the total trade of South America, possessed 42 per cent of the railway mileage and held 72.8 per cent of the gold reserves. The central importance of Argentina for Britain and its developing importance for the United States is well illustrated by the levels of capital investment in the republic.

Though it has recently been argued by William Appleman Williams that United States expansionism was originally due to agrarian

---

[1] F.O. 371/13459, 2 Oct. 1929. Enclosure in Lima despatch no. 129, 232. Michael Barratt Brown, *After Imperialism*, London, 1963, p. 125. Royal Institute of International Affairs Study Group, *The Problem of International Investment*, London, 1937, pp. 186-7, 270-2.

Table 2.1 Estimates of foreign capital in Argentina[2] (millions of gold pesos)

	1910	1913	1917	1920	1923	1927	1931	1934
Great Britain	1,475	1,928	1,950	1,825	1,975	2,075	2,100	2,285
United States	20	40	85	75	200	505	807	590
Germany	200	250	275	265	285	285	300	315
France	410	475	465	410	415	415	425	450
Others	150	557	575	575	325	320	468	660
Total	2,255	3,250	3,350	3,150	3,200	3,600	4,100	4,300

pressures, the need to find outlets for farm and plantation products,[3] it seems plain that the intensification of United States interest in South America in the early years of the twentieth century was due to the growth of industrial production beyond the capacity of domestic consumption. This growing interest in foreign trade prompted the formation of several organisations designed to promote overseas expansion. As early as 1893 the Pan American Union published a study entitled 'How the Latin American markets may be reached by the manufacturers of the United States'. The Bureau of Manufactures created in 1906 was expanded in 1912 into the Bureau of Foreign and Domestic Commerce with special trade commissioners and commercial attachés to implement governmental trade promotion. These activities backed up such organisations as the American Exporters and Importers Association (1911), the Chamber of Commerce of the United States (1912), and the National Foreign Trade Council (1914).

Within the Latin American area United States manufacturers showed growing interest in the lucrative Argentine market, and in the first decade of the twentieth century there was a significant expansion of North American trade with the River Plate. In 1900 U.S. imports from Argentina were worth 8,114,000 dollars and exports to the Republic totalled 11,558,000 dollars. By 1910 the corresponding figures were 33,463,000 and 40,695,000.[4] Thus a foundation had been laid for the spectacular progress of the U.S.A. in the Argentine market during the First World War when British links

[2] Vernon L. Phelps, *The International Economic Position of Argentina*, London, 1938, p. 99. The trade, railways and gold figures are from Dept. of Overseas Trade, *Report of the British Economic Mission to Argentina, Brazil and Uruguay*, London, 1930, p. 12.

[3] William Appleman Williams, *The Roots of the Modern American Empire*, London, 1971.

[4] Phelps, *op. cit.*, pp. 4, 176-7.

with the River Plate were weakened. This trading expansion gained strong support from the banking sector when the First National Bank of Boston and the First National City Bank both opened branches in Buenos Aires during the war years. The progress of North American export trade to Argentina compared to British exports appears in Table 2.2.

Table 2.2 Argentina's total imports from the U.S. and U.K. 1913-35 [5] (gold pesos)

	U.S. [5]	U.K.	Valuation
1913	73,012,668	154,053,513	E.R.V.
1918	169,506,948	125,091,483	E.R.V.
1919	232,868,392	154,478,509	E.R.V.
1920	310,395,308	218,605,483	E.R.V.
1921	200,860,141	173,899,864	E.R.V.
1922	85,442,740	86,182,745	1906 T.V. +20%
1923	104,941,773	104,960,739	1906 T.V. +20%
1924	136,456,022	139,644,829	1906 T.V. +60%
1925	155,153,696	150,247,624	1906 T.V. +60%
1926	175,766,544	143,575,367	1906 T.V. +60%
1927	194,360,508	146,339,640	1906 T.V. +60%
1928	192,766,465	164,247,438	E.R.V.
1929	227,174,938	151,968,782	E.R.V.
1930	163,118,192	146,562,600	E.R.V.
1931	81,539,636	108,489,466	E.R.V.
1932	112,656,000	180,004,000	E.R.V.
1933	107,371,000	209,850,000	E.R.V.
1934	151,824,000	230,330,000	T.V.
1935	161,000,000	237,000,000	T.V.

Faced with this growing North American challenge the British showed increasing concern about their post-war prospects, and even before the war ended a British mission led by Follett Holt and Sir Maurice de Bunsen was despatched to South America to make recommendations for a British comeback.[6] It concluded that although the past progress of British trade with South America was attributable to individual enterprise, post-war conditions would require a

5 U.K. Dept. of Overseas Trade reports for relevant years. E.R.V. is estimated real values, 1906 T.V. + 20 per cent is 1906 tariff valuations with 20 per cent added to bring the valuation nearer to real values as is 1906 T.V. + 60 per cent. If 1930 E.R.V. were given as T.V. the U.S. figure would be 166,301,945 and the U.K. 155,271,741. If 1931 E.R.V. were given as T.V. the U.S. figure would be 84,928,952 and the U.K. 106,536,833. From 1932 millions are rounded in the sources.

6 *British Diplomatic and Commercial Mission to South America, 1918.* Report by Follett Holt (with preliminary note by the Rt. Hon. Sir Maurice de Bunsen), HMSO, 1919.

determined governmental promotion effort and greater co-ordination in private enterprise. The institutional basis was felt to be there in the newly-created Department of Overseas Trade and in the excellent British Chamber of Commerce in the Argentine Republic. What was required from the government was a coherent policy and adequate finance. Neither, however, was forthcoming. In the late 1920s a prominent British official explained the government's conception of trade promotion in the following terms:

> The role of H.M. Government towards British firms is very largely that of the man who leads the horse to the water. The role of the horse is to drink the water but this must in the nature of things be left to the horse. All H.M. Government can do is to display the water as clearly, fully and appealingly as possible.[7]

What this meant in practical terms was that Britain had only three commercial secretaries and one assistant in the whole of Latin America, while the United States had at least one in every republic, usually with assistance.[8] Since the British government itself was so weakly represented in Latin American commerce, official exhortations to companies to strengthen their representation did not carry much conviction. The chief obstacle was, of course, the Treasury whose prime objective was to reduce personnel and expenditure to pre-war levels.

Until the beginning of the 1930s Anglo-U.S. trade rivalry in Argentina developed in the context of a relatively free economy and more or less equal treatment under Argentine commercial policy. The treaty basis for most of Argentina's foreign trade rested on most-favoured-nation (m.f.n.) clauses which fell into two types; unconditional m.f.n. clauses under which any concession made to a third party was automatically extended to others; and conditional m.f.n. clauses under which anything granted to a third party in exchange for a concession would be extended only to countries making the same or an equivalent concession. The first category did not operate on the principle of commercial reciprocity while the second applied it strictly.

The Republic's commercial relations with both Britain and the United States were based on the m.f.n. clause (unconditional with Britain, conditional with the United States) and a multilateral pattern became increasingly pronounced as the 1920s progressed. It

---

[7] F.O.371/13460. Minute by T.M. Snow on Robertson to Henderson, 17 June 1929, 28.

[8] F.O.371/13460, Snow's Minute, 17 June 1929, 28.

is notorious that North America was becoming increasingly protectionist in the 1920s. In 1913 eight of Argentina's major export commodities had enjoyed free entry into the United States market. As early as 1922 only hides remained on the duty free list and even they were to be removed by the Hawley Smoot tariff of 1930.[9] Products not totally excluded by heavy customs impositions were blocked by new sanitary regulations introduced in 1927. United States progress in the Argentine market was only attainable, therefore, within a multilateral system of payments under which currencies were freely convertible, so that sterling earned in Argentina's export trade to Britain could be readily changed into dollars to meet the rising imports bill from the United States.[10] Given that the multilateral framework was indispensable for United States progress in the Argentine market, what other factors contributed to North American success?

Recent studies of British international trade between the wars tend to imply that the generally disastrous export performance was primarily due to Britain's failure to defend overseas markets adequately with the existing export commodity structure in a general context of contracting world trade. Losses due to the inappropriateness of Britain's export products are deemed to have been relatively modest. This is broadly the view taken particularly by Maizels, Tyszinski, Baldwin and Aldcroft.[11] The validity of this thesis depends heavily on the commodity classifications adopted: excessively broad categories could conceal obsolescence in the commodity content. But with this qualification noted, the cautious conclusion of these studies is that the decline of British exports to the world in general in the inter-war period owed more to deficiencies in marketing than to an inappropriate structure of industrial output or an over-valued exchange rate. Britain seems to have been producing more or less the right goods but was failing to sell them effectively.

In contrast to this impression that Britain's poor export record

[9] This section has benefited greatly from the loan of an unpublished paper by R.A. Humphreys, 'British and United States Trade Policies in Latin America' (1941).

[10] Folke Hilgerdt, 'The Case for Multilateral Trade', *American Economic Review*, Vol. 33, no. 1, supplement, March 1943 for a useful discussion of multilateralism.

[11] A. Maizels, *Industrial Growth and World Trade*, Cambridge, 1963, especially pp. 198-202. H. Tyszynski, 'World Trade in Manufactured Commodities 1899-1950', *Manchester School*, 19, 1951. R.F. Baldwin, 'The Commodity Composition of Trade: Selected Industrial Countries 1900-1954', *Review of Economics and Statistics*, 40, 1958. D.H. Aldcroft, *The Inter-War Economy: Britain 1919-1939*, London, 1970, pp. 243-85.

generally between the wars was primarily due to distributive defects, it seems equally probable that the main problem for British exports to Argentina was an inappropriate production structure. It was calculated in 1927 that about two thirds of the Republic's total import trade could be considered non-competitive because of commodity specialisation among the five leading suppliers: United States, Britain, Germany, Italy and France. It was reckoned in 1929 that not more than 25 per cent of United States exports to Argentina were products competing with those of existing suppliers; 25 per cent were non-competitive by reason of natural advantages; 50 per cent were non-competitive by reason of production advantages.[12] Perhaps the most important feature of United States non-competitive exports to Argentina was the fact that they were generally new products, especially automobiles, office and household equipment, radios, films and machinery for new industries.[13] That is, the United States presence in the Argentine market seems to have rested to the extent of about 75 per cent on meeting a demand for goods which Britain did not supply. These circumstances point the finger at the inflexibility of British industry rather than the marketing system in assigning prime responsibility for Britain's decline in the import trade of the Republic.

In 1920 at least 2,170 British firms were supplying the Argentine market and a large proportion of these were represented by import agents or import-export agencies.[14] Where direct dealing was particularly necessary it was developed, notably by British-owned department stores in the Republic which normally controlled all stages of marketing from purchasing in Europe to retailing in Argentina.[15] But for most types of commodities exported from Britain the agency system was adequate and indeed the first wave of North American penetration of the market made some efforts to use these existing outlets. British agents were experiencing growing difficulty in surviving purely on the basis of distributing British

[12] Calculated by George Jackson Eder in *Studies in World Economy*, no. 4, 'International Competition in the Trade of Argentina', *International Conciliation*, no. 271, June 1931, pp. 403-5.

[13] J.F. Normano, *The Struggle for South America*, London, 1931, pp. 41-2. The introduction by Clarence Haring is also very interesting on the development of Anglo-U.S. rivalry.

[14] The Standard Directory Company, *The Argentine Standard Directory of National and Foreign Merchants and Manufacturers*, Buenos Aires, 1920. Though impressively comprehensive this count is certainly not complete, partly because a fire destroyed some of the company's records and appeals to the business community did not fill all the gaps.

[15] Roger Gravil, 'British Retail Trade in Argentina 1900-1940', *Inter-American Economic Affairs*, vol. 24, no. 2, especially 5-9.

products and so were willing to accept the marketing of United States goods.[16] The data for measuring this development are very imperfect but some rough indication may be derived from the following figures. Of 51 agents listed in a trade directory of 1914, 28 dealt exclusively in British goods; 13 handled both British and North American products; 1 dealt solely in North American goods. Of 73 agents listed in 1920, 33 dealt exclusively in British goods; 26 handled both British and North American; none dealt exclusively in North American goods.[17]

But North American business soon found that this form of commercial outlet was unsuitable for many of the articles being introduced into the Republic and new marketing techniques began to develop strongly by the middle of the 1920s.[18] It was widely thought that the U.S. recovery from the setbacks of 1923-4, when British exports to the Republic momentarily exceeded the North American, was mainly attributable to diverting trade from the old commercial system into new forms of sales outlet. Some commentators even speak of a revolution in United States marketing methods in Argentina in the 1920s mainly for the distribution of new products and, secondarily, for more effective competition in established lines.

One important development was the growth of direct dealing between manufacturers and retail distributors due mainly to increased sale by the United States of products requiring some form of after-sales service, especially cars and other consumers' durables.[19] The older commercial practice of placing annual orders with commission houses or general import agents was clearly unsuitable for this type of business. Where the volume of trade justified it, commercial representation was further strengthened by engaging full-time specialist representatives in Argentina and even opening

[16] F.O.371/13460, Robertson to Henderson, 17 June 1929, 46, notes examples of this dilemma.

[17] Robert Grant & Co, *The English Address Book of British and North American Residents, Business Houses, Institutions etc. in the Argentine Republic, 1914* and *1920*, Buenos Aires, 1914 and 1920. The main difficulty is that though the nationality of firms trading to the Republic is distinguished that of agencies is not. But contemporary comment leaves little doubt that it was largely a matter of British agents finding themselves obliged to handle North American goods rather than British products forcing their way through the few North American import agencies in the Republic.

[18] H. Hallam Hipwell, 'Trade Rivalries in Argentina', *Foreign Affairs*, vol. 8, Oct. 1929, pp. 151-4. On the setbacks see also American Bankers Association, *The River Plate Region*, New York, 1924.

[19] Julius Klein, 'Economic Rivalries in Latin America', *Foreign Affairs*, vol. 3, Dec. 1924, pp. 241-2. Phelps, *op. cit.*, 172-3.

branches in the Republic to organise distribution. The general effect was a speeding up of the selling process through smaller orders, prompt deliveries and more rapid turnover.

In sectors of the market where Anglo-U.S. competition centred on the same commodities it was essential to match price and quality exactly to consumers' needs. Though the high quality of British goods was rarely questioned, high production costs and high selling prices were frequently the cause of declining sales and in some cases even of total elimination from the market. The leading textile manufacturer and veteran of Anglo-Argentine trade, Sir William Clare Lees, explained:

> A further cause of loss of trade is due to the fact that Argentina is essentially a price market. Price is everything: durability, in a country changing and developing at such an astonishing rate, is naturally a secondary consideration. The result has been a steady drift towards standards deemed by the buyers to be good enough for the time being, though admittedly not so good as the high standards which we in this country seek to maintain.[20]

This did not mean that a developed market like Argentina, and especially not the ultra-sophisticated portion of it centred in Buenos Aires, could be regarded as a dumping ground for shoddy goods. What was really needed in many lines was a combination of reasonable quality and low prices. It seems clear that in directly competitive trade North American success was attributable to precisely that combination, though more comparative research is needed to establish the precise roles of production, the exchange rate and distribution in this process.

A further prominent feature of the North American export drive in Argentina was the extensive use of advertising and it is a testimony to the level of development of the Republic that outlets for advertising copy were so abundant. In 1911 there were 795 distinct journalistic publications mainly of dailies, weeklies, illustrated papers and trade journals. Of the principal language groups 724 were in Spanish; 16 Italian; 9 English; 6 German; 5 French; 25 included material in more than one language.[21] The channelling of foreign news and features into this range of national journalism was increasingly controlled by the North American syndicate, United

[20] Sir William Clare Lees, 'Some Aspects of Trade with South America', *Society of Arts Journal*, vol. 78, p. 461. Statistics for Anglo-U.S. trade rivalry in competing commodities may be obtained from the author.

[21] U.S. Bureau of Foreign and Domestic Commerce, Miscellaneous Series no. 10, *Foreign Publications for Advertising American Goods*, p. 48.

Press, which achieved a monopoly in South America comparable with that of Reuters in South Africa.[22] North American traders made effective use of these outlets not only to promote their products but to spread United States influence generally. For in a country populated by rapid immigration chiefly of non-Anglo Saxon people, the most important use of advertising was its educative role. The publicity problem was not merely of raising public awareness of new commodity lines but to a large extent of introducing consumers into North America's commercial orbit for the first time. In approaching this type of problem the North Americans had considerable advantages over the British, not only through the press monopoly, but also because they had previous experience of handling a market mainly composed of recent arrivals of a rather low cultural level to a pioneering country. The sort of people arriving in Argentina in the late 1920s had been settling in North America until immigration control was introduced in 1924. British traders had little comparable experience on which to draw.

The influence of national allegiances on consumption patterns in the Argentine market is usually most emphasised in the cases of Italians and Spaniards who were easily the largest elements in the population. But loyalty purchasing also had considerable significance in Anglo-U.S. trade rivalry in the Republic. The 40,000 strong British community may have been a mere fraction of the national population but at least it was considerably larger than the North American community and was for the most part prosperous.[23] Secondly, and much more important, British undertakings operating in the Republic made a virtually guaranteed market for renewals, spares and fuel. What this sector amounted to was a major branch of British export trade more or less impregnable to foreign suppliers. Anglo-Argentine enterprises were probably more likely to buy British than comparable businesses located in Britain. As long as Britain retained ownership of these undertakings a substantial British presence in the Argentine market was guaranteed. This was appreciated just as keenly, however, by the North Americans and consequently Anglo-U.S. rivalry in the 1920s increasingly took the form of a battle for control of capital assets in the Republic.[24]

[22] F.O.371/13459, Enclosure in Lima Despatch No. 129, 2 Oct. 1929, 241. F.O.371/13460, Robertson to Craigie, 11 March 1929, 125. Sir Malcom Robertson, 'The Economic Relations between Great Britain and the Argentine Republic', *Royal Institute of International Affairs Journal*, vol. 9, 1930, p. 227.

[23] Between 1906 and 1939 the British community seems to have maintained a level of about 40,000 passport holders.

[24] In purchasing British-owned assets the North Americans achieved double

The policy of purchasing undertakings which were major consumers of goods imported into the Republic was prosecuted fiercely
by the North Americans. One major United States victory was the
buying up of the Lacroze interests in the Buenos Aires Central
Railway, the tramways in the Federal Capital and a light and power
company in Buenos Aires.[25] The Harris Forbes group of New York
obtained for their subsidiary, Dwight Robinson and Co., the contract
for extending the underground railway. Electric power stations in the
provinces of Buenos Aires and Córdoba owned by the Compañía
Anglo-Argentina de Electricidad were similarly taken over by the
Electric Bond and Share Company of New York. The same
organisation also bought out the Atlas Light and Power Co., thereby
gaining control of tramways and power stations in Buenos Aires,
Córdoba and Tucumán. The Westinghouse Electric International Co.
was active purchasing the power stations of various towns in Santa
Fé. The International Telephone and Telegraph Company of New
York bought out Unión Telefónica, and similar strides were made
towards United States control in the glucose and tobacco industries.
Ford, General Motors and Chrysler were increasingly prominent in
the Republic, while Standard Oil was developing concessions from
1920, particularly in the north west.[26] Finally, by the late 1920s
British-owned railways in the Republic came under an attack even
more serious than the pre-war Farquhar Syndicate had threatened.[27]

North American assaults on the British railway system in the
1920s took two main forms. One type of North American strategy
was to develop road construction running parallel to the railways but
not feeding them. This activity prepared the ground for subsequent
massive sales of North American motor vehicles which would attract
both passenger and goods traffic from the railways. What could not
be ruined by competition was to be bought out. Considering the
strategic importance of the railways in the whole Anglo-Argentine
connection the directorates showed alarming complacency. Tracks
were badly maintained. Rolling stock was inadequately serviced.
Visits to the Republic by London-based directors seem to have been

---

victories in undermining British 'tied' trade and developing their own. But
even the purchase of local or other foreign-owned assets helped the United
States to create a 'tied' trade comparable to that in the Anglo-Argentine
connection.

[25] The enterprise of Teófilo and Federico Lacroze was the only privately-owned
railway system under Argentine management.

[26] F.O.371/13460, Report by Mr. Rongé, 13 March 1929, pp. 139-40.

[27] There is an excellent compilation of railway data in *The Times Book on
Argentina*, London, 1927, pp. 66-121.

unusual[28] and, above all, the companies were very slow to recognise the North American threat. British officials sensed the danger earlier than the companies. Ambassador Robertson said:

> I look upon them (railways) as the mainstay, the backbone of our whole position out here. If they go, we all go. Their loss would be a death blow to us out here and a serious one to our industry at home of which they are loyal supporters.[29]

The Buenos Aires and Pacific Railway Company, for instance, admitted that practically its only purchases inside the Republic were railway sleepers. Everything else was imported. In the worst year of the company's operations this had meant £300,000 worth of exports from Britain: in its best year £1,200,000. In addition an annual purchase of £500,000 worth of British coal was made.[30] The other railway companies followed much the same purchasing policy.

Against this general background of intensifying Anglo-U.S. rivalry in Argentina three specific pressures developed at the end of the 1920s to prompt a major trade promotion effort by the British. The first of these was growing alarm about the increasingly unfavourable trading balance for Britain in the Anglo-Argentine connection. Free trade interests in the Republic, through their major outlet *La Prensa*, estimated that Britain's invisible earnings in trade with Argentina totalled some £36m which placed the overall payments position near equilibrium.[31] But since the reduction of British overseas investments generally by 16 per cent as a result of the First World War there seems to have been a heightened appreciation of the vulnerability of invisible earnings and increasing unease about unfavourable balances on visible account. The adverse balance on visible account for Britain in the Anglo-Argentine connection was £35,542,106 in 1925; £41,788,505 in 1926; £46,241,380 in 1927; £42,884,007 in 1928.[32] The best overall estimates for both the U.K. and the U.S. appear in Table 2.3.

---

[28] Railway executives hotly denied this charge and even tried to obtain the dismissal of Ambassador Robertson when he criticised them. F.O.371/13459, St. Davids to Austen Chamberlain. 28 Dec. 1928, pp. 4-7. Same to same, 24 March, 1929, p. 117. Robertson's views were subsequently confirmed by the distinguished diplomat Sir David Kelly, *The Ruling Few*, London, 1952, pp. 293-4.

[29] F.O.371/13460, Robertson to Craigie, 10 May 1929, p. 283.

[30] F.O.371/13460, Memo, 10 May 1929, p. 261. See Colin Lewis's contribution for further details of the purchasing policies of British railway companies in Argentina (this volume, Chapter 5).

[31] F.O.371/14189, Macleay to F.O. 12 Aug. 1920, pp. 283-4.

[32] U.K. Department of Overseas Trade, *Economic Conditions in the Argentine Republic*, Nov. 1929, p. 20.

Table 2.3 Estimated major items in Argentina's balance of payments with the United States, the United Kingdom and other countries (in millions of gold pesos)[33]

	1914-20			1921-30			1931-34		
	U.S.	U.K.	Others	U.S.	U.K.	Others	U.S.	U.K.	Others
Commodity trade									
Exports	993	1,733	2,375	769	3,009	4,644	131	1,161	1,041
Imports	1,077	885	1,504	1,826	1,618	4,253	249	409	1,111
Surplus exports or imports (+) (−)	−144	+848	+871	−1,057	+1,391	+391	−151	+752	−70
Service items									
Immigrant remittances		180			340			95	
Tourist expenditures		20	60		50	160		20	60
Interest & dividends	35	560	416	221	1,021	414	160	400	223
Total service items	−35	−580	−656	−221	−1,071	−914	−160	−420	−378
Balances of payments	−179	+268	+215	−1,278	+320	−523	−275	+332	−448

33 Phelps, *op. cit.*, p. 190.

The second pressure for a British trade promotion effort in Latin America generally derived from the visit to ten republics of Herbert Hoover, president-elect of the United States, at the end of 1928. As a former Secretary of Commerce and Chairman of the Inter-American High Commission, Hoover was one of the few United States' presidents with some claim to experience in Latin American affairs. During his tour Hoover stressed the 'good neighbour' concept and repudiated earlier domineering policies.[34] Soon after assuming the presidency it was reported that Hoover began transferring the most capable United States diplomats to Latin American posts. The British ambassador felt that

> there can . . . be little doubt that Hoover is mainly out for trade and that he wishes to oust us from any position that we may hold. Hoover means serious business in South America and our sands are running out.[35]

Robertson became increasingly convinced of this:

> The United States under Hoover means to dominate this continent by hook or by crook. It is British interests that chiefly stand in the way. These are to be bought out or kicked out.[36]

The third pressure for a British trade drive came from Argentina itself. Promptly after Hoover's visit Senator Molinari, a confidant of President Yrigoyen, suggested to Robertson that a party of leading British industrialists should visit the Republic to discuss authoritatively with the president the whole field of Anglo-Argentine trade.[37] Yrigoyen even went so far as to suggest that Lord Melchett should be included in the mission. A number of influences may have prompted this overture by Argentina towards Britain. First, the change of administration from Alvear to Yrigoyen established a government in Buenos Aires more antagonistic towards the United States; secondly, the growing apprehension in Argentina of United States domination, while the British were 'regarded as less aggressive, less domineering and less inclined to use force in support of financial and commercial

[34] Gordon Connell-Smith, *The Inter-American System* (London, 1966), p.78.
[35] F.O.371/13460, Robertson to Craigie 11 March 1929, p. 125. F.O.371/13460, Robertson to Craigie 10 May 1929, p. 285.
[36] F.O.371/13459, Memo. 25 Oct. 1929, p. 230.
[37] F.O.371/13459, Memo. 18 Dec. 1928, p. 16. Lord Melchett, Alfred Mond, was president of the Empire Economic Union and the following year published a book entitled *Imperial Economic Unity*, London, 1930. In the event he did not go on the mission.

claims';[38] thirdly, the dependence of the meat trade in particular on the British market; fourthly, the threat to continuation of the Anglo-Argentine connection in proposals for imperial preference, and therefore the pressure on Argentina to reduce Britain's need to adopt such a course.

With these general influences inclining the Republic towards Britain, the contribution of Sir Malcom Robertson to what was intended as a new basis for the Anglo-Argentine connection was important.[39] The actual concept of the Anglo-Argentine connection was really equivalent to the so-called 'Imperial Idea' within Britain's formal empire. Both exploited sentiment to veil the realities of trading relations between primary production areas and the industrial centre. Robertson was a profound believer in the Anglo-Argentine connection and was capable of writing:

> Without saying so in so many words, which would be tactless, what I really mean is that Argentina must be regarded as an essential part of the British Empire.[40]

For him a central function of the Anglo-Argentine connection was to relieve unemployment in Britain. The slogan 'buy from those who buy from us' associated with Robertson's name readily became a plea for bilateral trade in the hands of the *Sociedad Rural*. But Robertson personally maintained that this was a bad adaptation of his original phraseology 'buy from us that we may buy from you' implying not preferential treatment for Britain but simply that if Argentina imported more British manufactures, unemployment would be reduced in Britain bringing improved living standards and greater consumption of Argentine products.[41] At the level of general declarations Robertson more or less consistently maintained that he was against pressing for any concessions from the Republic which

[38] F.O.371/13459, Memo, 15 Oct. 1929. Lord D'Abernon's words.

[39] Malcom Robertson, 'Argentina and Great Britain', *Institute of Hispanic Studies, Lectures and Addresses No. 2* Liverpool, 1935, p. 1. Sir Malcom Arnold Robertson (1877-1951) was a career diplomat who had served in Berlin, 1903-4; Peking, 1905; Madrid, 1907; Bucharest, 1910-11; Montevideo, 1912-13; Rio de Janeiro, 1913-15; Washington, 1915-18; The Hague, 1918-19; Rhineland High Commission, 1919; Tangier, 1921-5. He was Envoy Extraordinary and Minister Plenipotentiary at Buenos Aires, 1925-7 and Ambassador, 1927-9. He resigned at the age of 52 with no pension apparently in connection with a dispute over delay in getting the D'Abernon agreement signed.

[40] F.O.371/13460, Robertson to Henderson, 17 June 1929, 42.

[41] F.O.371/13460, Robertson to Henderson, 17 June, 1929, p. 41. F.O.371/ 13460, Robertson to Craigie, 10 Aug. 1929, p. 58.

would be denied to other countries.[42] In this he kept himself in line with the government he represented which also professed to be against any departure from the established principles of British commercial policy.[43] In the three or four years before 1931 a great deal of intellectual ingenuity was, in fact, expended in developing trading formulae which gave effective preference without completely discarding the unconditional m.f.n. clause.[44] The mission of Edgar Vincent, Viscount D'Abernon, to Argentina, Brazil and Uruguay in August and September 1929 was one such endeavour.

Viscount D'Abernon had been British ambassador in Berlin from 1921 to 1926 and in retirement was chiefly engaged in preparing his diaries for publication when approached to lead the proposed trade mission to South America.[45] His view of the world economic crisis in general was that it was mainly due to gold shortages, particularly the absorption by India of about one half of South African production. Beyond that (and more correctly), he blamed North American tariff policies which impeded debt service and amortisation through trading earnings. Further he connected the low price levels of primary products with the worsening political instability of South America.[46] The others selected for the mission were Sir William Clare Lees, a prominent cotton textile manufacturer and member of the Bleachers Association who had previously served on the Balfour Committee, Julian Piggott of the firm Roland and Piggott, nominated by the National Federation of Iron and Steel Manufacturers; W. Howard-Williams of the Agricultural Engineers Association; H.W. Wiswould, an official of the Department of Overseas Trade; H.O. Chalkley, the outstanding commercial counsellor of the British Embassy in Buenos Aires.[47] These appointments were made

[42] F.O.371/13460 Robertson to Craigie, 10 Aug. 1929, pp. 55, 57, 58.

[43] F.O.371/14190, F.O. to Millington Drake, 11 April 1930. 'You must on no account suggest to the Argentine Government, or in other quarters, that it would be desirable from His Majesty's Government's point of view that the Argentine Government should take any action with a view to the revision of Argentina's commercial treaties', for instance.

[44] Sir Andrew McFadyean, 'International Repercussions of the Ottawa Agreements', *International Affairs*, vol. 12, 1933, pp. 39-45, shows how the unconditional m.f.n. clause was gradually drained of meaning.

[45] Edgar Vincent, *An Ambassador of Peace: Pages from the diary of Viscount D'Abernon*, Berlin 1920-26, 3 vols, London, 1929-30. He was 72 at the time of the trade mission.

[46] Edgar Vincent, *The Economic Crisis: Its Causes and the Cure*, London, 1930, pp. 8-10.

[47] Sir Herbert Gibson 'happened' to return from London to Buenos Aires on the liner 'The Alcantara' which took the mission to Argentina. British Chamber of Commerce in the Argentine Republic, *Monthly Journal*, vol. 9, 31 Aug. 1929, p. 21.

under Stanley Baldwin's Government. But the idea of a trade mission, its intent and even its membership were acceptable to the Labour Party, and Ramsay MacDonald approved all these arrangements when the Labour Government assumed office in June 1929.[48]

As the Mission progressed in its work its official announcements developed from general attempts to disarm suspicion such as,

> We are not coming with the exclusive intention of selling English products. We come to stimulate commerce and to stimulate in both directions the flow of human necessities which binds us:[49]

to open threats of a possible change in British policy,

> In particular, Argentina cannot permanently rely on the open British market, still less on British capacity and willingness to absorb an even greater volume of her products unless she entrenches herself there by offering us facilities for doing a reciprocal trade . . . We endeavoured to bring home to the Argentines the importance of keeping the British market open and the obvious danger to them of increased imperial preference which might arise from the indiscriminate adoption by Argentina of augmented customs duties which, in effect, penalise British goods.[50]

What in concrete terms did the Mission expect to achieve in that area of Argentine's import trade which was competitive?[51] The centrepiece was the arrangement by which Argentina undertook to purchase British manufactures up to the value of £8,700,000. In return Britain agreed to purchase foodstuffs up to the value of £8,700,000 from Argentina. There was, however, a crucial but unpublicised difference between the two sides of the bargain.

[48] British Chamber of Commerce in the Argentine Republic, *Monthly Journal*, 31 Aug. 1929, pp. 17-19.

[49] F.O.371/13459, 6 Sept. 1929, p. 178. The mission remained in Argentina from 20 August to 8 September 1929 and finally left South America on 25 September, 1929.

[50] U.K. Dept. of Overseas Trade, *Report of the British Economic Mission to Argentina, Brazil and Uruguay*, London, 1930, pp. 14, 20-1. The agreement was dated 8 November 1929.

[51] This article is concerned solely with the significance of the D'Abernon agreement in the context of Anglo-U.S. rivalry in Argentina's import trade. There was also fierce Anglo-U.S. rivalry in the conduct of the Republic's export trade and the D'Abernon report commented on it. But the subject falls outside the scope of this article. See Roger Gravil, 'State Intervention in Argentina's Export Trade between the Wars', *Journal of Latin American Studies*, 2, 2, pp. 147-73.

Argentina's purchases from Britain were additional to existing trade; Britain's purchases from Argentina were incorporated in existing trade and were purely an accounting arrangement.[52]

Strictly speaking, therefore, the D'Abernon agreement was not bilateral but unilateral. The British government apparently accepted *La Prensa*'s estimate that on invisible account Britain's surplus totalled £36 millions and since Britain's deficit on visible account averaged roughly £45 millions in the later 1920s, it seems a reasonable surmise that the object of the D'Abernon mission was to secure sufficient additional export trade for Britain to put the overall balance of payments in the Anglo-Argentine connection into equilibrium. What were the details of the agreement?

There was, first, the question of grain elevator construction. Sporadically, since the 1890s and more frequently in the 1920s proposals were aired in the Republic for the building of a national network of grain elevators. Under the D'Abernon agreement President Yrigoyen promised favourable consideration of the proposal to entrust the firm Henry Simon Ltd., with the construction. Secondly, similar terms were obtained for the firm Pauling and Co., for roadbuilding in the Republic.[53] Indeed, Yrigoyen is reported to have stated without reserve that in public works other than those carried out directly by the government, preference would be given to English contractors.[54] Thirdly, the Argentine state railways habitually placed their orders for rails with France or Belgium; D'Abernon obtained an assurance that they would subsequently be placed in Britain.[55] Fourthly, there was the question of the passenger tax. When the British government tried to press British businessmen to make more frequent visits to the Republic it was often retorted that the tax on travellers imposed by the Argentine government was a deterrent. D'Abernon obtained a promise that this would be abolished.[56] Fifthly, a further promise was extracted that certain anomalies in Argentine customs collection would be ironed out.[57] The agreement was initially for two years but it was felt that prospects of an extension was good.[58] Thus Britain seemed destined

---

[52] This is clearly explained in F.O.371/13461, Argentine Agreement, Note for Lord Privy Seal, 17 Oct. 1929, pp. 242-3.

[53] F.O.371/13461, Chalkley to Crowe, 9 Sept. 1929, p. 97.

[54] F.O.371/13459, Memo, 25 Oct. 1929, p. 232.

[55] F.O.371/14188, Millington Drake to F.O. 23 Jan. 1930, p. 83.

[56] F.O.371/13461, Chalkley to Crowe, 9 Sept. 1929, p. 97.

[57] F.O.371/13461, Robertson to F.O., 10 Sept. 1929, p. 98.

[58] F.O.371/13459, Memo, 25 Oct. 1929, 231. F.O. 371/13461, Robertson to F.O. 7 Nov. 1929, p. 4.

to derive considerable benefit from the D'Abernon agreement. Of what possible advantage was it for Argentina?

Argentina's paternity of the mission should be remembered. Yrigoyen is reported to have said, 'I should like to see a British mission every week'.[59] When it duly arrived he assigned Espeche, chief permanent official of the Ministry of the Interior, to assist and promised full co-operation, adding significantly that this was 'a promise I should not make if it came from elsewhere [the U.S.A.]'.[60]

Robertson remembered Yrigoyen saying, 'I do not care at all about the details. I want this to be a great moral gesture towards your country.'[61] Foreign Minister Oyhanarte amplified this attitude:

> We are not much concerned whether the treaty benefits the other party more than ours. We are under a great moral obligation to Great Britain for when this country was nothing more than a geographical expression she gave us the benefit of her science and experience.[62]

At the social level Yrigoyen treated D'Abernon more like a visiting head of state than the leader of a trade mission. This attitude is all the more striking when compared with the dealings of Uruguay and Brazil with the D'Abernon Mission. The Uruguayans demanded that Britain should purchase the entire output of their National Meat Factory in exchange for the placing of orders for manufactures in Britain. The Brazilians wanted British import duties removed from their coffee in exchange for British participation in the development of Brazil's coastal fleet.[63] But neither of these republics had much to lose compared with the importance of the Anglo-Argentine connection to Yrigoyen.

Their comparatively spirited approach to the D'Abernon Mission

[59] F.O.371/13460, Robertson to F.O. 16 May 1929, p. 220.

[60] F.O.371/13460, Robertson to F.O. 16 May 1929, p. 220.

[61] Sir Malcom Robertson, 'The Economic Relations between Great Britain and the Argentine Republic', *Royal Institute of International Affairs Journal*, vol. 9, 1930, p. 228.

[62] In the Argentine congressional debate on the agreement. F.O.371/13462, Millington Drake to F.O. 14 Dec. 1929, p. 204. There is no wholly satisfactory treatment of Yrigoyen and the Radicals. Luis V. Sommi, *Hipólito Yrigoyen, su época y su vida*, Buenos Aires, 1947, deals with his early life. Felix Luna, *Yrigoyen*, Buenos Aires, 1964, is useful but concentrates almost entirely on internal politics. Eduardo F. Guiffra, *Hipólito Yrigoyen en la historia de las instituciones argentinas*, Buenos Aires, 1969, is uncritical; David P. Rock, *Radicalism and the Urban Working Classes in Argentina* (unpublished Ph.D. Cambridge, 1971) is a thorough treatment of Yrigoyen's first administration.

[63] F.O.371/13459, 25 Oct. 1929, p. 233. F.O.371/13459, 16 Oct. 1929, p. 208.

made Argentina appear more supine than ever and this may well help account for Yrigoyen's growing nervousness about the agreement. One cause for anxiety was that it was illegal. Clause 5 gave the Argentine government the option of buying directly from British factories without inviting tenders on the open market. These provisions contravened Argentine Law No. 423 article 22 and Law No. 775, article 3.[64] Apart from the legal issue Yrigoyen's opposition soon realized that the £8m worth of produce to be purchased from Argentina by Britain was not additional to existing trade and that meat exports alone were worth vastly more than that. In a bid to fudge the issue Yrigoyen proposed to alter the convention so that it applied only to cereals, but in the event the Chamber of Deputies approved the agreement on 13 Dec. 1929 by 84:4.[65]

There then seemed to be every ground for optimism and the agreement was hailed as a tremendous success. Robertson reported from Buenos Aires that the D'Abernon Mission, 'has been so stupendous a success that people here are simply flabbergasted . . . the draft convention which in point of fact makes a present of £8m or £9m sterling to our industries with no apparent advantage to Argentina was the culminating act.'[66] Another official view was that 'the agreement will in itself be an achievement of the highest importance. Indeed, if the Argentine example is followed by other countries, or even by our own Dominions, the agreement may well prove epoch-making.'[67]

It was also seen as a personal triumph for Lord D'Abernon. Ramsay MacDonald assured him that 'the mission has opened a new era in our relations, political as well as economic, with the three countries which you visited and I do not doubt that your work will have important effects throughout the South American continent.'[68] D'Abernon's social success in Buenos Aires was attributed in roughly equal proportions to his strong interests in horse racing and his urbane personality, and he was seriously considered for the now vacant post of British ambassador in Buenos Aires.[69]

[64] F.O.371/13461, Robertson to F.O. 12 Sept. 1929, p. 104. F.O.371/13461, Robertson to Henderson, 7 Oct. 1929, p. 258.

[65] F.O.371/14188, Millington Drake to F.O., 24 Dec. 1929, pp. 74-8.

[66] F.O.371/13461, Robertson to Lindsay, 10 Sept. 1929, pp. 202-5.

[67] F.O.371/13459, Memo, 25 Oct. 1929, p. 232.

[68] F.O.371/13461, Macdonald to D'Abernon, 26 Oct. 1929, p. 209. D'Abernon's diary includes a warm appreciation of Ramsay Macdonald, Edgar Vincent, *An Ambassador of Peace*, London, 1929-30, vol. 3, pp. 29-32.

[69] D'Abernon was chairman of the Thoroughbred Horsebreeders Association and a member of the Racecourse Betting Control Board. On the ambassadorship see F.O.371/14188, 8 Jan. 1930, p. 17.

The general excitement over the agreement naturally encouraged demands that Britain should press home the advantage, and this was attempted in two ways. First, the prospects of equivalent agreements with other South American republics were explored. The British legation in Lima reported that President Augusto Leguía would welcome a British mission which might prove even more fruitful than the Argentine one. A mission to Chile was also in prospect and it was once again proposed to raise Santiago from legation to embassy status. From Buenos Aires Eugene Millington Drake appealed for a second mission to be followed up with a royal visit.

The second approach was to press for further concessions and assistance from the Argentine government in Britain's struggle with the United States. The opportunity was seized to enlist Yrigoyen's help in keeping the railways under British ownership. The president assigned Dr Montes de Oca to assist the railway companies resisting a North American takeover and he travelled to England at once for briefing from the company head offices.[70] It occurred to Ambassador Robertson that it would assist the railway companies if the Argentine government prohibited the sale of public utilities without official authorisation, though it cannot be proved that he suggested this move directly to the president.[71] Yrigoyen did announce, however: 'I have authorised the British railways to undertake several extensions. If they fall into other hands I shall withdraw those authorisations.'[72]

Matters even reached a point where the Argentine authorities asked could not the British government act to prevent a North American takeover of the railways in the Republic? It had to be explained that under British company law shares circulated freely on the open market and that the government was unable to alter this state of affairs.[73] In the event the companies at last began to defend themselves. In the summer of 1929 the Buenos Aires and Pacific Railway created a special register of stock owned by or on behalf of foreigners, or foreign corporations, or corporations under effective

---

[70] F.O.371/13460, Robertson to F.O., 10 May 1929, pp. 210-12. Montes de Oca was an Argentine lawyer who specialised in conducting relations between British enterprises and the Argentine authorities, a common type in pre-war Buenos Aires.

[71] F.O. 371/13460, Robertson to F.O., 16 May 1929, p. 226.

[72] F.O.371/13460, Robertson to F.O., 16 May 1929, p. 225.

[73] F.O.371/13460, Robertson to F.O., 16 May 1929, pp. 225-6. The British government had acted in this vein to preserve British control of shipping companies, but in that case there were major strategic interests to protect. The author is indebted to Dr Robert Greenhill for this comparison and for other help and encouragement.

foreign control. Stock transferred to this register relinquished voting rights at general meetings. This procedure was widely acclaimed and the Buenos Aires Western, the Entre Ríos, the Córdoba Central and the Central Argentine Railways soon took similarly effective steps to safeguard British control.[74]

Closely associated with the D'Abernon agreement was the attempt to improve sales of artificial silk in Argentina which were greatly hindered by the fact that under Argentine customs classification artificial silk appeared in the same category as real silk.[75] The British view was that goods made wholly or partly from artificial silk were much closer in purpose and value to fine cotton articles than real silk goods. Roughly speaking, for textiles of equivalent weight an article containing up to 40 per cent artificial silk would pay 5 or 6 times more duty than a similar article made entirely of cotton. There was little doubt that this customs classification accounted for the impressive development of an artificial silk industry in the Republic. At the end of the 1920s there were 54 local factories producing articles made of artificial silk.[76] Yet Yrigoyen seemed willing to reduce import duties to the level of local production costs. The intention was to extend this tariff concession only to Britain in a reciprocal convention in which Britain also made some concession.[77]

There were two main difficulties in this proposal. All existing Argentine exports entered Britain duty free so that on the basis of existing trade it was not obvious what form reciprocity should take. One possibility was that Argentina might develop a trade in fruit to Britain on which tariff concessions could then be granted 'for the sake of appearances which is all that is required'.[78] A second problem was that the declared British policy was to operate on the unconditional m.f.n. clause. But a formula was found to circumvent this principle. Argentina would grant a tariff preference on silk to all countries which placed no restrictions on the importation of Argentine goods. Technically this was not an exclusive preference for

---

[74] F.O.371/13460, Dalton to Wedgewood, 20 June 1929, p. 15. *The Times*, 13 May 1929; ibid., 21 June 1929.

[75] British Chamber of Commerce in the Argentine Republic *Monthly Journal*, vol. 10, November 1929, pp. 22-3. F.O.371/13461, Robertson to F.O. 10 Sept. 1929, p. 98. F.O.371/13461, Memorandum on the Subject of the duty on goods containing artificial silk. 3 Sept. 1929, p. 180.

[76] F.O.371/13461, Robertson to F.O. 25 Sept. 1929, pp. 132-4. F.O.371/14189 Millington Drake to F.O. 3 Jan. 1930, p. 329.

[77] F.O.371/13461, Robertson to F.O., 25 Sept. 1929, p. 134. It was felt that home industry would suffer less from an exclusive preference to Britain than from a general tariff reduction obtainable by all foreign producers.

[78] F.O.371/13461, Robertson to F.O., 25 Sept. 1929, p. 134.

Britain: in practice it was because Britain was the only country with that policy.[79]

Further pressure for the reclassification of artificial silk came from the *Unión Comercial Argentina* which urged that the high duties were proving counter-productive by encouraging extensive contraband.[80] A decree came into operation on 1 January 1930 but it did not cover mixed fabrics of artificial silk with cotton or wool which was a major portion of the trade. Furthermore, for the brief period when the decree was in operation it failed to grant the intended exclusive preference even for wholly artificial silk articles from Britain because the customs officials neglected to read their instructions carefully and extended the concession to imports from the United States.[81] Following this fiasco the British Chamber of Commerce in Buenos Aires took up the issue and foolishly entered a confrontation with the protectionist *Unión Industrial Argentina*.[82] The Buenos Aires press turned the silk duties issue into a *cause célèbre* thereby creating an atmosphere in which it was impossible for Yrigoyen to grant the concession without obtaining something substantial in return.

By something of a paradox Yrigoyen was now in a significantly stronger position for dealing with Britain. He had two agreements in his hands which the British were very anxious to see finalised. And he faced enough opposition within the Republic to convince the British that some substantial concession would have to be made. He felt strong enough, in fact, to approach Baring Brothers for a loan of £5m. This request came at a very awkward moment since Philip Snowden, the British Chancellor of the Exchequer, had recently appealed for a drastic reduction in loans and credits to overseas borrowers. The British Government, however, was most anxious that this particular application should be met and equally anxious that it should be kept secret.[83] Through the agency of Leng Roberts and Co., £5m was raised by Baring Brothers assisted by Morgan Grenfell. The loan was left on deposit at interest in London and credited to the account of the *Caja de Conversión* which had been out of operation since the Republic suspended gold payments in December 1929.[84] Fired with this success Yrigoyen approached Barings for a further £30m. The British Embassy in Buenos Aires urged that this

[79] F.O.371/13461, Memo on Robertson to F.O., 25 Sept. 1929, p. 132.

[80] F.O.371/13561, Robertson to F.O., 22 Oct. 1929, 298.

[81] Phelps, *op. cit.*, 183.

[82] F.O.371/14190, Millington Drake to F.O., 10 Feb. 1930, p. 372.

[83] F.O.371/13462, Wellesley to Hamilton, 8 Nov. 1929, p. 39.

[84] F.O.371/14188, Millington Drake to F.O., 8 Jan. 1930, p. 16.

second application should also be granted since it might assist in reopening the *Caja de Conversión* and restoring the Republic to the gold standard.

It transpired, however, that there were more immediate claims on the Yrigoyen administration than the building up of national reserves. The government owed about £37m to the *Banco de la Nación* and a further £13m was due to various firms working on government contracts.[85] A £30m loan to a country in this economic condition seemed an exceedingly high price to pay for the D'Abernon agreement and the artificial silk preference and there was great hesitation in Britain. The North Americans, by contrast, did not hesitate. At the beginning of April 1930 two U.S. banks, the Phoenix Corporation and Chatham, loaned Yrigoyen 50m dollars for six months renewable on maturity.[86] The fact that the sum was substantially less than the £30m requested from Barings suggests that this overture towards the United States was intended to hurry up the British rather than replace them as lenders, for the North Americans would surely have supplied the full amount if asked. Further, the North American loan did not extinguish President Yrigoyen's determination to give preferential treatment to the British as his handling of the oil question seems to show.

Since 1922 the Shell Group, through their subsidiary La Diadema Argentina S.A., had been exploring concessions in Chubut and Comodoro Rivadavia drilling about 60 wells. Oil was struck in these concessions in 1925 and eventually a refinery was needed which obtained authorisation for construction from the Alvear government on 1st October 1928. A site on South Dock, Buenos Aires was purchased for about £300,000, and £500,000 worth of equipment was delivered to the site. Over the same period the Standard Oil company had been active in north western Argentina developing concessions obtained from the provincial governments of the region, particularly Salta and Jujuy. While out of office Yrigoyen had grown increasingly apprehensive about the growing influence of Standard Oil in the Republic and on regaining the presidency he began to prepare legislation for nationalisation of the oil industry. A side effect of this project was a decree suspending construction of the Shell refinery on South Dock pending the enactment of the new oil legislation. With 15,000 tons of equipment deteriorating on the quayside the Shell Group grew increasingly restive until, at Lord D'Abernon's request, Yrigoyen received Sir William Foote Mitchell and other Shell representatives who learned that the main reason for

[85] F.O.371/14188, Millington Drake to F.O., 3 Jan. 1930, p. 8.
[86] F.O.371/14188, Millington Drake to F.O., 9 April 1930, p. 52.

their discomfiture was that the president could not appear to expedite Shell's operations while engaged in proceedings against Standard Oil.[87] He nevertheless relented ultimately and construction of the Shell refinery was authorised on 24 May 1930 with the explanation that Yrigoyen did not consider these British operations a threat to his national oil policy.[88]

Yrigoyen was finally forced to resign on 7 September 1930 and allegations have lingered on that the Standard Oil Company was in some sense responsible for his deposition.[89] The influence of business on government is not a subject which historical inquiry should avoid. But on an issue of this type it seems unlikely that firm evidence could ever be produced. It was reported that 'American businessmen here are very jubilant at the fall of Yrigoyen and . . . urging instant recognition'[90] of the provisional government of General Uriburu. In his first press interview Uriburu promised close co-operation with the United States, a renewal of Argentine interest in Pan-American activities and that the long-vacant post of Argentine ambassador to Washington would be filled.[91] Asked about the D'Abernon Agreement by 'The Times of Argentina' Uriburu said, 'You may say that it is archived.' 'Dead?' queried our representative. 'Yes', said the President, 'you may call it that.'[92] It looked as if Britain was to be confronted with a less amenable government in Buenos Aires. But then the revision of British economic policy at the beginning of the 1930s changed everything.

British scholars have customarily thought of the D'Abernon agreement in the same context as the general run of commercial missions and trade fairs designed to promote exports by a sheer intensification of competitive effort. A link with the British Trade Exposition in Buenos Aires in 1931 was a particularly obvious one to make in treating the D'Abernon mission as a straightforward exercise in trade promotion. North American scholars have generally been more sceptical and regarded the D'Abernon mission as an attempt to undermine the multilateral system of trading on which the growth of United States' exports to the republic depended. It now appears

---

[87] F.O.371/14191, Memo on desire of the Diadema Company to construct a refinery in Argentina, 24 Feb. 1930, p. 176. Same 19 March 1930, p. 181. F.O.371/14191, Millington Drake to Henderson, 27 May 1930, pp. 209-13.

[88] F.O.371/14191, Macleay to F.O., 12 June 1930, pp. 220-2.

[89] Most notably perhaps by the outstanding publicist, Raúl Scalabrini Ortiz, *Política británica en el Río de la Plata*, Buenos Aires, 1965, pp. 165-9;

[90] F.O.371/14191, Macleay to F.O., 10 Sept. 1930, p. 345.

[91] F.O.371/14191, Macleay to F.O., 10 Sept. 1930, pp. 345-8. *La Nación*, 10 Sept. 1930.

[92] F.O.371/14189, Macleay to F.O.29 Oct. 1930, pp. 320.

clear from newly-available British Foreign Office documents that the North American view is nearer the truth. The D'Abernon agreement was not simple trade promotion but an attempt at trade diversion. It was a precocious instance of a policy which Britain applied elsewhere in the 1930s, notably in trade with Australia. It did not work in Argentina in 1929 and it did not work in Australia in 1936-7.[93] But it did work in Argentina in the 1930s because, whereas the D'Abernon agreement was attempted under the old liberal trading system, the introduction of high tariffs and exchange controls created the conditions under which a substantial diversion of Argentina's import trade away from the U.S. towards the U.K. could be achieved.

[93] Noel F. Hall, 'Trade Diversion — An Australian Interlude', *Economica*, n.s. vol. 5, 1938. He concludes: 'What seems to have lain behind the trade diversion policy was the numb fear in official quarters that if they allowed Japan to rout Lancashire in the sale of textiles to Australia, then they would be subjected by the Government of the United Kingdom to a further substantial contraction of the British market for all types of agricultural produce' (p. 7).

3

Radical Populism and the Conservative Elite, 1912 - 1930

DAVID ROCK

The period between 1890 and 1930 in Argentina is significant for a number of reasons. It coincided with the first expressions of popular nationalism and anti-imperialism. The university problem became a serious political issue, and for the first time there were attempts to bring the urban working class into formal political participation. It also marked the rise to a position of national dominance of one of Argentina's leading political parties, the *Unión Cívica Radical*, or Radicalism. However, one of the central issues of the period revolved round the failure of liberal representative government and its abandonment following the military coup d'etat in 1930. The problem is to what extent was a political system based on popular elections incompatible with the type of society which had emerged in Argentina early in the twentieth century.

To deal with this issue I have chosen to make a general reappraisal of the relationship between the Radical Party and the 'conservative elite', which supported the revolution of 1930. By this term 'conservative elite' I mean the major landowners of the Argentine littoral region, dependent economically on their position as exporters of cereals and beef to the European market, principally to Great Britain. Before 1916 the conservative elite also controlled the State and during this period it was commonly known as the 'Oligarchy'. At the same time the conservative elite also embraced a number of subsidiary pressure groups, the chief of which were the British business groups which controlled the transportation system and much of the organisation of Argentina's overseas trade, and the army. My intention is not to examine the coup of 1930 itself, but to point to some of the main factors which led to conflict and political polarisation. I shall also point to some of the inadequacies of the 1912 representative system in terms of the elite. I have left out most of the details — the structure of power within the elite, and a precise analysis of the way in which motivations for political action emerged.

The complexity of this problem stems from the fact that there was no clear opposition of interest between the Radical Party, which controlled the National Government between 1916 and 1930, and the landed interests, which made up the core of the conservative elite. At one time it was thought simply that Radicalism was the political vehicle for the Argentine middle classes. However, more recently it has been shown that the party's origins are to be traced to a coalition between the middle classes and segments of the land-based elite.[1] Moreover, another study emphasises the close continuities between policies adopted by the Radical governments and the conservative administrations preceding them.[2] This makes the revolution of 1930 rather less than intelligible. Apparently the state of incompatibility between the Radicals and the conservatives in 1930 is not to be found simply in any basic conflict of economic interest between them.

The social and political corollaries of the primary exporting economy

In view of these conclusions it is important to note some of the conditions which encouraged the emergence of Radicalism as a coalition of landed groups and middle class sectors. Argentina's primary export economy meant that there was no openly perceived struggle at this time between the two groups over structural questions of economic development. Both had a certain vested interest in the avoidance of structural change. For their part, the landowners wished to retain their exporting position for the same reasons that had led them in the latter half of the nineteenth century to support Argentina's participation in a British-led 'international division of labour'.

Also the primary export economy was the framework in which a large proportion of both the urban middle and working classes had emerged as social entities. Although there was an important industrial sector in Argentina by 1914, the urban class structure was rooted in the international commercial and service sectors. This reflected a situation where industrial activities had been restricted to

---

[1] Ezequiel Gallo and Silvia Sigal, 'La formación de los partidos políticos contemporáneos: La U.C.R. (1891-1916)', Torcuato S. Di Tella *et al.* (eds.), *Argentina, sociedad de masas*, Buenos Aires, 1965, pp. 124-76.

[2] Peter H. Smith, 'Los radicales argentinos y la defensa de los intereses ganaderos, 1916-1930', *Desarrollo económico*, vol. 7, no. 25, April-June, 1967, pp. 795-829.

a narrow framework established by the leader primary sector.[3] Thus the urban middle class had evolved lacking the normal traits of the urban bourgeoisie in the industrial West: a commitment to the overthrow of agrarianism for the sake of its own class interests. On the contrary it appeared as a social appendix to the agrarian system, and a reflection of its development in an advanced capitalist form.

Reinforcing this was the position of the urban sectors as consumers. While a reliance on a large quantity of imported manufactured goods had its drawbacks during periods of depression, industrial dependence, which the primary export economy implied, generally provided a painless flow of low cost industrial goods. During periods of economic expansion, by raising domestic levels of consumption, this apparently assisted the expansion of mobility avenues through which the middle classes emerged. Once this process had begun and an advanced urban social system had appeared, industrial development on an ambitious scale became correspondingly more unattractive. The Argentine urban sectors always showed themselves extremely hesitant in supporting a programme of industrialisation. When the country's industrial sector began to expand significantly in the 1930s, it was prompted not by the middle classes but by the landed elite, which, as a means to correct recurrent deficits in the balance of payments during the Great Depression, began to advocate a programme of import substitution.[4]

Until 1930, however, there was a broad state of consensus between the landed interests and the middle classes over the need to uphold the basic framework of the primary exporting economy. This led to considerable popular support for such caveats of traditional policy as free trade. This was the consensus which Radicalism reflected. Not surprisingly the party supported leader interests such as the beef producers, but also rejected any real commitment to industrialisation.

On the other hand, the stability of this system was undermined by the inherent tendency of the primary export economy to concentrate economic power and opportunities narrowly in the hands of the landed groups and foreign capital. Although the true nature of the situation was rarely recognised, the uneven distribution of

---

[3]   For a further development of this theme see Ezequiel Gallo, 'Agrarian Expansion and Industrial Development in Argentina', Raymond Carr (ed.), *Latin American Affairs: St. Antony's Papers* no. 22, Oxford, 1970, pp. 45-61. Also Eduardo F. Jorge, *Industria y concentración económica*, Siglo XXI, Buenos Aires, 1971.

[4]   Miguel Murmis and Juan Carlos Portantiero, 'Crecimiento industrial y alianza de clases', *Estudios sobre los origines del peronismo*, Siglo XXI, Buenos Aires, 1971.

control over the means of production led to the appearance of structural unemployment among the urban sectors. So far as the workers went, who at this time were mostly European immigrants, this was evident in the presence of a large indigent floating population, and in the heavy re-migration rate among the immigrants up to 1914. It was also the source of the so-called *golondrina* system of labour recruitment for the land, the practice of contracting labour annually in Mediterranean Europe. For the middle classes, it was the cause of a peculiar form of disguised unemployment, which led to a heavy concentration of occupations in the bureaucracy and in professional activities. As the following table shows, in the city of Buenos Aires in 1914, this 'dependent' middle class, composed of rentiers, bureaucrats and professional men, was numerically almost as large as the entrepreneurial and white-collar groups.

Table 3.1 Occupational structure in the city of Buenos Aires (natives and foreigners, 1914)[5]

Total male employed population 626,861

Middle classes and above		% of total employed
Rentier, bureaucratic and professional groups	97,345	15
Entrepreneurs and proprietors	53,438	8
Salaried employees in the private sector	52,443	8
Working class		
Skilled labour and artisans	202,768	32
Unskilled labour	206,028	33

(Source: *Tercer Censo Nacional*, 1914).

There is also some evidence of an association between such dependent roles and status within the middle class. Generally, the immigrants made up the working class. Within the middle class the immigrants were the entrepreneurs, while the creoles and the native-born sons-of-immigrants represented an overwhelming proportion of the dependent groups. Studies of mobility patterns suggest that upward mobility was directed not towards ownership and entrepreneurial roles but towards the professions and the bureaucracy. This

---

[5] For a full account of the compilation methods for these figures see D.P. Rock, 'Radicalism and the Urban Working Classes in Argentina, 1916-1922', Unpublished Ph.D. dissertation, Cambridge University, 1971.

reflected the dominance of small units of production outside the fields controlled by foreign capital. For example, the average number of workers per firm in Buenos Aires at this time was no more than eight. By the same token positions of political leadership within the middle class were also controlled by the dependent group.[6] How-ever, although dependent roles held the promise of greater wealth and higher status, they were also subject to greater insecurities. Large sections of the urban middle class were in a weak and exposed economic position. This led in turn to the politicisation of these groups. Another feature of the dependent middle class was its close relationship of dependence upon the State. The State controlled directly access to the bureaucracy, and its supervisory role over the universities meant that it also had discretional control over access to the professions. In effect the State controlled the social mobility process.

It was this which underlay expressions of friction between the landed elite and the middle-class groups before 1916. Since the landed interests controlled the State, they became a target for the frustrations of the middle-class groups seeking upward mobility and positions of relative stability. This was the background to the political changes which occurred in 1912, when a system of represen-tative government was introduced. However, the important thing about this was that because of the parallel position of leader groups among the middle classes as consumers and occupants of dependent roles, the political struggle developed quite separately from any latent economic conflicts. Rather it revolved around the issues of distribution: access to high status positions and to the opportunities which stemmed from control over the state apparatus. The primary object of the urban middle classes was to increase the rate of public spending and thus to expand the supply of dependent roles.

The advent of representative government in 1912

During its early period the Radical Party, which was founded in 1891, attempted to manipulate the frustrations of the urban groups. For much of its first twenty-five years of existence the party was little more than an aristocratic faction, composed of disenchanted aspirant politicians of landed origins, seeking a means to win power through the creation of a popular coalition. In the early 1890s conditions appeared to be propitious for this, since the economic

[6] Oscar E. Cornblit, 'Inmigrantes y empresarios en la política argentina', *Desarrollo económico*, vol. 6, no. 24, 1967; Gustavo Beyhaut *et al.*, 'Los immigrantes en el sistema ocupacional argentina', in Di Tella *et al.* (eds.), *op. cit.*, pp. 85-123.

collapse of 1890 created widespread unrest among the urban sectors. The Oligarchy survived this first challenge by dividing the leadership of the opposition groups through a more strategically efficient distribution of government offices. Nor was there at this time any sustained political mobilisation among the urban groups. Between 1891 and 1900, the Radical Party, first under the leadership of Leandro N. Alem, and then of Hipólito Yrigoyen, thus oscillated between periods of activity and periods of decline, depending upon the unity and stability of the Oligarchy.[7]

This picture changed at the turn of the century with the emergence of further political unrest. This came from two main sources, from the immigrant working class in Buenos Aires and from the dependent middle-class groups. Whereas before 1900 the urban sectors had only manifested themselves politically during periods of depression, afterwards they became politicised on a permanent basis. This process may be traced directly to the manner in which the primary exporting economy discriminated against urban society. Among the workers between 1900 and 1910 a militant Anarchist movement led a series of revolutionary strikes against different governments. Although these were put down by force without much difficulty, the Oligarchy began to contemplate seriously the possibility of an immigrant rebellion.[8] One of the effects of this was that it encouraged the search for political changes which would wean the working class away from supporting a revolutionary movement.

Among the middle-class groups there were similar expressions of political frustrations, which, as in 1890, the Radicals attempted to take advantage of. In the universities there was unrest among the middle-class groups of immigrant origin against the control of the creole elite groups.[9] This was to persist for almost twenty years until the first Radical government introduced the famous university reform of 1918. There were also hints of similar conflicts in the army, which Yrigoyen attempted to exploit when he organised an abortive revolt in 1905.[10] Finally after 1905 the Radicals began to

---

[7] Cf. David Rock, 'The Rise of the Argentine Radical Party, 1891-1916', *Working Papers No. 7*, Cambridge University Centre of Latin American Studies, 1973.

[8] Carl Solberg, *Immigration and Nationalism in Argentina and Chile, 1890-1914*. Latin American Monographs No. 18, Institute of Latin American Studies, University of Texas, 1970.

[9] Tulio Halperín Donghi, *Historia de la universidad de Buenos Aires*, Buenos Aires, 1962, pp. 110-20.

[10] For accounts of the 1905 revolution see Ricardo Caballero, *Yrigoyen, la conspiración civil y militar del 4 de febrero de 1905*, Buenos Aires, 1951.

make substantial progress in the recruitment of popular support among the middle classes. In 1909 the party's local committees were established on permanent basis in many parts of the Littoral region.

In this way Radicalism had come to reflect both the factors working in favour of a coalition between the landed and middle-class groups, and those which worked in the opposite direction and which had led to increasing political instability. What the leaders of the Radical Party wanted was a form of limited institutional change which would maintain the political power of the landed groups, while providing wider opportunities to the middle classes without which there was no chance of organising a popular political party. This meant not so much a change in the economic structure but wider access to the middle-class groups to professional and bureau-cratic positions. This was apparent in the Radicals' ideology, which called simultaneously for a change in the 'system', but attacked the Oligarchy because of its failure to expand the primary export economy rapidly enough. The same anomaly was also enshrined in the party's organisation and structure, which, in spite of its pro-visions for the free election of office-holders, maintained up to 1916 the dominance of the patrician groups by a system of cooptation. In this sense the alliance with the middle-class groups was merely a means of circulating control over the State within the traditional elite groups.

The reaction of the Oligarchy to this was to seek to eliminate the possibility of successful rebellion by means of strategic political concessions. As the threat of rebellion increased, a group emerged within the Oligarchy committed to political reform. This was led by Roque Sáenz Peña, who in 1910 became President of the Republic. His view was that continual political instability was becoming a serious barrier to the country's economic expansion, and a threat to the economic interests of the conservative elite:

> If our self-aggrandisement has begun, it is because we hâve been able to demonstrate the overriding power of the National Government, inspiring a sense of security, peace, and confidence. I shall not support oppression, but I condemn the revolutions . . . I do not believe we can consolidate our present position, except by a process of perfecting ourselves in a climate of order.[11]

Out of this came the reforms of 1912 known as the Sáenz Peña Law, which introduced the secret ballot and gave the vote to all

[11] Roque Sáenz Peña, *Discursos del Dr. Roque Sáenz Peña al asumir la presidencia de la Nación*, Buenos Aires, 1910, p. 40.

native-born males. This meant in effect the enfranchisement of the dependent middle-class groups as well as that of an increasingly important number of workers in the city of Buenos Aires. The prime objectives of the reform were referred to by speakers in Congress. So far as the workers went, it was necessary, as one leading conservative in the National Senate confessed,

> ... to open up an escape valve and allow two or three socialists into Congress, especially at this time of working-class unrest when legislation on strikes and working regulations is about to be discussed.[12]

Referring to Radicalism one of Sáenz Peña's supporters declared:

> For twenty years there has existed in the country an organised popular, dynamic party, which has had as its banner the liberty of the suffrage and which has openly supported revolution as the only way to fulfil its ideals ... For a generation both government and nation have lived in a constant state of having either to suppress rebellion or in fear that rebellion is about to break out ... A change in the electoral system is not only a change in policy, it is to adopt at this critical hour the only policy which the country is united upon: the policy of disarmament, to eliminate abstention from the elections and rebellion; to incorporate each active political force into the electoral process.[13]

Finally came a growing recognition of the limited scope of the Radicals' objectives and a perception of their usefulness to undermine the appeal of the genuine revolutionary groups:

> Why is it that the conservatives are bent upon preventing the Radicals from taking over the administration? They represent the same interests and principles as we do. We should let the People have its way, because if not we run the risk of attracting it to the really advanced parties.[14]

Yrigoyen and the Radical Party: objectives and strategies, 1916-1930

As a result of the Sáenz Peña Law, Hipólito Yrigoyen was elected to the presidency in 1916. However, the introduction of the suffrage

---

[12] *Diario de sesiones*, Senadores, 1911, vol. 2, p. 338 (Benito Villenueva).

[13] *ibid.* Cámera de Diputados, 1911, vol. 2, p. 160 (Ramón J. Cárcano).

[14] Quoted in Jorge A. Mitre, 'Presidencia de Victorino de la Plaza', Academia Nacional de la Historia, *Historia argentina contemporánea, 1862-1930*, vol. 1, section 2, Buenos Aires, 1965, p. 241.

did not imply any decisive break with the past. Yrigoyen had won his position as much by courtesy of the conservative elite as by his own efforts. He had received a conditional mandate to rule circumscribed by two central objectives: the preservation of the elite's economic position and the elimination of popular unrest which had led to previous political instability. He was thus to placate the middle class and the working class, but at the same time to perpetuate the economic system which underlay their expressions of discontent.

What led to the initial friction between Radicalism and the conservative elite was not these objectives in themselves, since the Radicals shared them. There were two major elements in their conception of popular democracy. The first was liberal in inspiration, reflecting the common attitude of the landowners and the middle classes on the economic front. It attacked the Oligarchy because it had set authoritarian barriers against what the Radicals defined as 'distributive justice'. The second was more pluralist in tone. It reflected the problems of mass party organisation in a heterogeneous social environment. It saw the community as a quasi-biological entity. Thus 'democracy' became a means to establish a national commonwealth of class harmony and reconciliation. These conceptions only differed in detail and style from those which the elite had adopted. Whereas the elite conceived a multi-party system emerging after the Sáenz Peña Law, Radicalism aimed for maximum active popular support for the single party. The following party propaganda claims appeared with great frequency and they signalled the new populist atmosphere which developed in Argentina after 1916:

> The U.C.R. is not hostile to any legitimate interest, and on the contrary there is room in its ranks for all those who wish to put themselves sincerely at the service of their country.[15]

> In assiduous and direct contact with the People, and with the progressive activities of the Nation, President Yrigoyen, the true democrat, has managed to win something which the presidents of class (the Oligarchy) were never able to win — the love and confidence of the citizenry.[16]

Much of this contact with the 'People' took the form of an interchange of individualised favours between the government and the electorate, or what might be called direct incentive participation. In return for the vote in municipal, congressional and presidential

[15] Party manifesto, 30 March, 1916. Quoted in Roberto Etchepareborda, *Hipólito Yrigoyen: pueblo y gobierno*, Buenos Aires, 1951, vol. 1 'Abstención', p. 405.

[16] *La Epoca*, 11 January, 1920.

elections the party, organised on a geographical basis in local committees, provided government patronage usually in the form of positions in the administration, or local charity activities. On many occasions and in many areas the party would provide cheap food-stuffs and systems of free medical and legal advice. One of the leading features of Radicalism until 1930 was the manner in which it expanded the range of such methods of politicisation to cover wide sections of the electorate. This was exploited to win mass popular support. For example, in the annual internal party elections in the city of Buenos Aires in the mid-1920s, it was not unusual to achieve a turnout of 40,000. This illustrates the importance of the party's middle level leadership in the committees.[17]

This was buttressed by Yrigoyen's plebiscitarian and charismatic notions of his role as president and party leader. Although the appeal to charismatic authority was generally employed as a smokescreen to preserve a facade of party unity during periods of extreme political crisis, Yrigoyen often projected himself as a kind of apostle-harbinger of democracy and the symbol of national reconciliation. 'There are', he roundly announced on one occasion, 'lives through which shine all the qualities and conditions of an epoch, and such is my own.'[18] This blend of illuminism and caesarism was largely again a reflection of the party's extreme heterogeneity in regional and interest group terms, as it developed after 1916. In the absence of any developed common interest among its members, the appeal to charismatic authority became a necessary component of party unity.

Conflict between Yrigoyen and the conservative elite stemmed initially from the government's attempts to consolidate its authority among the middle and working classes and thus to establish overall political supremacy free from the constraints of the opposition groups. In practical terms this added up to an attempt to trim the privileges of the landed groups to the benefit of the urban sectors. The conflicts began when these trespassed on the elite's economic interests. At first between 1916 and 1918 Yrigoyen attempted to steer a number of moderate reforms through Congress, designed to benefit the Radicals' popular supporters in the Littoral region. Among them were proposals for an agricultural bank to help colonisation schemes, a temporary tax on agricultural exports for the relief of wartime unemployment, and later an income tax.[19] But few of these

[17] David Rock, 'Machine Politics in Buenos Aires and the Argentine Radical Party, 1912-1930', *Journal of Latin American Studies*, vol. 4, no. 2, pp. 233-256, November, 1972.
[18] Message to Congress. Quoted in *La Epoca* 24 October, 1921.
[19] For a full account of the Government's legislative proposals see Roberto Etchepareborda, *Yrigoyen y el congreso*, Buenos Aires, 1956.

proposals passed through Congress successfully. The conservative majority in the Senate, where members enjoyed a nine year term, proved unassailable.

This led to a prolonged struggle for control over Congress. Here the big obstacle was the provinces in the Interior, where the local legislatures elected representatives to the National Senate. As a means to win control over the interior provinces, the government became increasingly dependent upon a procedure known as Federal Intervention, a takeover of the provincial administration by the National Government. This was intended to be used only in very specific cases, though Yrigoyen employed it frequently as a means to establish Radical Party control. In the backward interior provinces control over the provincial executive often meant undisputed political dominance. The provincial governor controlled the sources of patronage which could be used to buy the support of key groups. Once each governor had established this position, and was prepared to supervise the system effectively, he was virtually immoveable except by federal intervention.

Yrigoyen's weakness in the Interior and his reliance on Federal Interventions to win seats in the National Senate for his supporters reflected the fact that his main axis of support lay in the province of Buenos Aires and the federal capital. This meant that it embraced both agrarian and urban groups. The problem emerged when the interests of the two diverged. An example of this came in 1920 during the post-war boom. Heavy demand for Argentina's main agricultural exports in Europe had a severe inflationary effect on local prices. The price of wheat, for example, doubled in 1920. While this favoured the producers and the exporting interests, it had an adverse effect on the urban consumers, for whom the cost of living increased rapidly. The pressure mounted on the government to take steps to bring down prices. However, instead of attempting to deal seriously with the principal consumer staples, wheat and beef, the government turned to the sugar producers in the north-west and proposed the expropriation of a large proportion of the sugar available. This was a scapegoat measure, since the consumption of sugar was unimportant in terms of the cost of living. Its advantage was that it gave the impression to the urban consumers that the government was doing something to cope with inflation without affecting the producer interests in the province of Buenos Aires.

The exploitation of the Interior in this fashion led to accusations that the Interior was being reduced to a tributary economic status. There were pointed criticisms of the manner in which the new political system undermined the delicate interregional balance which had emerged under the Oligarchy. Referring to what he described as the government's general discrimination against the Interior, a spokesman in the National Senate asked:

> Can it be because the interests of the Littoral add up to larger numbers than those of the Interior? . . . Thus we see the parties and the Government in constant competition with one another to satisfy the appetites of the electoral masses.[20]

This was the nub of the problem: the government tended to frame its actions to conform with the structure of the electorate.

By the early 1920s the regional question had become an important issue. Measures like the sugar expropriation proposals of 1920 and Yrigoyen's exploitation of the client regimes he had created in the interior by Federal Interventions led to the formation of several anti-*yrigoyenista* local populist movements. The chief of these was *bloquismo* in the province of San Juan. This owed its origins to the systematic manner in which the National Government had discriminated against provincial interests. It was said later that the groups in the Littoral were monopolising credit from the National Mortgage Bank, that the National Government had failed to develop local hydro-electricity and oil resources and to provide funds for local developmental investment.[21]

Government, the workers and the elite, 1916-1922

Nevertheless it was not these expressions of regional rivalries which led to the most serious expressions of tension between the government and the conservative elite during Yrigoyen's first period of office up to 1922. It was not until the late 1920s that the Interior organised a united political movement which had a sustained impact at the centre. A far more important issue, until 1922 at least, was the working class problem. This impinged directly on the elite's economic position, since it threatened its relations with foreign capital.

From the beginning in 1916 the Radicals were vitally concerned to win political support among the urban working class in Buenos Aires. This stemmed in part from their commitment to 'class harmony', but also from their need to outflank the Socialist Party. However, this objective had certain inherent difficulties. It was difficult to adapt the party machine and its essentially individualistic technique of political recruitment to a situation where strong specialised interest groups associations intervened. The working class was more likely to give its allegiance to the unions, which as class-based organisations,

[20] *Diario de sesiones*, Senadores, vol. 1, 1920, pp. 789-90 (Carlos Zabala).
[21] See the Cantoni debates. Senadores, vol. 1, 1929, pp. 138-337.

were more geared to securing class benefits, than to a party machine which operated on the basis of charity and state patronage. The Radicals' attempt to overcome this problem was to expose not only the real power structure to which the primary export economy had given rise but also the incapacity of the primary exporting economy, given its close dependence on foreign capital, to provide a scheme to overcome extremes of economic inequality.

In their approach to the labour problem the Radicals were not impelled by any sympathy or recognition for the workers as a class:

> Nor do we accept class differences, or that there are any classes in the Argéntine Republic . . . We do not fail to see that there are conflicts between Capital and Labour, but we do not accept that there is a proletarian or a capitalist class, even if 95% of the Argentines were to fall into what in Europe is called the proletariat. Nor is it right to bring into our new America, where new ideals of human solidarity are being formed, such sentiments of hate on account of differences of race, religion or class.[22]

During the First World War and up till the end of the post-war boom in 1921 there was a period of acute inflation. This reflected first the interruption of imports during the War, and then after 1917 rising European demand for Argentina's exports. The result was a marked decline in real wages and a great expansion in the trade union movement. This was accompanied by a sudden efflorescence of strikes. The most important of these affected the core areas of the country's economic system: the port, the railways and the meat-packing plants.[23]

The government, impelled by its need to support its electoral majority in the city of Buenos Aires, began to intervene in the strikes. Its aim was to help the strikers just enough to win for itself a reputation of favour towards working class interests and to establish a working relationship with the unions which would prevent them moving over towards the Socialist Party. The Radicals presented this as democracy in action. Instead of the working class having to be repressed, as had happened under the Oligarchy, it was being 'civilised' through its contact with the formal political system:

> Only when President Yrigoyen took over the Government were the directions of a forward-looking, modern administration charted. Excessive capitalist privileges disappeared . . . Organis-

[22] Cámara de Diputados, vol. 5, 1918-19, p. 293 (Francisco Beiró).
[23] A full account of the strikes appears in D.P. Rock, 'Radicalism and the Urban Working Classes', *op. cit.*

ations among the working classes ceased to be dark and menacing hives of anti-social outcasts . . . They were converted into a living part of Argentine society, worthy of being listened to and attended to.[24]

Conflict appeared when this policy was opposed by foreign capital. Lockouts and blackleg unions were organised and every attempt was made to involve the landed interests in the strikes. By May, 1918 an employers' federation had appeared which was supported by the major cattle and agricultural associations. This quickly grew into an organised political campaign against the government, which the supporters of foreign capital manipulated to their advantage by reviving the old spectre of working class revolution. This culminated in the famous *Semana Trágica* of January, 1919. Following an abortive general strike, para-military groups, composed of members of the conservative elite, including the Army and members of the middle class, organised a bloody roundup of alleged communist sympathisers.[25] This brought the Radical Government very close to a coup d'etat. It made evident how little in reality the power structure had changed since 1912. Soon afterwards the conservative elite formalised the alliance which emerged during the general strike through the creation of the Argentine Patriotic League, (*Liga Patriótica Argentina*). During the next two years, until the strikes finally subsided and the unions declined during the post-war depression after 1921, the League became the country's most powerful political association. It forced Yrigoyen to abandon his hopes of winning working class support by intervening in the strikes and instead on several occasions forced the government into taking repressive measures.

This pattern continued until 1930. The working class and the unions continued in a state of complete subordination until, with the rise of Peronism in the 1940s, a further attempt was made to revive Yrigoyen's objectives. The success won by the conservative elite before 1922 thus made it apparent that 'democracy', in the form of institutionalised conflict and changes in the distribution of income, was a myth in Argentina during this period. It was impeded by the power structure to which a narrowly based agrarian structure had given rise, and by the dependence of local power groups, including the middle classes, upon the services provided by foreign capital. This meant that, unlike during the later *peronista* period, the workers had

[24] *La Epoca*, 27 June, 1918.
[25] For an account of the *semana trágica* from a sociological perspective see David Rock, 'Lucha civil en la Argentina Semana Trágica de enero de 1919', *Desarrollo económico*, 11, 42, 4, July, 1971, 165-215.

no support from within the bourgeoisie. Before 1922 the strikes led to a state of simple class polarisation. Attempts to support the workers by the government thus resulted in its complete political isolation.

The urban middle-class groups

The structure of the urban middle class, the lack of an influential and independent industrial bourgeoisie, and the association of social mobility and status with the bureaucracy and the professions, meant that its relations with the landed elite were dominated by the issue of state spending. At first Yrigoyen attempted to control this demand by supporting change through legislation. However, by 1919 the failure of legislation, plus the paralysing loss of middle-class support during the strikes, forced the government into a much greater reliance on patronage systems of control. From this time forward the 'machine' character of party control intensified. The number of Federal interventions increased and there was a succession of purges in the national administration to make room for party supporters. This was accompanied by a marked increase in public spending. Between 1916 and 1922 this rose from 375 million paper pesos to 614 million. Two thirds of the rise occurred after 1919 as the government grew to depend more on its patronage system. The increase in public spending was accompanied by a rise in the annual budget deficit and this led to the creation of a vast floating debt. Between 1913 and 1922 the floating debt rose from less than 100 million paper pesos to over 800 million.[26]

During the period of boom between 1917 and 1920 increased state spending raised no difficulties for the landed interests. The government was compelled to finance its deficits through short-term treasury bills with high interest rates which were drawn mainly on local banks. Between 1916 and 1919 the value of such treasury bills in circulation rose from 99 million paper pesos to a little under 300 million.[27] This favoured at least some of the landed sectors because they were one of the few sources of credit. This would suggest that lending to the government became a profitable business during the War and immediate post-war years. It also points to one of the great anomalies of the Radical Government. In rewarding its middle-class supporters with sinecure positions in the bureaucracy, it penalised the rest of the urban sectors, since the tax system was based on

[26] Figures from E. Tornquist and Co. Ltd., *Business Conditions in Argentina*, Buenos Aires, quarterly, 1915-22.
[27] *ibid.*

tariffs on imported goods. At the same time it favoured business capital.

The difficulties emerged during depression periods such as between 1921 and 1924 and, more acutely, in 1930. Here a clear division of interest emerged between the landed sectors and the urban middle-class groups. Under depression conditions demand for credit among the landed interests increased, but their access to it was impeded by the government and the effect its burrowing had on interest rates. The problem was compounded by the fact that during depression periods the rate of government spending tended to rise. This reflected the increase in the demand for patronage jobs during a period of growing unemployment. As a Radical Party worker commented in 1922:

> There has developed among our fellow party members a contagious desire to acquire positions in the administration. The cost of living, the restriction of credit, the paralysation of certain industries and the decline in employment opportunities in others — the general crisis in a word — have left a large number of people either without work or with very poorly paid work.[28]

Another serious problem which came from high government spending during depression periods was the effect it had on the balance of payments and the government's debt services overseas. By maintaining the level of demand, government spending encouraged imports at a time when exports were declining. Since too between 1914 and 1927, and again in 1930, the Argentine peso was allowed to float on the international exchange, the deficit in the balance of payments led to the depreciation of the peso. Between 1921 and 1924 the value of the peso fluctuated between 20 per cent and 40 per cent below par in terms of the U.S. dollar. Since also the government had come to rely on the New York banks during this period for a substantial proportion of its overseas loans, the cost of servicing the debt increased by the proportion which the peso depreciated in value. However, in 1921 and 1922 this did not prevent the government from continuing to increase its spending in readiness for the presidential elections of 1922.[29]

By 1922, when Yrigoyen left power, the landed interests had

---

[28] Unión Cívica Radical, Circunscripción 11, *Rendición de cuentas*, Buenos Aires, 1922, pp. 9-10.

[29] Cf. Vernon L. Phelps, *The International Economic Position of Argentina*, University of Pennsylvania, Philadelphia, 1937; Harold E. Peters, *The Foreign Debt of the Argentina Republic*, Johns Hopkins Press, Baltimore, 1934.

become the opponents of increased state spending. They wanted more credit for themselves at cheaper rates and they were also concerned that the government might be running towards a cessation of payments on its international debts.[30] This problem eventually led to the collapse of Radicalism as a coalition between the landed groups and the urban middle classes. It was also a vital factor impinging upon the coup d'etat of 1930.

In 1922 Yrigoyen selected as his successor Marcelo T. de Alvear, who had no personal following in the party and who it was thought could be expected to rely on that of the former President. However, Alvear proved, at least until the end of the depression in 1925, less committed to the middle-class groups, who made up the party's rank and file, than he was to the relief of the landed groups by easing the pressure on credit. His attempts to control government spending led quickly to the collapse of Yrigoyen's patronage system. This exposed the delicate fragility of party unity and by 1923 the party was completely divided. Finally in 1924 there was an attempt to usurp Yrigoyen's control over the party by a dissident group led by the Minister of the Interior, Vicente C. Gallo. This resulted in the party split of 1924. The bulk of the middle class groups continued to follow Yrigoyen and became known as the *yrigoyenistas*. The party's old elite wing organised a new party known as the *Unión Cívica Radical Antipersonalista*, thus called as a sign of its opposition to the 'personalist' or patronage methods of control embodied by Yrigoyen. In fact this claim was inaccurate since Gallo made every effort to employ patronage techniques to win control over the party. He failed because of Alvear's resistance to rechannelling the flow of public spending once more in the direction of the middle class groups.

This meant the failure of Antipersonalism. The only popular following the party acquired was in the provinces of Entre Rios and Santa Fe, where there was a tradition of hostility towards Yrigoyen because of his close links with the province of Buenos Aires. In Buenos Aires, however, the party split ran broadly along class lines. Whereas in the past, the landed groups had retained overall control over the party, now the rump which remained supporting Yrigoyen moved into a subordinate position. *Yrigoyenismo* thus became in the mid-1920s the party of the dependent middle-class groups, which had benefited most between 1919 and 1922 from the rapid increase in government spending.

This may be illustrated by comparing the origins of Radical and *yrigoyenista* members of the National Congress in 1916 and 1928. In 1916 almost all the Radical members of Congress were recruited

[30] Cámara de Diputados, *op. cit.* vol. 1, 1923, passim.

from among the traditional elite groups.[31] By contrast in 1928 a large proportion were of middle-class background and of immigrant family origins.[32] But the great symbol of the change which occurred in the mid-1920s was the strong commitment developed by the *yrigoyenistas* between 1926 and 1928 to the nationalisation of oil. This new positive programme contrasted strongly with the situation ten years earlier when the Radicals had done little more than reiterate vague platitudes over the need to restore 'the Constitution' and 'Democracy'. Ideological amorphousness was a reflection of the party's structure as a coalition movement. As soon as this coalition identity declined, the party's programme became clearer and more explicitly geared to middle-class interests.

The nationalisation of oil became a middle-class cause primarily because it offered a means to justify increases in state spending without the tremendous waste which had occurred before 1922. But its significance was that it represented the first step taken by the middle class groups in support of domestic industrialisation. State control over the power system was seen as a means to siphon internal growth into new fields and thus supersede the country's narrow dependence on the primary exporting economy. In this fashion the urban middle-class groups began to acquire some of the traits of an industrialising bourgeoisie. If in part their advocacy of nationalisation reflected the need of the new oil technology for the concentration of investment resources, it also reflected their own background of dependence on the State. They framed their objectives not in the traditional conventional form of support for *laissez-faire* and individual enterprise, but in the form of support for state intervention. Finally the oil nationalisation programme had a number of political advantages. Although the foreign oil companies were already actively campaigning to be allowed to expand their explorations and their production, this was the only major field where foreign capital had not yet won for itself a dominant vested interest. It thus promised to avoid the situation which had occurred before 1922 with, for example, the railway companies. Here attempts by the Radical Government to increase state control had led eventually to the events of 1919. The difference between the railway companies and the oil companies before 1930 was that the former had shown themselves capable of mobilising in their support core groups among the conservative elite. The allies of the oil companies had were much

---

[31] Darío Cantón, *El parlamento argentino en épocas de cambio: 1890, 1916 y 1946.* Instituto Torcuato Di Tella, Buenos Aires, 1966, pp. 37-66.
[32] Rock, 'Machine politics . . .' *op. cit.* p. 248.

less powerful than this.[33] Thus the *yrigoyenistas* could support nationalisation and promote the interests of the urban sectors while minimising the risk of a political reaction from the conservative elite.

The end of representative government

Between 1925 and 1928 *yrigoyenismo* became by far the most popular political party in the country. It weathered the party split and vastly expanded the range of its support. In 1928 Yrigoyen won an overwhelming victory in the presidential elections. The primary aim of the new government was to secure the nationalisation of oil. Its plan of action was to conserve its popular support by reintroducing the patronage system which had been used before 1922. In 1928 conditions were relatively propitious for this as the country was in the middle of an economic boom. There was thus no immediate pressure on state finances. Secondly the new government aimed to protect its position among the various pressure groups which had emerged through the Patriotic League in 1919. It gave strong support for British capital and made a determined effort to weed our Yrigoyen's oppenents in the Army.[34] The labour policies which had been the major source of difficulty during Yrigoyen's first government were now abandoned.

The main problem with the oil legislation stemmed from the opposition to it in the Interior. Since each of the Interior provinces had two representatives in the National Senate, the opposition groups still enjoyed control over the Congress. The struggle for control over the Senate led to a serious political crisis in 1929. This culminated in the prolonged dispute between the *yrigoyenistas* and the supporters of Federico Cantoni, who was Senator-elect for the province of San Juan. Behind this was the old regional problem which had emerged during Yrigoyen's first presidency. However, towards the end of 1929 there were signs that the *yrigoyenistas* were winning. They achieved their objective of excluding Cantoni and his

[33] It has been said that Standard Oil played an important part in the coup d'etat in 1930. However, the political influence of the American oil companies was more marked among the groups in the Interior than it was among the more powerful landowner interests in the Littoral. The Interior provinces opposed nationalisation on the grounds that it meant the expropriation of their resources by the middle class groups in Buenos Aires. Although they formed part of the alliance supporting the coup, they were not its leaders. This suggests a more subsidiary role for Standard Oil than has generally been acknowledged.

[34] Robert A. Potash, *The Army and Politics in Argentina 1928-1945*, Stanford University Press, 1969, pp. 29-54.

supporters from the Senate on the grounds that they had employed fraudulent methods to secure their election. Also Congress proved itself quite unable to stem the new spate of Federal Interventions which Yrigoyen used to remove the opposition parties from their control over the provinces. It was similarly unable to control government spending and prevent it being used to conserve Yrigoyen's popular support. The pressure groups had been successfully neutralised. The British were kept happy with the provisions of the D'Abernon Mission.[35] The dissidents in the Army remained isolated. By the end of 1929 it seemed possible that a successful start could be made with the oil legislation in 1930 and 1931.

At this point the Great Depression began to make its effects felt in Argentina. Within a short time Yrigoyen's political strategy had collapsed completely and the government was engaged in an effort for survival. Opposition to the government from the conservative elite stemmed directly from the question of public spending. By 1930 the floating debt had reached over 1200 million paper pesos, and discounted treasury bills held by local banks amounted to over one third of total credit outstanding. This was the same situation as during the post-war depression, except that its effects this time were more marked. At the beginning of 1930 pressure on credit resources increased following a disastrous harvest and the parallel collapse of agricultural prices and exports.

In an effort to release local funds the government attempted to contract new external loans, but with the depreciation of the peso in 1930, this simply led to further increases in its total overseas debts. Finally to avoid defaulting on its overseas debt services, the government was compelled early in 1930 to reduce the rate of state spending. Administrative positions were left vacant and personnel were left unpaid. The result of this was the complete collapse of the links between the government and the electorate through the party machine. As unemployment and bankruptcies mounted, there a sudden expansion of support for the opposition parties. Party morale declined and it became evident in the elections of March 1930 that the middle-class groups, which had given Yrigoyen such strong support between 1926 and 1929, had now moved over towards the opposition. It was significant that when the military coup came in September, 1930 it followed upon street demonstrations against the government by the students. Before they, as a group keenly interested in the type of benefits which *yrigoyenismo* had traditionally conferred, had been among the government's leading supporters.

[35] See this volume, Chapter 3.

There can be little doubt that the key to the collapse of Yrigoyen's second government, which brought to an abrupt end the process which had begun in 1890, may be traced to the Great Depression. The situation which developed in 1930 had been fore-shadowed during the post-war depression with evidence of the breakage of the ties linking the middle classes to the traditional elite groups. However, in 1921 and 1922 Yrigoyen had managed to defray the effects of the depression on the middle classes by maintaining the rate of expansion in public spending. Attempts to control spending had only come in the period of his successor, Alvear. The antagon-isms to which this gave rise among the middle class groups had thus been directed against him rather than against Yrigoyen. In 1930 Yrigoyen was unable to repeat this. As a result of the conflicts over the oil legislation and the struggle with the interior provinces, he was now much more dependent on patronage as a means of maintaining his popular support. Recalling the effects of the depression on the government's position in 1930 some years later Yrigoyen's vice-president, Enrique Martínez, declared:

> The economic crisis was the great factor which made the revolution possible. Those who instance purely political causes or matters of personal standing should remind themselves of the country's situation. The value of our money had been eroded by depreciation, the cereals had been left in the soil, misery was knocking at the door of every household. History teaches us that poverty among the People is the worst enemy of the stability of government.[36]

At the same time the government's dependence upon political patronage ran counter to the interests of the landowning groups. They demanded deflation, a balance of payments equilibrium and the protection of the exporting interests. This was precisely what was aimed for under Yrigoyen's successors after 1930. It also points to the central reason for the abandonment of representative government in 1930. All these policies which were carried out in the 1930s ran directly counter to the interests of the middle class groups. Whereas in 1912 it was possible for a coalition to emerge between the landed interests and the urban middle classes, this ended with depression. Under approximate zero-sum conditions, if comparable benefits to those in the past were to be distributed to the middle classes, these could only come at the expense of the elite. For this reason the elite moved to impose an undissimulated form of open class rule.

[36] Quoted in Roberto Etchepareborda, 'Breves anotaciones sobre la revolución del 6 de setiembre de 1930'. *Investigaciones y ensayos*, no. 8, 1970, p. 82.

Also the political history of Argentina during these years can be seen to have been largely determined by conditions arising out the primary exporting economy. A dependence on overseas export markets and overseas credit led first to the coalition between the landed and urban groups and then to its destruction. The salient features of this economy were responsible for the emergence of a simple power structure dominated by the elite. They determined the basic weaknesses of the middle classes, their lack of any autonomous economic base and their narrow dependence upon the State.

4

Plantations and Peasants in Northern Argentina: the Sugar Cane Industry of Salta and Jujuy, 1930-1943

IAN RUTLEDGE

The expansion of the sugar cane industry in the provinces of Salta and Jujuy

The sugar cane industry of Argentina underwent its great period of growth in the late nineteenth century, but because of adverse climatic conditions, Argentina remained a marginal zone from the point of view of world sugar production and the industry could only prosper as a protected, import-substituting sector serving the internal market. However, the political power achieved by the provincial oligarchies of north-west Argentina (see Map·4.1) in the 1870s and 1880s enabled them to exert pressure on the National Government and obtain a high tariff barrier which practically cut off the external supply completely. Behind this tariff wall the provincial oligarchies of Tucumán, Jujuy and Salta were able to expand their new source of revenue up to the point that, by the turn of the century, the sugar industry was one of the most important in the country.[1]

It was in the small but heavily populated province of Tucumán that the industry enjoyed its major development in the late nineteenth century. The railway, which was the key factor making possible the industry's expansion, reached Tucumán in 1876, but did not extend as far north as Salta and Jujuy until 1890. In 1894, Salta had only one sugar *ingenio*[2] and Jujuy three, whereas there were thirty-six in Tucumán.[3]

---

[1] According to the 1914 census, there were 44 *ingenios y refinerías* in the country, with an average factory size (in terms of labour employed) which was second only to that of the *frigoríficos* (meat-packing plants).

[2] *Ingenio* means sugar factory, but it will be used here to refer to the joint factory-plantation complex.

[3] Emilio Schleh, *Noticias históricas sobre el azúcar en la Argentina*, Buenos Aires, 1945, p. 258.

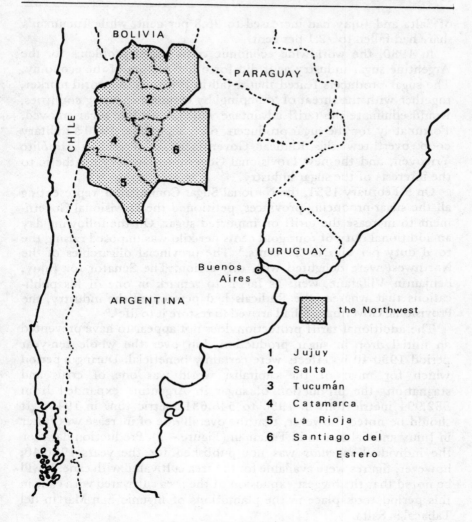

1   Jujuy
2   Salta
3   Tucumán
4   Catamarca
5   La Rioja
6   Santiago del
        Estero

the Northwest

Map 4.1

However, in the 1920s the sugar industry began to develop much
more rapidly in Salta and Jujuy, at which time a new and very large
ingenio called Ingenio San Martín del Tabacal, was added to the
existing one in Salta. The sugar output of Salta and Jujuy began to
increase at a faster rate than in Tucumán; in 1920, Salta and Jujuy
only contributed 15.7 per cent of total national sugar production
(compared with Tucumán's 82.3 per cent[4]) but by 1930, the share

[4]   The remainder in these calculations is the contribution of the Littoral region,
whose production was minimal.

of Salta and Jujuy had increased to 25.8 per cent, while Tucumán's share had fallen to 72.1 per cent.

In 1930, the worldwide economic crisis posed problems for the Argentine sugar industry as it did for other sectors of the economy. The sugar producers feared that a fall in prices in the world market, together with the threat of 'dumping' by certain exporting countries, would eliminate the tariff advantage which Argentine sugar enjoyed. Fortunately for the sugar producers, on 6 September 1930 a military coup overthrew the Radical Government of President Hipólito Yrigoyen, and the new Provisional Government was sympathetic to the interests of the sugar industry.

On 5 February 1931, the National Sugar Commission, representing all the sugar-producing provinces, petitioned the Provisional Government to increase the tariff on imported sugar. On the following day an additional duty of four gold cents per kilo was imposed raising the total duty per kilo to 25 cents.[5] The provincial oligarchies of the Northwest were delighted with this action. The Senator for Jujuy, Benjamín Villafañe, went as far as to remark in one of his publications that whereas the Radicals had persecuted the industry, the Provisional Government 'had arrived to restore it to life'.[6]

The additional tariff protection does not appear to have prevented an initial drop in sugar production, but over the whole ten-year period 1930-40 its effects were certainly beneficial. During a period which for most of the capitalist world was one of crisis and stagnation, the production of sugar in Argentine expanded from 382,994 metric tons in 1930 to 540,631 metric tons in 1940.[7] It should be noted, however, that the overall rate of increase was faster in Jujuy and Salta than in Tucamán (Figure 4.1). Production data for the individual *ingenios* was not published for the years 1930-40; however, figures were available for the area cultivated with cane. It will be noted that the biggest expansion of the area cultivated with cane in this period took place in the plantations of Ingenio San Martín del Tabacal in Salta.

This period of expansion of the sugar industry coincided with the growth of the political power of the sugar oligarchy of the Northwest. The Provisional Government which seized power in 1930 was strongly representative of the conservative forces of the Northwest and was headed by General José Felix Uriburu, a prominent member of the oligarchy of Salta whose family had been among the pioneers

---

[5]   Deputy Américo Ghioldi, *Diario de sesiones*, Cámara de Diputádos, 26 April, 1932, p. 787.

[6]   Benjamín Villafañe, *La región de las parias*, Buenos Aires, 1934, p. 145.

[7]   *Estadística azucarera No. 7*, Centro Azucarero Argentino, Buenos Aires, 1957.

Table 4.1. Area cultivated with sugar cane per ingenio, 1930 and 1940 (hectares)

Province	Ingenio	1930	1940
Jujuy	La Esperanza	4,110	5,371
Jujuy	Ledesma	6,699	7,207
Jujuy	Rio Grande	2,810	2,346
Salta	San Martín del Tabacal	4,805	7,616
Salta	San Isidro	1,032	1,262
	Total	19,456	23,802

Source: *Estadística azucarera No. 7*, Centro Azucarero Argentino (Buenos Aires, 1947).

of the sugar industry.[8] In addition the power of the sugar oligarchy was amply displayed by the political positions and offices held by the owners of the two largest *ingenios* in Salta and Jujuy.[9] Herminio Arrieta, owner of Ingenio Ledesma in Jujuy, was the National Deputy for Jujuy in the Congress from 1934 to 1938, and from 1938 to 1943 he represented Jujuy in the Senate. Robustiano Patrón Costas, owner of Ingenio San Martín del Tabacal, enjoyed even greater political status. From 1932 until 1943 he was Senator for Salta in the Congress; he was also President of the Senate in the same period, interim President of the Nation in 1942, and President of the Partido Demócrata Nacional (Conservative Party) between the years 1931 and 1935. In 1943 he was the Conservative candidate for the Presidency and would probably have been elected President but for the military coup of 1943.[10]

At the local level, the political power of the *ingenios* showed itself

---

[8] Schleh mentions that, in 1832, Vicente de Uriburu acquired the Misión de Zenta in Orán, Salta, and set up a primitive sugar factory. (Schleh, *op. cit.*, p. 322). This establishment was still in the hands of the Uriburu family in 1952 (Schleh, *op. cit.*, p. 328). In 1882 Pio Uriburu formed a company to operate the *ingenio* and plantations of La Esperanza in Jujuy together with Miguel Aráoz and Angel Ugarizza (E. Schleh, *Cincuentenario del centro azucarero argentino*, Buenos Aires, 1944, p. 242). In the 1880s the brothers Pio and Antonio Uriburu also had a share in the *ingenio* San Isidro in Salta, and in 1896 this *ingenio* was owned by the company Dorado y Uriburu (*ibid.*, p.179).

[9] Strictly speaking the *ingenios* were owned by companies, but these two individuals had a controlling interest in the companies and in addition were responsible for the management of the *ingenios*. For this reason they have been referred to as the 'owners' of the *ingenios* here and in the remainder of the paper.

[10] During this period the sugar oligarchy of Tucumán was also strongly represented in the national political power structure; Juan Simón Padros, owner of Ingenio Aguilares, was Deputy for the province from 1932 to 1936.

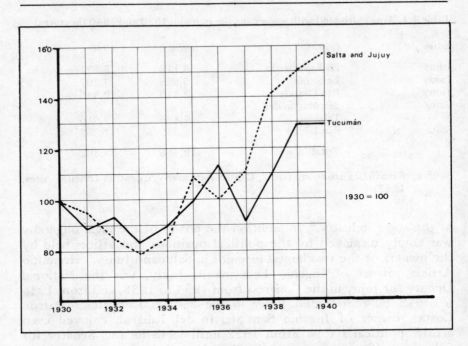

Figure 4.1 Percentage changes in sugar production 1930-1940. Source: *Estadistica azucarera* no. 7, 1947

in two ways; first in the relationship between the *ingenio* owners and the provincial governments, and secondly in the relationship between the *ingenios* and the provincial legislatures.

In both cases the *ingenios'* most important political instrument was the political party. In Salta the Partido Demócrata Nacional, a strongly conservative organisation, was dominant throughout the 1930s. From 1932 until 1943 all the Governors of Salta were members of the Partido Demócrata Nacional. As was pointed out earlier, the party's President from 1932 to 1935 was Robustiano Patrón Costas, owner of the Ingenio San Martín del Tabacal.

Jujuy was very similar. After the military coup of September 1930, the Conservatives, and a few Radicals who resented the reforming tendencies of Hipólito Yrigoyen, banded together to form the so-called Partido Popular.[11] This followed a common practice in the province where the anti-Yrigoyen Radicals tended to ally with the Conservatives.[12] The alliance lasted until 1940 when the

[11] Benjamín Villafañe, *El asesinato de Rafael Tauler, perpetrado por las autoridades*, Buenos Aires, 1938, pp. 35-6.
[12] See B. Villafañe, *El yrigoyenismo*, Jujuy, 1927.

Radicals of the province reunited and a Radical Governor was elected. The leader of the local Conservative party during the 1930s was Herminio Arrieta, owner of Ingenio Ledesma.

In Salta the Ingenio San Martín's relationship with the Provincial Government came to be at its very closest in 1936 with the election of Luis Patrón Costas, the brother of Robustiano, to the Governorship of the province, a post he held until 1940. In Jujuy the relationship between the *ingenios* and the Provincial Government, although equally close, appeared to be complicated somewhat by the existence of the powerful mining interest. In fact, however, the mining and sugar interests were closely intertwined. An important group of businessmen had interests in both industries and at the same time enjoyed the close cooperation of the Provincial Government.[13] The extent of this cooperation was amply demonstrated in the mid 1930s when the Governor of the province, Peréz Alisedo, was accused of instructing the provincial police to assassinate a Spanish miner who was obstructing the speculations of these businessmen in the tin industry. In a subsequent debate on the affair in the Senate, Herminio Arrieta came strongly to the defence of the Governor of Jujuy.[14] Precisely what Arrieta's role was in the affair is not clear, but he was generally regarded as being closely related to the Pichetti company. The national newspaper *Crítica* echoed the sentiments of many when it stated that:

> Jujuy is not in the risk of falling into the hands of a specific political group, but into the trammels of a rapacious combination of dubious interests linked to the speculative mining industry and to the position of power which one of the *ingenios* of the province wants to create for itself: Ingenio Ledesma.[15]

[13] This was the company 'Pichetti, Pirquitas y Compañía Limitada' to which the following individuals belonged: Alberto Pichetti, Andrés Galinski, Pérez Alisedo (the Governor of Jujuy) and the brothers Walter and Stephen Leach (Villafañe, *El asesinato de Rafael Tauler*, p. 105). Walter and Stephen Leach were co-founders (with their four other brothers) of the firm 'Leach Hermanos' which owned Ingenio La Esperanza, and continued as major shareholders in the limited company 'Leach Argentine Estates'. They were, as partners in the 'Pichetti, Pirquitas' company, part-owners of the tin mines of Pirquitas in the Puna (high plateau) of Jujuy, and they also possessed asphalt mines in the department of San Pedro. Alberto Pichetti and Andrés Galinski, who also owned part of the Pirquitas tin mines, expanded into the sugar business in 1940 when they installed a new *ingenio*, Ingenio San Andrés, in the department of Santa Barbara, Jujuy; however, this does not appear to have been a successful venture as the *ingenio* ceased operation after a few years.

[14] See Senator Herminio Arrieta, *Diario de sesiones*, Cámara de Senadores, 19 May, 1938, pp. 125-39.

[15] *Crítica*, 7 May, 1942.

The influence of the *ingenios* on the Provincial Governments was undoubtedly an important way in which they protected and promoted their interests in these provinces, but of equal importance was their relationship with the provincial legislatures. The *ingenios'* control over vast tracts of land throughout the provinces of Salta and Jujuy, together with the control they thereby exercised over the local Indian peasantry, made it easy for them to gain the election of their own nominees in the elections for the provincial legislatures. This political control was exercised largely through the *ingenios'* agents, the *contratistas* (labour contractors). In the rural areas of the provinces, the *contratistas*, who were frequently also store-owners, enjoyed a position of local power and authority. They recruited seasonal labourers for the *zafra* (cane harvest) often by securing a dependent clientele of peasants who were indebted to them for goods bought at their stores.[16] However, according to Deputy Juan Solari's Congressional report of 1934, 'in addition to workers', the *contratistas* 'also recruit votes'. Indeed, the *contratistas* were themselves frequently nominated as candidates and duly elected. For example, one of the most important *contratistas* of Ingenio Ledesma, Lázaro Taglioli, was deputy for the department of El Carmen, Jujuy, in the 1930s,[17] and the *contratista* and administrator of Patrón Costas' estates in the department of Yaví, Mamerto Salazar, was also deputy for that department between 1932 and 1942.[18]

The recruitment of seasonal labour in Salta and Jujuy

The relationship between economic power and political power is frequently a complex and subtle one which resists one-sided determinist arguments, whichever viewpoint they are taken from. It could no doubt be argued that the great wealth accumulated and enjoyed by the sugar oligarchy of the Northwest had facilitated their acquisition of an important degree of power and influence in the national political structure; but it could also be pointed out that this political power itself enabled them to promote their own economic interests and increase their accumulation of wealth.[19] Similarly, at

[16] See the Congressional report of Deputy Juan Solari, *Trabajadores del norte Argentina*, Buenos Aires, 1937, especially pp. 78-9.

[17] Nicolas González Iramáin, *Tres meses en Jujuy*, Buenos Aires, 1942, p. 142.

[18] *ibid.*

[19] Since the late nineteenth century, the political influence of the sugar producers had enabled them to expand the industry far beyond the limits which were desirable for the national economy as a whole, by massive tariff protection, export premiums to finance the disposal of surpluses, credits from the banking sector and the provision of railway transport. In the nineteen-

the local level, the *ingenios'* economic power as the largest employers of labour in the area gave them the political power to engineer the election of their own nominees. However, the *ingenios'* political power did in turn facilitate their acquisition of labour for the cane harvest, especially in areas where a landless rural proletariat had not yet emerged, and where the *ingenios'* increasing demand for seasonal labour had to be provided for by non-economic forms of coercion. The way in which this occurred will now be explained.

As distinct from the pampa area of Argentina, the land tenure structure of north-west Argentina acquired its basic form under Spanish colonial rule. In Salta and Jujuy vast tracts of land were handed out to individual owners as *mercedes* (royal property grants) which contained within their territory a settled and relatively pacific Indian population of agriculturalists and herdsmen. Some of the biggest estates created in this way were in the Puna (high plateau) of Jujuy and in the Calchaquí Valley of Salta.

In 1874-5 a rebellion of Indian peasants took place in the Puna which spread to some of the neighbouring departments of the province of Salta. The Indians refused to pay their rents to the absentee landlords who between them owned the Puna lands. The Indians demanded the return of the lands to the collective ownership of their own communities, but the revolt was bloodily suppressed by government troops of the provinces of Salta and Jujuy. After the defeat of the Indians, their economic burdens were maintained. The Swedish anthropologist Eric Boman, who made a study of the Puna in 1903, gave the following description of the *latifundio* systems prevailed at this time:

> The land is divided among a small number of landlords almost all of whom live in the town of Jujuy. Each property has an enormous extent and is occupied by a hundred or more Indians who must give up to the landlord the greater part of the production of their small herds of sheep, and in addition, give personal service when it is required. The greater part of the owners never visit their lands in the Puna but are content from time to time to send an agent to settle Indian problems and return with supplies.[20]

This situation seems to have persisted throughout the first two

thirties, there was added to this list the provision of state financed irrigation works in the provinces of Salta and Jujuy, as well as the extension of tariff protection.

[20] Eric Boman, *Antiquités de la region andine de la République Argentine et du Désert d'Atacama*, Paris, 1908, 2, p. 472.

decades of the twentieth century, although there is some evidence
that the Indians' conditions improved a little during this time.[21]
However, the Indians never abandoned their belief that the lands
they rented were rightfully theirs. 'If they live in eternal protest,'
remarked an ex-Governor of the province in 1927, 'it is because they
want to be owners of the land . . .'[22]

Around 1930 this situation changed. The *ingenios* started to buy
up or rent the lands of the great *latifundios* of the Puna and the
Calchaquí Valley. The biggest acquisitions were made by the Patrón
Costas family, owners of Ingenio San Martín del Tabacal. It appears

Table 4.2 Latifundios in the provinces of Salta and Jujuy controlled by the
Patrón Costas Family and associates c.1930-1949

Latifundio	Size (hectares)	Department and province	Owned or rented	Owner
Rodero y Negra Muerta	164,550	Humahuaca, Jujuy	owned	Ingenio y Refinería San Martín del Tabacal, S.A.
Yaví	100,000	Yaví, Jujuy	rented	Hortensia Campero de Figueroa
Hornillos	16,000	Santa Victoria, Salta	owned	Ingenio San Martín
Santa Victoria	223,496	Santa Victoria, Salta	rented	Hortensia Campero de Figueroa
San Andrés	129,247	Orán, Salta	owned	Ingenio San Martín
Santiago	171,943	Iruya, Salta	owned	Compañía Territorial del Norte, S.A.[23]
Lurucatao y Entre Rios	125,000	Molinos, Salta	owned	Abel Ortíz and Robustiano Patrón Costas

Total amount
of land controlled *930,236 hectares*

Source: *Diario de sesiones*, Cámara de Senadores, August 10th 1949, pp.
1177-8; *Diario de sesiones*, Cámara de Senadores, September 21st 1949,
p. 1891.

[21] See Villafañe, *El yrigoyenismo*, pp. 28-31.
[22] *ibid.*, p. 31.
[23] This was a 'front' company for the Ingenio San Martín del Tabacal.

that the owners of the *latifundios* found the traditional rental arrangements with their Indian *arrenderos* (tenants) to be less and less profitable, and the terms offered by the *ingenios* considerably more attractive.[24] Table 4.2 gives a list of the *latifundios* which were controlled (either owned or rented) by the Patrón Costas family and their associates during the period 1930-49. This list had been drawn up from a plan for the expropriation of these estates, which was presented by the Peronist Senator for Jujuy in the Congress in 1949. It can be seen that the total area of land in the provinces of Salta and Jujuy controlled by Patrón Costas in this manner amounted to 930,236 hectares (that is, over two million acres). Map 4.2 shows the departments in the provinces of Salta and Jujuy which were brought under the economic and political control of the Patrón Costas family and the Ingenio San Martín del Tabacal, as a result of this policy of land monopolisation.

It should be pointed out that much of the land acquired by the *ingenios* was of little value from the point of view of agricultural production. In the Puna the lands acquired were at an altitude of around 10,000 feet, at which height only small amounts of potatoes, maize and alfalfa could be grown in sheltered gullies, and sheep and llamas raised, largely for their wool. These economic activities provided subsistence for the Indian peasantry as well as providing a modest fund of rent to the landlords, but they could hardly be of any interest to a powerful entrepreneur like Robustiano Patrón Costas. Why then did the *ingenios* monopolise this land?

In 1949 this same question was raised in the Senate in connection with a plan to expropriate these estates in the Puna and Calchaquí Valley and turn them over to the Indians. In long and detailed discussions in August and September of 1949, the Peronist Senators

---

[24] This is a conjecture based on the available evidence. The decision of the *latifundio*-owners to rent their lands to Patrón Costas and his associates was probably made simply on the grounds that Patrón Costas' rental was higher than the annual rental payments of their *arrenderos*. Alternatively the latifundists may have been offered some share in the profits of Ingenio San Martín del Tabacal. One of the *latifundios* in Table 4.2, Santa Victoria in Salta, was still being rented by Patrón Costas in 1959, (*Santa Victoria y Iruya*, Dirección de Estadística de Salta, Salta 1959). I have been informed that in return the owner enjoyed a shareholding in the company 'Ingenio y Refinería San Martín del Tabacal, S.A'. With regard to the estates which were sold directly to the *ingenio*-owners, the decision to sell was probably motivated by similar factors. One *latifundio*, 'Rodero y Negra Muerta' in the department of Humahuaca, Jujuy, was sold to Patrón Costas and his associates for the sum of 41,000 pesos. (Leopoldo Abán, 'Cruenta y larga lucha por la reinvindicación de la Puna', *Pregón*, San Salvador de Jujuy, 4 March, 1970.)

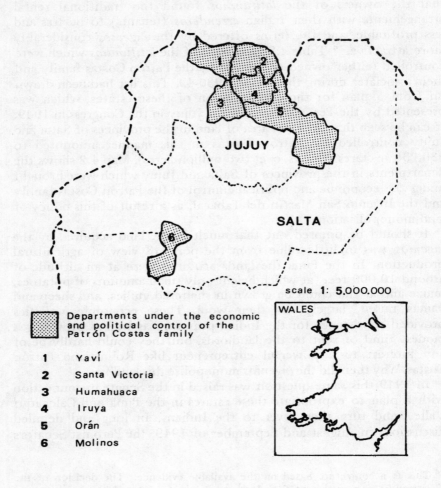

Map 4.2

for Salta and Jujuy explained the rationale behind the *ingenios'*
massive acquisitions of land. They showed that it was not as much
the land itself which the *ingenios* required but the potential labour
force which lived in the territory they had acquired and which could
be coerced into performing seasonal labour services in the cane
harvest:

> Why — I say — have these great industrialists of the *ingenios* of
> the North made these investments? Because in these same lands

they have the human material which can be transported to the *ingenios*, and in abnormal and inhuman conditions.[25]

They (the Indians) constituted the cannon-fodder of the *ingenios*; this was the principal motive for the monopolisation of these vast tracts of land.[26]

This system worked like this. In the *latifundios* which had been rented by the *ingenios*, the Indian *arrenderos* became the *ingenios'* sub-tenants. In the *latifundios* which had been bought outright, the Indians simply received a new landlord. In both cases the Indians' rental payments were transformed from payments in money or goods into payments in labour.[27] The Indians had to pay their rent in labour services in the plantations of the *ingenios*, working for six months as cane cutters in the *zafra*.

An example of this system is provided by the *latifundio* of Yaví in Jujuy. This *latifundio* constituted part of a royal *merced* or land grant which had been made to the Marqués de Tojo (also known as the Marqués de Yaví) in the eighteenth century. It had remained in the hands of the descendants of the Marqués up to the early nineteen-thirties when the owner, Hortensia Campero de Figueroa, let the estate to Robustiano Patrón Costas. Patrón Costas installed his own administrator in the *latifundio*, a man named Mamerto Salazar who was also given the job of *contratista* (labour contractor) for the area. Mamerto Salazar soon became an important and powerful figure in the area and was in due course elected deputy to the provincial legislature for the department of Yaví, a position he enjoyed from 1932 to 1942. At the beginning of the *zafra* Salazar's task was to round up all the Indians who owed labour services to Patrón Costas, load them into cattle trucks and ship them off to the plantations. The most brutal methods were used to ensure that the maximum number of Indians fulfilled their 'obligations' in the *zafra*. The manner in which they were transported to the *ingenio* was well documented by contemporary writers, officials and politicians. In 1942, for example the Federal Interventor in the province of Jujuy described how the *contratista* and his agents forced the Indians into trucks for the long journey to the *ingenio*, using 'the whip and other fearsome means of flagellation'.[28] Salazar was himself personally

[25] Senator Ernesto Bavio, *Diario de sesiones*, Cámara de Senadores, 8 September 1949, p. 1660.

[26] Senator Ricardo Durand, ibid., p. 1661.

[27] Robert Riguelet, Guillermo Ruben, Carlos West Ocampo, and Mario Murias, *Migración y organización social en Yaví*, an unpublished thesis of the School of Anthropology of the National University of La Plata, 1970.

[28] Iramáin, *op. cit.*, p. 134.

denounced by the Federal Interventor for putting his political powers as deputy at the service of the Ingenio San Martín del Tabacal.[29] Once delivered to the plantations the Indians were set to work under a rigid and harsh discipline which was meted out by armed overseers.[30] With regard to wages, the various accounts of the system are unclear as to whether the Indians received any payment for their work. It seems certain, however, that if they did receive any payment it was no more than sufficient to pay for the food they bought at the notoriously extortionate *proveeduría* (company store).[31] Indeed the whole intention of the policy of land monopolization was to acquire seasonal labour at a 'price' which was well below the wage level required to attract free wage workers.

Whether or not all the *ingenios* of Salta and Jujuy adopted the policy of land monopolisation is uncertain. The speakers in the Senate debates clearly refer to 'the *ingenios*' (plural) in their accusations. However, some of the *ingenios* may have acquired their labour force in a somewhat different manner (see below, section 3). For example, the Ingenio La Esperanza does not appear to have used Indians from the Puna or Calchaquí Valley during the nineteen-thirties; according to an ex-administrator of the *'lote'* La Cienaga (one of the individual plantations of the *ingenio*) at this time most of their seasonal labour was performed by *Mataco* Indians from the Argentine Chaco.[32] One thing that is absolutely clear, however, is that the *ingenio* which practised the policy of land monopolisation on the largest scale was Ingenio San Martín del Tabacal.

A number of economic factors may account for this *ingenio*'s policy of land monopolisation. First it should be remembered that sugar production is a highly labour intensive industry requiring very large numbers of cane cutters during the *zafra*. Figure 4.2 shows the numbers of permanent and seasonal field-workers employed in the four main sugar-producing departments of Salta and Jujuy in 1937. It will be noted that the number of seasonal workers is roughly double that of permanent workers. It will also be noted that it is in the department of Orán (Salta) where the greatest number of seasonal field workers are employed. It was in this department that Ingenio San Martín del Tabacal was situated.

[29] *ibid*. pp. 134, 142.
[30] Carmen Paula Muñoz, *La desintegración de la communidad Chiriguana en el Ingenio San Martín del Tabacal*, School of Anthropology of the National University of Buenos Aires, 1964 (mimeo), p. 27.
[31] See remarks of Senator Ernesto Bavio, *Diario de sesiones*, Camara de Senadores, 8 September 1940, p. 1660.
[32] Personal Communication from Sr. P.H., ex-administrator of a *lote* of Ingenio La Esperanza. Interview of December 16th 1969, Belgrano, Buenos Aires.

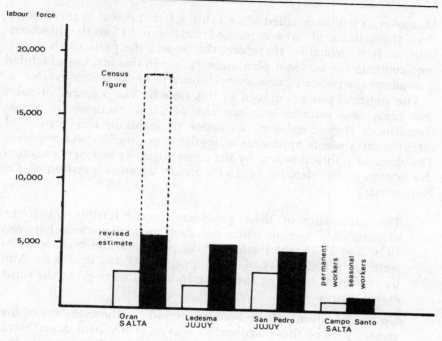

Figure 4.2 Permanent and seasonal labour in sugar cane plantations, Salta and Jujuy, 1937. Source: National Agropecuarian Census 1937.

The Censo Agropecuario of 1937 gives the number of seasonal plantation workers in the department of Orán, Salta as 18,232, compared with a permanent labour force of 2,978. In my view the number of seasonal workers given here must be extremely inflated. As far as I know there were at this time no major differences of agricultural technology between this department (i.e. the department in which was situated Ingenio San Martín) and the others which might account for this extremely high proportion of seasonal workers. It is therefore concluded that the figure given in the census is in error. To obtain a more realistic estimate of the number of seasonal workers, an average ratio of seasonal workers to cultivated cane land has been calculated from the remaining three departments, and the number of hectares cultivated in cane in the department of Orán has then been multiplied by this factor, giving a seasonal plantation labour force of 5,483 which seems much more reasonable.

The amount of seasonal labour employed in the sugar-cane *zafra* is proportional to the area harvested. The large numbers of seasonal workers employed by Ingenio San Martín del Tabacal simply reflects the fact that this *ingenio* had the largest area of land in sugar cane.[33]

[33] In 1937, San Martín had 7,618 hectares in cane, Ledesma 6,129, La Esperanza 4,740, Rio Grande 1,919, and San Isidro 1,744 (*Estadística azucarera* no. 7, 1947). These are figures for area cultivated in cane. Strictly

Moreover, it will be recalled from Table 4.1 that it was in this *ingenio* that the cultivated area expanded most rapidly in the nineteen-thirties. It is probable, therefore, that it was the particularly heavy requirements for seasonal plantation labour in this *ingenio* which led it to adopt the policy of land monopolisation on such a vast scale.

The political power enjoyed at this time by the *ingenios* of Salta and Jujuy was intimately connected with the methods of labour recruitment they employed. In order to maintain this system of recruitment a whole apparatus of legalised oppression was required. The abuse of political power by the sugar oligarchy was denounced in the Senate in the debates of 1949 on the agrarian question of the Northwest:

> The authorities of these provinces, in the terrible era of the oligarchies, above all when the dark ages reappeared between 1930 and 1943, the justices of the peace and the municipalities were all in the service of the big capitalists and landlords. And by choice or by force they (the Indians) had to go to the sugar *ingenios* to work.[34]

> Up to the advent of the Peronist period . . . the overseers of the greater part of these *latifundios* — even in my own department of Rosario de Lerma — were employed as police; so that the orders of the landlord also had political force, the force of law.[35]

It has already been noted how the provincial Governors of Salta and Jujuy collaborated closely with the *ingenios* (and the mining interest) and how the departmental deputies were frequently employees of the *ingenios*. It can now be seen that there existed a hierarchy of political power which ran parallel to the hierarchy of the plantation system itself, making the agrarian social structure of this area a system of social relations based largely on coercion and repression. Figure 4.3 presents a schematised version of the agrarian social structure of Salta and Jujuy in this period.

---

speaking my argument requires data for area *harvested* which are not available. However, I believe that there would be little difference between the two sets of data since climatic conditions in Northwest Argentina make it risky to leave grown cane over the winter period, or stagger harvesting as occurs in Peru.

[34] Senator Ernesto Bavio, *op. cit.*, p. 1660.

[35] Senator Ricardo Durand, *op. cit.*, p. 1661.

Figure 4.3 Schematic diagram of agrarian social structure of Salta and Jujuy 1930-43

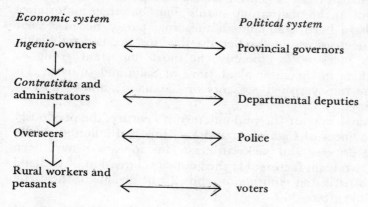

Note: The vertical arrows represent relationships of domination and subordination; the horizontal arrows represent relationships of cooperation between social actors or the same social actors playing different roles.

The recruitment of seasonal labour in the provinces of Catamarca and La Rioja

In the first and second sections of this paper attention has been focused on the recruitment of labour within the provinces of Salta and Jujuy. It was mentioned that not all the *ingenios* acquired their seasonal labour by the process of land monopolisation which has just been described. Indeed it is probable that of the total number of seasonal labourers employed in the plantations only a minority came from within the territory of Salta and Jujuy. In the case of Jujuy, for example, the Provincial Department of Labour reported that in 1933 the 19 *contratistas* registered in the province recruited 5,544 men, of whom 1,761 came from the province of Catamarca and a large but unspecified number consisted of Bolivians living in the province.[36]

The employment of Bolivian labour was at this time quite important to the industry; large numbers of Bolivians from the departments of Potosí, Chuquisaca and Tarija had begun to migrate to the sugar plantations after the termination of the War of the Chaco between Bolivia and Paraguay (1932-5).[37] However, this source of seasonal labour was as yet fairly limited in comparison with

[36] Solari, *op. cit.*, p. 80.
[37] Avila Echazú, 'Las migraciones de braceros bolivianos a la Argentina', *Mundo nuevo*, no. 30, 1968, p. 28.

what it was to become in the nineteen-forties and fifties. The *Mataco* and *Toba* Indians of the Argentine Chaco also provided a source of seasonal labour in the plantations at this time, but their importance appears to have been gradually diminishing, partly because their number was decreasing and also because they were considered highly unsatisfactory workers.[38] Probably the most important group of seasonal workers in the sugar plantations of Salta and Jujuy at this time were the impoverished peasants of Catamarca, and to a lesser extent, La Rioja.

Since the civil wars of the mid-nineteenth century, the previously rebellious provinces of Catamarca and La Rioja had fallen gradually into extreme poverty and backwardness. This appears to have been the result of two main factors: (1) the gradual subdivision of the land in the areas of irrigated *minifundio*, and (2) the decline of the cattle trade with Chile after 1930.

In various departments of Catamarca and La Rioja the growth of population in areas where the amount of cultivable land was strictly limited by the lack of irrigation water led to the extreme subdivision of the peasant plots by inheritance (*herencias*), bringing about the gradual impoverishment of the peasant population. This occurred especially in the departments of Santa Maria, Andalgalá and Belén in Catamarca and in Famatina in La Rioja; in this last department, for example, the vast majority of properties were less than half a hectare in size by the mid-nineteen-thirties.[39]

In other areas of these provinces, the population had enjoyed a certain degree of prosperity based on the raising and fattening of cattle for the Chilean market. According to Senator Alfredo Palacios, in 1901 the province of La Rioja exported 25,000 head of cattle to Chile.[40] However in 1930, the Chilean Government, seeking to defend its own landlord class in the face of economic depression, imposed a high tariff on imports of live steers from Argentina which reduced Argentina's cattle trade with Chile from 114,848 head of cattle in 1929 to 2,270 in 1931.[41] This economic catastrophe affected all the provinces of north-west Argentina to some degree, and was particularly disastrous to the areas which were dedicated to the growing of alfalfa for the fattening of cattle in transit. But the

---

[38] Many contemporary reports on the sugar industry describe the *Matacos* and *Tobas* as being 'lazy'. This was also the expressed opinion of Sr. P.H. ex-administrator of the *lote* La Cienaga in Ingenio La Esperanza (personal communications).

[39] Ing. Gabriel Ocampo, *Diario de sesiones*, Cámara de Senadores, 1941, p. 378.

[40] Alfredo Palacios, *Pueblos desamparados*, Buenos Aires, 1944, p. 119.

[41] Silvio Pascale, 'El intercambio comercial argentino-chileno', *Revista de ciencias económicas*, April, 1932, pp. 255, 257.

provinces of Catamarca and La Rioja appear to have suffered the most. It is interesting to note that whereas in the other provinces of the north-west the stock of cattle increased between 1922 and 1937, in Catamarca and La Rioja the stock declined considerably.[42]

These two factors, the extreme subdivision of the peasants' lands and the decline of the cattle trade with Chile, brought extreme poverty to the provinces of Catamarca and La Rioja. The situation in La Rioja was described vividly in 1941 by the Senator for the province, who was speaking in support of state aid for the provinces of Catamarca and La Rioja:

> This general poverty of the population, now revealed in the compulsory exodus in search of work, in the propagation of diseases which were hitherto unknown, in the state of malnutrition of the proletarian classes . . . in the high infant mortality figures, constitutes a deep-rooted evil which the province cannot remove by itself alone.[43]

In the midst of this poverty the *contratistas* arrived, seeking seasonal labour for the plantations of Jujuy, Salta and Tucumán.[44] The system of recruitment was described in detail by the Deputy Juan Antonio Solari in his Congressional report on working conditions delivered in the Congress in 1934:

> The traders or *conchabadores*[45] operate like this: in the small villages far from the railway stations, they set up grocery stores in which they sell almost exclusively maize and salt, the staple necessities of the poor, which are extremely cheap but which nevertheless give a profit of 50 per cent. The sale of these commodities continues all year and is conducted on credit (*a libreta*), the bill at the end of the year amounting to, say, eighty or a hundred pesos. The purchaser promises, almost always in writing, to pay the bill with what he earns in the *zafra*

[42] Stock of cattle in the provinces of north-west Argentina 1922 and 1937 (thousands of head):

Year	Jujuy	Salta	Sgo. del Estero	Tucumán	Catamarca	La Rioja
1922	118	488	630	336	307	188
1937	125	626	651	356	249	141

Source: Agropecuarian Censuses 1922, 1937.

[43] Senator Hector González Iramáin, *Diario de Sesiones*, Cámara de Senadores, 26 August 1941, p.401.

[44] The *ingenios* of Tucumán employed mainly workers from Catamarca, Santiago del Estero, and from the province of Tucumán itself.

[45] *Conchabador* is another name for *contratista*.

and he also promises to accept the store owner as an intermediary (*contratista*) between himself and the *ingenio*. When the period of the harvest arrives, each *contratista* sends his workers to the *ingenio* in goods trains and the exploitation enters into another phase. The *contratista* sells the labour he commands at piece rate and he also pays his workers in the same way. But he retains as profit the difference between the price he is paid by the *ingenio* for the labour and what he pays the workers, in addition to the profit arising from his grocery trade throughout the whole year . . .[46]

According to another report, the amount deducted from the workers' true wages (the 'official' wage-bill paid by the *ingenios*) by the *contratista* varied between 15 per cent and 30 per cent,[47] and bearing in mind that in addition were deducted the sums owing to the *contratista* in his capacity as store-owner, it is not surprising that about 60 per cent of the workers coming from Catamarca, who had been the subject of an official study, returned from the *zafra* absolutely penniless.[48] However, the situation of these workers was even more desperate. The *contratistas* maintained a permanent hold on their workers by arranging that they remained indebted to them from year to year so that they became more or less attached to the *ingenios* in a type of debt-bondage. Juan Solari describes this practice as follows:

I have . . . the pass-book (*libreta*) of a man who works all one year and who, by chance, as in almost all the other cases, has to return (to the plantation) the next year even though he doesn't want to, since it so happens that he has a debit balance of 12.2 pesos, which allows the *contratista* to hold him subject, bound to work in the next harvest, for the next *zafra*.[49]

It should be noted that in the case of Catamarca around eight thousand workers made the annual journey to the *ingenios* under conditions similar to those described above, this figure being about one third of the economically active population of the province.[50]

[46] Solari, *op. cit.*, pp. 78-9.
[47] Palacios, *op. cit.*, p. 122.
[48] *ibid.*
[49] Solari, *op. cit.*, p. 119.
[50] Palacios, *op. cit.*, p. 117.

The role of coercion and the contratista *system in the formation of a seasonal plantation proletariat*

The pattern of agrarian change which has been briefly studied in this paper might be described as the historical process whereby two interior provinces of Argentina have become integrated into the national capitalist market via the spread of commercial agriculture. In recent years it has become popular among development theorists, especially those dealing with Latin America, to attribute to this kind of integration process a fundamental role in bringing about economic development in the region's backward, interior areas. The study of the sugar industry in Salta and Jujuy presents a much more sombre view of this type of process.

The expansion of commercial agriculture in Salta and Jujuy brought with it, neither an open system of modern social relationships nor a spread of economic benefits to the mass of the rural population, but on the contrary a reversion to forms of social organisation reminiscent of the colonial *mita* and *encomienda* which had once prevailed in this area.[51] Instead of generating 'modern' work relations and encouraging the growth of a free labour market by offering sufficiently attractive wages, the *ingenios* in Salta and Jujuy resorted to direct coercion based on political power in order to acquire a work force. Nor did the system of labour recruitment in Catamarca and La Rioja approximate at all closely to the 'modern' worker-employer relation which is usually taken for granted by the supporters of the capitalist development model; the worker-peasants of these two provinces enjoyed little more freedom than the Indians of the Puna and the Calchaquí Valley, tied as they were to the *contratistas* in economic and social dependence. Moreover in this case too the system was buttressed by the political power of the *ingenios*, since their control of the provincial legislatures in Salta and Jujuy effectively blocked any serious attempts to reform the system of labour recruitment.[52]

However, these repressive forms of work relations were not part of a feudal or precapitalist economy. The *ingenios* were highly capitalised and technologically advanced enterprises, and their brutal methods of obtaining labour can hardly be blamed on a 'traditional mentality' or 'feudal outlook'. Indeed, their behaviour appears to have been based on quite rational capitalistic criteria, as I shall now try to show.

[51] The *mita* and *encomienda* were systems of forced labour imposed on the Indians by the Spaniards in the sixteenth century. They were formally abolished by the Primera Junta on 1 September, 1811.

[52] See Solari, *op. cit.*, pp. 81-2.

It has already been pointed out that the sugar cane industry demanded extremely heavy inputs of seasonal labour during the six-month *zafra* or cane harvest. Since the early nineteenth century the cane-growing areas of the provinces of Salta and Jujuy had been notorious for their shortage of labour.[53] The continued expansion of the sugar industry in the 1930s consequently required not only tariff protection but also an ample supply of seasonal labour. The Puna and the Calchaquí Valley contained considerable numbers of potential labourers, but their attachment to the land as peasant producers presented a serious obstacle to their conversion into wage labourers. The principal desire of the Indian inhabitants of these areas was not to become salaried workers but to obtain the ownership of the lands they rented from the latifundists,[54] a preference which was intensified by the Indians' traditional belief that the lands of the Puna and Calchaquí Valley justly belonged to their own communities. In this situation the *ingenios* were faced with the necessity of *creating* a work force, by coercion, and they accomplished this by monopolising the lands on which the Indians lived and worked and using their political power to dragoon the population into working for them. To this extent the system was quite similar to the historical pattern of capitalist development in other parts of the world.[55] However, one important difference from the 'classical' pattern of proletarianization should be noted. The Indians were not totally 'divorced from the means of production' in the manner described by Marx.[56] They were permitted to remain on their lands on the condition that they worked in the plantations during the *zafra*. It is this pattern of labour services alternating with subsistence activity on their own lands which makes it tempting to interpret this system as a type of feudal serfdom, but it has already been indicated that such a conclusion would be misleading. The question we must ask is: would it have

[53] Many nineteenth-century commentators remarked upon the shortage of labour, and the obstacle this presented to the development of the sugar industry in Salta and Jujuy. See for example, G.A.H.y P., 'Causas del atraso de las cinco ciudades de la carrera de Buenos Aires al Peru', *Seminario de agricultura, industria y comercio*, 3, Buenos Aires 1804, quoted in Manuel Lizondo Borda,.*Historia del Tucumán (Siglos 16 y 17)*, Tucumán, 1941, p. 165, where the solution seen was the importation of negro slaves; also see E.W. White, *A Young Naturalist in the Argentine Republic*, 2, London, 1882, 292-3, and Schleh, *op. cit.*, pp. 332-4.
[54] Villafañe, *El yrigoyenismo*, p. 81.
[55] See for example, Giovanni Arrighi, 'Labour supplies in historical perspective: A study of the proletarianization of the African peasantry in Rhodesia', *Journal of Development Studies*, 6, 3, 1970.
[56] Karl Marx, *Capital*, I, London, 1970, pp. 713-16.

served the *ingenios'* interests to expel the Indians completely from their lands and create a totally landless proletariat, as occurred for example in parts of Great Britain in the eighteenth and nineteenth centuries? The answer, probably, is 'no'. The type of labour force required by the *ingenios* had the following two very specific characteristics: (*i*) it was only to be employed for, at the most, half the year,[57] and (*ii*) it needed to be on hand and ready to start production en masse at the precise time decided by the *ingenios*, since delays in harvesting could result in enormous losses once the sugar factories had commenced operation. Under these conditions a completely landless proletariat would not necessarily be the best kind of labour force. In particular there would always be the risk that after the harvest season, it would drift away to the cities and fail to return the following year. In the last extremity, of course, the *ingenios* could have paid the seasonal workers high enough wages to maintain them for the rest of the year and thereby ensure their loyalty to the sugar industry. However, a much more economic solution lay open to them. By permitting the Indians to remain on their lands the *ingenios* not only assured that they would remain in the area, ready for work when required, but also placed upon them the burden of supporting themselves during the 'dead season' by their own subsistence activities.

The argument, then, is that the direct coercion practised by the *ingenios* against the Indians of the Puna and the Calchaquí Valley does not signify the existence of a feudal or precapitalist economy based on a kind of serfdom. The brutal methods of labour recruitment constituted the primary phase in the proletarianisation of the Indian peasantry of this area, a phase which in other countries has frequently involved a similar degree of direct coercion. That this proletarianisation remained partial or incomplete is to be explained not by any 'feudal outlook' on the part of the *ingenios* but by the specific technological requirements of the sugar cane industry, which created a pattern of demand for labour with extremely heavy seasonal variations.

The same technological requirements determined the system of labour recruitment in Catamarca and La Rioja (and later in Bolivia), although in a somewhat different manner. As we have seen, in these provinces there was no need for the *ingenios* to adopt measures to divorce the peasants from their means of production since this had already occurred to a large extent by the impoverishment of the local agrarian economy. However, the problem of maintaining a secure and

---

[57] I am speaking here of the majority of the labour force; there are, of course, some permanent workers.

reliable work force, which could be counted on to arrive en masse for the *zafra*, remained. In this case, the solution adopted by the *ingenios* was the widespread use of the *contratista* system which tied the peasants to the plantation system indirectly, via the labour contractors and the system of debt-bondage which they employed. In this area, then, as in the Puna and the Calchaquí Valley, the repressive social relationships arising from the system of labour recruitment should not be regarded as 'feudal' or 'precapitalist' but as an outcome of the specific historical form in which agrarian capitalism developed in this area.[58]

Finally, let us briefly consider this pattern of development from a spatial or geographical point of view. The study of the sugar industry in Salta and Jujuy strongly suggests that the spread of economic development into the Northwest during this period was only partial and incomplete. The immense wealth created by the expansion of the sugar industry remained concentrated in the plantation zones and main towns of Salta and Jujuy and the same occurred in the province of Tucumán. A certain amount of this wealth was probably reinvested in the sugar industry, but there can be little doubt that a larger part was either converted into luxury consumption or channelled off to finance development elsewhere — invested in the more prosperous Littoral region, or, as in the case of Leach's Argentine Estates (Ingenio La Esperanza), remitted to a rich foreign country. Certainly, the growth of income in the sugar producing zones did not encourage any general process of diversified, self-sustaining growth throughout the Northwest as a whole. Provinces like Catamarca and La Rioja, as well as certain areas of the sugar-producing provinces themselves, like the Puna of Jujuy and the Calchaquí Valley in Salta (or the Valley of Tafí in Tucumán), remained permanently on the margin of development (see Map 4.3).

Thus the development of agrarian capitalism in this region of Argentina produced a kind of 'core-periphery' spatial distribution of economic growth, but one in which there existed a structural unity between the backward and the more developed parts of the region.

[58] In this respect my findings support some of the general conclusions expressed in the writings of A.G. Frank. (See for example, *Capitalism and Underdevelopment in Latin America*, New York, 1967, especially Chapter 4.) However, Frank's approach to the problem is not entirely satisfactory. In particular he tends to interpret all situations of commercial orientation and market relations as evidence for the existence of a capitalist economic system, which leads him to conclude that even Spanish colonial society was thoroughly capitalist, a conclusion which is not shared by this writer. (See the critique of Frank's views on Spanish colonial society which is contained in the essay by Ernesto Laclau, 'Feudalism and Capitalism in Latin America', *New Left Review*, 67, 1971.)

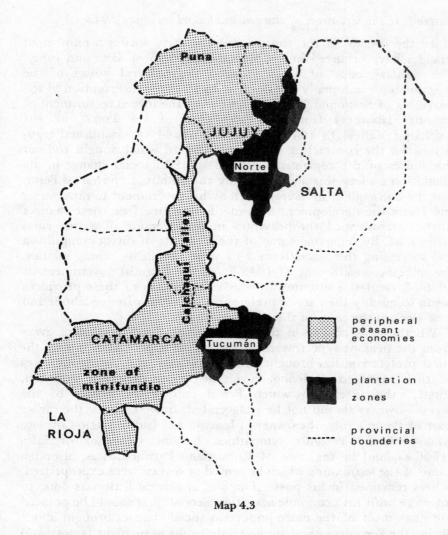

Map 4.3

In this system the continuing poverty of the backward areas was in a large part a consequence of their mode of relationship with the more developed areas. In this particular case the particularly harsh exploitation of the inhabitants of the peripheral peasant zones by the *ingenios* and their *contratistas* contributed considerably to the expansion of the sugar industry, while perpetuating the grievous poverty of the Puna, the Calchaquí Valley and parts of Catamarca and La Rioja.

Postscript: the situation of the seasonal workers since 1943

Since the decade of the thirties and the early forties a number of changes have occurred in the plantation system of Salta and Jujuy. The military coup of 1943 reduced the political power of the *ingenios* both nationally and locally. In 1943 the intervention of the provinces of Salta and Jujuy put an end to the forced recruitment of seasonal labourers from the *latifundios* of the Puna and the Calchaquí Valley. In 1944 Decree no. 10.644/44 established regulations for the contracting of seasonal labour, which sought to limit the abuses of the *contratista* system. In 1946 social change in the plantation society was accelerated by the coming, to power of Perón and the consequent measures taken by his government to raise wages and foster the development of trade unions. In effect, these changes further transformed the peasantry in the direction of a true rural proletariat. By removing some of the elements of direct compulsion and increasing the attractiveness of wage labour by raising salaries, the military government of 1943-5 and the Peronist government of 1946-55 created a situation in which the Indians of these provinces began to modify their set of preferences in favour of wage labour and seek work in the *zafra* of their own volition.

Whether this change in the status of the direct producers, away from the peasant type towards a more close approximation with the rural proletarian, has brought about significant and lasting increases in their standard of living, is a much more debatable question. Firstly, the extent to which Perón curbed the power of the *ingenio*-owners should not be exaggerated. Indeed, during the earlier part of Perón's rule, the owner of Ingenio San Isidro, Lucio Cornejo, who professed Peronist sympathies, became Governor of Salta (1946-8), and in the case of Robustiano Patrón Costas, although some of the *latifundios* which he rented or owned were expropriated, others remained in his possession, and in general little was done to interfere with his economic activities. Secondly, it should be pointed out that most of the more important social changes brought about during the Peronist period applied only to the permanent factory and plantation workers; this was especially the case with regard to the formation of trade unions which to date do not include the seasonal plantation workers. Thirdly, the seasonal immigration of vast numbers of Bolivian peasants, which commenced in the late forties and early fifties, brought with it the perpetuation of repressive and socially-backward work relations in the plantations; this occurred because many of the immigrants lacked the official documents and registration which were supposed to guarantee them the same conditions as Argentine workers.[59]

In 1960 the Agropecuarian Census calculated that there were 21,791 transitory or seasonal agricultural workers in the provinces of Salta and Jujuy. However, this figure almost certainly underestimates the number of Bolivian migrant workers employed in the provinces which a representative of the sugar industry calculates to be as high as 20,000.[60] Most of the transitory workers in these provinces are employed in the sugar cane plantations. The standard of living of these workers continues to be extremely low. In 1964 the report of the National Council for Economic Development (CONADE) on the land tenure structure of Argentina described in detail the miserable living conditions of the transitory workers in the plantations of Salta and Jujuy — low nutritional levels, illiteracy, coca-chewing, alcoholism, and a fatalistic attitude to everyday life being among the most common conditions of these workers.[61] In 1960 the provinces of Jujuy and Salta had, respectively, the highest and the fifth-highest infant mortality rates among the 24 provinces of Argentina.[62] Even the *ingenio*-owners themselves have admitted the miserable living conditions of the transitory workers, although they blame this on the workers' 'lack of education'.[63] Significantly, while mentioning its modern techniques and type of economic organisation, the CONADE report states that the sugar plantation complex, with its floating population of seasonal workers, 'is similar to the type of situation prevalent in areas of Latin America which are less economically developed'.[64]

[59] According to Avila Echazú, 'Las migraciones de braceros bolivianos a la Argentina', *Mundo nuevo*, 30, 1968, p. 28, the *ingenios* have conspired to bring about the clandestine immigration of Bolivian peasants without correct documents, in order to obtain a passive and easily exploited workforce.

[60] Martínez de Hoz, President of the Centro Azucarero del Norte, *Diario de sesiones*, Cámara de Diputados, 31 March, 1965, p. 8848.

[61] Consejo Nacional del Desarrollo (CONADE) and Consejo Federal de Inversiones (CFI), *Tenencia de la tierra, aspectos de la estructura agraria y su incidencia en el desarrollo agropecuario argentino*, Buenos Aires, 1964, vol. 1, part 3, p. 239.

[62] Juan Octaviano Taire, *Azúcar para el monopolio*, Tucuman, 1969, p.104.

[63] Carlos Blaquier, *Diario de sesiones*, Cámara de Diputados, 31 March, 1965, p. 8917. ·

[64] CONADE and CFI, *op. cit.*, p. 239.

5

Anglo-Argentine Trade, 1945-1965

COLIN LEWIS

When Argentina's trading performance since the Second World War is considered, it is invariably contrasted unfavourably with the situation that prevailed during earlier periods. Whatever criteria are adopted, the picture painted is generally a gloomy one. Commenting on his country's foreign trade since 1945 the president of the Argentine Chamber of Commerce stated that until the early 1960s exports had run at approximately $1,000 million a year (1968 dollars). Some improvement had been observed since 1962 when that figure had climbed to approximately $1,500 million p.a. Nevertheless, this improvement, he said, compared unfavourably with the position of Argentine trade between the end of the First World War and the Wall Street Crash. Indeed, it represented little more than a return to the 1918-29 situation, when Argentine foreign trade had run at some $1,500 million (1968 dollars), and could not compare with the peak year, 1928, when trade had reached $1,700 million (1968 dollars).[1]

If these words brought little comfort to Argentine traders, they had even less to offer their British counterparts. For few of Argentina's trading partners can this period bear a less favourable comparison with earlier developments than for the British. If total Argentine trade since the 1920s has exhibited little improvement in real terms, British trade with Argentina has witnessed an absolute decline, while Britain's role as Argentina's major trading partner has been usurped by others.

Since the turn of the present century Britain had become accustomed to her position as Argentina's most important market and

[1] Jorge S. Oria, *Disertación del presidente de la Cámara Argentina de Comercio, Dr. Jorge S. Oria, en el centro de altos estudios del ejército argentino*, Buenos Aires, 1968, pp. 10-11.

supplier of manufactures. True, this position had been challenged by other nations, particularly during periods of international stress when traditional trading patterns had been disrupted. Generally, however, such competition had been short-lived. Moreover, there had always existed within the Argentine trading community a section conscious of Britain's importance. Thus, until the Second World War, Britain had remained Argentina's major trading partner, taking between one-fifth and one-third of her exports and supplying a similar proportion of Argentina's import requirements.

Table 5.1 Argentine trade [2]

	Imports from			Exports to		
	U.K.	U.S.A.	Germany	U.K.	U.S.A.	Germany
	%	%	%	%	%	%
1910	31.1	13.8	17.5	21.8	6.8	12.1
1913	31.0	14.7	17.0	24.9	4.7	11.2
1916	28.3	29.2	0.1	29.4	20.9	—
1919	23.6	35.5	0.2	28.7	18.4	0.9
1921	23.3	26.9	9.5	30.6	8.9	7.5
1924	23.4	22.0	12.5	23.1	7.1	10.0
1927	19.4	25.4	11.2	28.2	8.3	16.5
1930	19.8	22.1	11.8	36.5	9.7	8.8
1933	23.4	11.9	10.0	36.6	7.8	7.7
1936	23.6	14.4	9.2	35.0	12.2	5.8
1939	22.2	16.4	9.2	35.9	12.0	5.7

Subsequently this dominant position was lost. During the early 1950s Britain was providing less than 10 per cent of Argentina's import requirements. Not only was the U.S.A. supplying a greater proportion of Argentina's imports than Britain, but also France and Germany. Nor was Britain Argentina's best customer. On several occasions during the decade the U.S.A. purchased a greater proportion of Argentina's exports than did Britain.[3]

1. The Argentine economy: industrial development and overseas trade

These comparisons of post and pre-war statistics are valuable, for they allow current developments to be seen in their historical perspective, and, moreover, they do serve to indicate the poor performance of the Argentine economy since 1945. Nevertheless, a too frequent use of such statistics does tend to blur the realities of

[2] *Revista de la economia argentina*, Year 23, no. 268, October 1940, vol. 39, pp. 304-5.

[3] A.H. Tandy, *Overseas economic survey: Argentina, Economic and Commercial Conditions in the Argentine*, H.M.S.O. 1956, p. 105.

the current situation. Despite the undoubtedly slow rate of growth which has occurred in Argentina since 1945, irrespective of comparisons with earlier periods, the Argentina of today – or rather, the period under consideration – is not the Argentina of the 'golden era'. Neither is the world situation analogous. To compare glibly statistics pertaining to the post-war era with those for periods prior to, and including, the 1920s is to ignore the changes which have taken place in Argentina since the 1930s. Argentina is still a major supplier of primary produce, which continues to provide that vital commodity, foreign exchange, but import requirements are somewhat changed.

The middle third of the present century has seen a rapid expansion in the capacity of local industry. Stimulated by war-time shortages, exchange difficulties, and favoured by government policy, domestic industrial production in Argentina has expanded and diversified until the greater part of effective local demand for consumer goods, and some capital goods, can be met domestically.

Table 5.2 Consumption of industrial production in Argentina[4]

Import coefficients %

	Total consumption	Consumer goods	Importation		Total imports	Domestic production
			Capital goods	Raw material & semi-finished		
	%	%	%	%	%	%
1920/24	100.0	20.2	8.4	20.6	49.2	50.8
1925/29	100.0	18.9	11.1	21.0	51.1	48.9
1930/34	100.0	14.6	5.2	17.5	37.3	62.7
1935/39	100.0	12.3	7.0	17.4	36.7	63.3
1940/44	100.0	5.9	1.9	11.6	19.5	80.5
1945/49	100.0	6.2	6.3	13.4	25.9	74.1
1950/54	100.0	2.7	4.4	14.1	21.2	78.8

As can be seen from the far right-hand column, total consumption of secondary goods in Argentina has been increasingly satisfied by local production, while imports have suffered a corresponding decline. This situation represents a reversal of the pre-1914 position when importation satisfied some two-thirds of effective demand in Argentina for manufactured commodities. Of particular significance is the change in the composition of imports. The decline in imports of consumer goods is much greater than, and is sometimes offset by, the trend observed among imports of capital goods and semi-finished

[4] U.N., E.C.L.A., *Análisis y proyecciones del desarrollo económico, V: El desarrollo económico de la Argentina, Parte II (Primera Parte), Los sectores de la producción,* Mexico, 1959, p. 160.

goods and raw materials. While imports of consumer goods never recovered after 1929 those of capital goods, on the other hand, were maintained and increased when conditions allowed; an indication that industrialisation was taking place. In this context the data pertaining to the quinquennium 1945/9 is of special relevance. It can be seen that while imports of consumer goods are hardly affected by the ending of the war, capital imports virtually regain their pre-war position.

This changing pattern of importation could not fail to have an effect upon Argentina's trading position in the long term. By definition, a policy of import substitution, if it is successful, must inevitably lead to at least a relative decline in certain categories of imports. Equally obvious, in the short-term one would expect imports to increase or the structure of importation to alter as capital goods are imported to provide the means of increasing domestic production. This phenomenon can be observed in the case of Argentina. To render Table 5.2 in money terms:

Table 5.3 Argentine importation of secondary produce (millions of 1950 pesos)[5]

	Total imports	Consumer goods	Capital goods	Raw material & semi-finished goods
1930/34	4,985	1,951	700	2,334
1935/39	5,884	1,983	1,118	2,783
1940/44	2,956	902	292	1,762
1945/49	5,605	1,339	1,363	2,903
1950/54	4,614	586	969	3,059

If the figures pertaining to the war years are ignored it can be seen that total imports of industrial goods for the period 1930-54 are maintained at quinquennial averages of approximately 5,000 million pesos a year. Imports of consumer goods, however, fall away after the war; the level of total importation being maintained by the increase which occurs in the field of capital goods and raw materials and semi-finished goods. Argentina's increased demand for the latter category may be seen as a further indication of industrialisation. Thus the continued growth in imports of raw materials and semi-finished goods during the quinquennium 1950-4, when total imports falter, is worthy of note.

Import substitution also tends to exert other pressures upon the domestic economy; the repercussions of such a policy are not limited

[5] U.N. *Análisis y proyecciones... Parte II, Los sectores de la producción,* p. 159.

to merely changing patterns of importation. The changes in the structure of a country's economy, from an agricultural to an industrial base, that are implied in these developments occasion important re-alignments with regard to sectoral balance. The higher wages generally commanded by industrial workers must inevitably lead to increased consumption of exportable produce. Furthermore, in competing for resources, domestic and foreign, the process of industrialisation tends to drive up the costs of agricultural production. The agriculturalist invariably faced increased competition for — and consequently increases in the cost of — the factors of production. Paradoxically, increases in the cost of production are likely to lead to greater agricultural efficiency, and can reduce the final cost of the product.

This is, however, but one side of the argument. For if import substitution and industrialisation altered Argentina's import requirements, and affected her performance, she still remained an important world supplier of primary materials, particularly foodstuffs, which had a vital importance to her continued economic development. At this juncture it is perhaps as well to recall the economists' 'model'. The basic international trade model consists of two countries, A the producer of primary goods which trades with country B, the secondary producer. The purchases of A from B, all other things being equal, are determined by B's purchases from A, and *vice versa*. Argentina and Britain are not trading in a perfect world, neither are they each other's sole trading partner. Nevertheless, the lessons taught by model building are of relevance. Argentina's capacity to import has notoriously been limited by her ability to export; a sensitive balance at best, the relationship between the country's export performance and ability to import was likely to be further upset by the process of industrialisation with the consequent increased domestic consumption of the exportable surplus. Failure to maintain the exportable surplus would mean a reduction in imports with the resulting adverse effect upon other nation's ability to import from Argentina. Again, this phenomenon has been observed in the case of Argentina. Tariff protection apart, exchange shortages have been one of the greatest hindrances to the expansion of her trade. Balance of payments problems due to a decline in the yield of exports relative to the country's import requirements have been an almost constant feature of Argentina's recent history. Indeed, it has been a further spur to import substitution.

Finally, when considering Anglo-Argentine trade, it must be remembered that the two countries have not suffered a mutual degree of dependence. While, during the earlier period, Britain might have been Argentina's major trading partner, Argentina never assumed the same function for Britain. Argentina was but one of many — admittedly an important one — of Britain's trading partners. For one or two commodities Britain might depend upon the Argentine source of supply, but in general she was less committed to one market or source of supply.[6] Although this dependency has been reduced, Argentina still finds Britain a more important market for her produce than does Britain Argentina. Many of these factors are self-evident, but bear reiteration, and should be borne in mind when considering Anglo-Argentine trade during the post-war era.

2. The structure of trade, 1945-1965

The fillip administered to the process of import substitution/industrialization during the early period of the twenty years under review was merely one facet of a policy which sought to achieve the radical alteration of Argentina's traditional trading patterns. In her commercial policy Argentina attempted to secure a high level of balanced trade. To obtain this objective she looked for new trading partners and favoured a system of bilateral trade agreements. In this way she hoped to broaden the pattern of her trade and wean the economy away from dependence upon a limited range of commodities and markets. Subsequently, the latter half of the period saw a return to multilateral trade and a dismantling of some of the checks and controls which had been established earlier, though not necessarily any alteration of the underlying policy.

In 1946 Latin America in general, and Argentina in particular, found itself in a favoured situation. Few would dispute the assessment that 'at the end of the Second World War, Latin America faced the outside world from a position of considerable strength. The demand for its exports was high; it could trade on much improved terms, new merchant fleets had been constructed, reserves of foreign exchange had been accumulated, and there were good prospects of a resumption of large-scale foreign investment.'[7] There were indeed markets for Argentina's produce. The terms of trade were moving in her favour, and were to continue to do so for some time.

Table 5.4 Argentina's terms of trade[8]

1935/9	100	1945/6	107
1940/4	100	1947/9	129

[6] U.K., Dept. of Trade and Industry, *Report on Overseas Trade*, 1, 1, 1950, p. 6.

[7] U.N., *A Study of Trade between Latin America and Europe*, Geneva, 1953, p. 8.

[8] Carlos F. Díaz Alejandro, *Essays on the Economic History of the Argentine Republic*, 1970, p.88.

The countries of western Europe, after the destruction wrought by the war, were unable to supply total food requirements from domestic sources. Post-war uncertainties served to maintain demand at a high level. Also, as a consequence of the war, many of Argentina's competitors in eastern Europe were no longer in a position to rival her. She possessed too, valuable blocked balances of foreign currency. However, if we look at Argentina's subsequent trading performance, a rather disappointing picture emerges.

Table 5.5 Argentine Trade (millions of dollars at current prices)[9]

| | Imports | | | Exports | | |
	From G.B.	From U.S.A.	Total	Total	To U.S.A.	To G.B.
1945	30	41	301	720	158	189
1946	77	167	587	1,154	173	254
1947	111	609	1,343	1,599	159	479
1948	195	577	1,563	1,630	158	451
1949	183	175	1,178	1,144	112	238
1950	113	157	965	1,177	240	211
1951	111	310	1,480	1,169	206	200
1952	70	216	1,179	688	174	97
1953	49	135	795	1,125	213	218
1954	72	128	979	1,027	105	188
1955	76	154	1,173	929	118	201
1956	53	230	1,128	944	118	212
1957	101	307	1,310	975	112	237
1958	102	203	1,233	994	128	237
1959	90	191	993	1,009	107	235
1960	113	327	1,249	1,079	91	221
1961	140	383	1,460	964	84	174
1962	119	396	1,357	1,216	88	204
1963	78	242	981	1,365	150	200
1964	81	255	1,077	1,410	91	154
1965	73	273	1,198	1,493	93	153

The significance of the above trading figures can only be completely understood when it is recalled that until the end of the 1940s the terms of trade were markedly in Argentina's favour, and that they began to move against Argentina after 1951. Moreover, as can be seen, there was a decline in the Anglo-Argentine trading partner-

[9] Compiled from Díaz Alejandro, *op. cit.*, pp. 461, 465-6, 476, 483. Peso/dollar conversions effected in accordance with exchange rates which appear upon p. 485.

ship at precisely that time when an improvement could have been anticipated.

Few commodities mirror this adverse trend in Anglo-Argentine commercial relations more faithfully than the meat trade. Since the 1920s when it had obtained its prominence, chilled beef had been one of Argentina's major exports to Britain. No little sacrifices had been made to retain the important British market during the 1930s, then virtually the only outlet for the product. Given a continuance of established patterns, meat exports to Britain could have been expected to remain an important item of trade between the two countries, even when allowing for British imports of Commonwealth meat.

Meat, however, was one of the first commodities to respond to the changed circumstances brought about by the industrialisation of the Argentine economy. As domestic real incomes increased so local demand for meat began to affect the exportable surplus adversely. This trend had been discernible for many years; it did not originate during the post-war era. Since the First World War the greater portion of animals slaughtered in Argentina had been sold on the internal market. But during the immediate post-war period the pace of the trend towards increased local consumption quickened with unfortunate results for the export market.

Table 5.6 Cattle slaughterings[10]

	Home consumption %	Export %		Home consumption %	Export %
1914	59	41	1951	86	14
1928	60	40	1952	85	15
1938	68	32	1953	87	13
1949	77	23	1954	87	13
1950	79	21	1955	80	20

Such a trend need not have affected Argentina's export performance if the volume or value of exports could have been maintained in absolute terms; this was not the case. Total meat exports which during 1940-4 had averaged 1,295 million pesos a year declined in value to a little over 1,000 million pesos p.a. during the following quinquennium, and for 1950-4 were half the previous annual rate, standing at 566 million pesos.[11] An increase in local demand was not

[10] Compiled from *Revista de la economía argentina*, year 21, no. 257, November 1939, 38, p. 333, and Tandy, *op. cit.*, p. 96.

[11] U.N., *Análisis y proyecciones . . . Parte I, Los problemas y perspectivas del crecimiento argentino*, p. 115.

the sole cause of this drastic reduction in exports, but the large volume of domestic consumption made the industry less flexible, less able to maintain the volume or value of exports in the face of a natural disaster. At precisely the time when domestic demand was increasing at its greatest rate the volume of cattle being presented for slaughter was declining.

Table 5.7 Cattle slaughtering (millions of tons)[12]

1939	1.8	1952	1.7
1949	2.0	1953	1.7
1950	2.0	1954	1.8
1951	1.8	1955	2.0

This decline can be accounted for partly by the state's policy with regard to the camp which had made investment less attractive, and partly to nature. As so often in the history of Argentina, natural disaster coincided with and reinforced the prevailing economic trend. In this instance it was the drought of 1950-1. The resultant effect upon exports has already been observed. The effect upon Anglo-Argentine trade was as can be expected.

On 18 July 1948, the two countries had signed a meat agreement which was due to last for five years, but could be terminated by either party on the 1 July of any year. Argentina undertook to supply Britain with 300,000 tons of meat in the first year, and, if possible, 400,000 tons subsequently. In 1948 Argentine meat exports stood at 509,000 tons (684,000 tons if exports of live animals are included). The following year meat exports stood at approximately the same figure, 497,000 tons; total exports, however, had fallen to 550,000 tons (i.e., including exports on the hoof). For 1950 the reduction in the exportable surplus was even more spectacular. Total exports, both slaughtered and live, amounted to only 422,000 tons — barely the amount that Argentina had promised to send to the British market alone.

In July 1950, shipments to Britain were suspended due to the failure of the two governments to arrive at an agreed price. The agreement was amended in August 1951, and shipments resumed, although at the reduced rate of 200,000 tons p.a. The total exportable surpluses for 1951 and 1952 were 369,000 and 294,000 tons respectively.[13]

Meat was not alone in experiencing a decline during these years. Partly as a result of the government's policy with regard to agri-

[12] Tandy, *op. cit.*, p. 96.
[13] Díaz Alejandro, *op. cit.*, p. 478.

culture, the effects of industrialisation, and natural disaster, virtually every sector of agriculture witnessed a decline in economic activity and a falling-off in production.

Table 5.8 Major Argentine grain exports [14]

Year	*Area sown (000 hectares)	*Production (000 tons)	Exportable surplus (000 tons)
	WHEAT		
+ 1935/40	7,553	6,036	3,270
1953	6,066	7,386	2,527
1954	6,354	6,200	2,943
1955	5,937	7,690	3,617
1956	5,210	5,250	2,526
1957	5,947	7,100	2,660
	MAIZE		
+ 1935/40	6,458	7,671	5,322
1953	3,354	3,550	1,083
1954	3,268	4,450	2,185
1955	3,002	2,546	362
1956	2,888	3,870	1,065
1957	2,740	2,698	789
	LINSEED		
+ 1935/40	2,961	1,513	1,378
1953	1,020	584	10
1954	732	410	11
1955	739	405	—
1956	675	238	—
1957	1,285	620	—

+ = Averages   * = Crop years

The above table, however, does not present a complete view of arable production, as the arable sector was being diversified at this period. Experimentation with new cash crops was undertaken. The production of barley and rye, until then relatively unimportant, had been rapidly expanded during the thirties; oats had also become a major crop in terms of the area of land devoted to its cultivation. Even more dramatically, the production of sunflower seeds threatened to rival linseed as an oil producer. In addition, another

[14] Compiled from Tandy, *op. cit.*, p. 95, and Díaz Alejandro, *op. cit.*, pp. 437, 441 and 478.

newcomer, the fruit industry, exhibited dynamic growth potential. Yet these new products could not usurp the function of Argentina's more traditional crops. They remained relatively minor items of trade and their production was influenced by precisely the same factors which occasioned a reduction in the output of more established products.

By the early and mid-fifties the export of these newer crops was also declining.

Table 5.9 All, non-grain, arable exports[15]

	Volume (millions of metric tons)	Value (millions of dollars)
1953	1.0	170.2
1954	0.9	130.3
1955	0.4	78.0
1956	0.8	88.2
1957	1.0	126.6

This decline in agricultural output was essentially an indication of the underlying malaise. As the state pursued its industrialization policy investment in agriculture became less attractive. The rural sector was unable to compete with industry for the allocation of the factors of production: the government system of prices and marketing was extremely disadvantageous. Capital investment fell off and labour inputs declined. Initial improvements in productivity were not maintained and were insufficient to counteract the prevailing trends. Inevitably the area under cultivation was reduced and animal stocks were run down.

Despite the attention devoted to the industrial sector it was unable to meet the growing requirements of the country as was witnessed by the creeping paralysis which overtook transportation. An added hindrance to foreign trade at this time was not merely the falling off in rural production, but also the difficulties involved in moving the exportable surplus to the ports for shipment overseas. By the mid-1950s some 30 per cent of Argentina's locomotive park of approximately 4,000 engines was out of service, undergoing repair. In normal circumstances this percentage should have been 10. Some 3,000 of these locomotives were over 25 years old, of which 1,500 were over 48 years old. Only 1,000 engines could be described as 'modern', that is, with less than 25 years service. Due to the deficiency of traction the average wagon run had declined from some

[15] *The Review of the River Plate*, 17 March 1961, 129, p. 23.

25,000 Km. p.a. before the war to only 12,000 Km. p.a. by 1955.[16]

A similar situation existed with regard to farm tractors. At the time when increased mechanisation on the land was required to offset the decline in labour, Argentina experienced a chronic tractor shortage. Argentine agriculture was one of the least mechanised in the world.

While the country's ability to trade was thus impaired the government sought to implement a new commercial policy which involved the establishment of a national purchasing agency, multiple rates of exchange and bi-lateral trading agreements. Rarely were these policies successful in achieving their objective. The state trading agency which was charged with purchasing in Argentina the exportable surplus was a contributing factor to the agricultural decline. Paying the producer less than the world market price, the agency in the early years of its existence contrived to make a profit at the expense of driving the agriculturalist out of production and indirectly discouraged investment in the rural sector. Subsequently, at a time when world prices were declining, the agency attempted to counteract the adverse effects of its earlier operations, and stimulate agricultural production by offering a more attractive price to the producer. As a consequence of this reversal of policy, the agency succeeded only in accumulating large deficits which in turn served to give the inflationary spiral in Argentina a further twist.

Multiple exchange rates were necessitated by the need to reduce the effects of the government's theoretically completely elastic monetary policy, and the very nature of Argentine industrialisation. Between 1945 and 1955 money supply increased at an average of 23.4 per cent per annum.[17] During the same period gross production increased by only 3.5 per cent per annum.[18] Multiple rates of exchange were partially successful in that they prevented the full effects of inflation being passed on directly to the price of Argentina's secondary exports.

Nor did bi-lateral trade succeed in maintaining a high level of balanced trade. Argentina did not always obtain her imports in the cheapest market, neither did she necessarily obtain the commodities that she required. Traditional trading partners lost interest in Argentina and were not easily regained. In addition, the country accumulated large balances of blocked currencies which were not always universally acceptable, viz. the Spanish peseta.

---

[16] *The Review of the River Plate*, 31 March 1956, 119, pp. 13, 16.
[17] Tandy, *op. cit.*, p.110.
[18] U.N. *The Economic Development of Latin America in the Post-War Period*, New York, 1964, p. 85.

With the change of government which occurred in the middle of this period there was a return to freer trading patterns, a trend, which had been re-introduced during the last years of the Perón era. But to a large extent Argentina had missed many opportunities.

As can be seen in Table 5.5, Argentine trade registered an increase. during the late 1950s which was continued, through a balance of payments crisis, to the mid-1960s, by which time the value of exports was rising at a greater rate than the increase in total trade. The terms of trade also exhibited a marginal improvement by the mid-1960s. New policies such as the ending of price controls had some effect upon exports. Yet the pressure of domestic demand continued to exert an adverse influence upon the exportable surplus. Meat production exhibited a marked recovery during the late 1950s which was sustained into the early 1960s when adverse climatic conditions caused a temporary retardation; recovery was resumed by the mid-1960s. Meat exports, however, reacted rather differently. Showing an equally spectacular recovery during the mid-1950s, exports began to fall off at the same time as production declined, but continued to decline after production picked up again. Grain production also began to increase around the middle of the decade — indicating the slack that existed in the rural sector — and maintained a steady increase through to the mid-1960s. Exports, on the other hand, after an initial increase, became relatively static.

Britain's role as Argentina's major trading partner had by this time been irretrievably lost. Not only had she been out-distanced by the U.S.A., but also by several of her European rivals. By the mid-1960s both Germany and Italy were exporting more to Argentina than Britain. Nor did Britain hold her position as Argentina's main customer; again by the mid-1960s that position had been claimed by Italy. By 1965 Britain was not even able to hold her position behind Italy, and in that year Holland became Argentina's second best customer. Indeed, during 1965 Argentina's trade with Brazil was more important than her trade with Britain.[19]

3. Industrialisation and Anglo-Argentine commerce

It was Argentina's misfortune to have suffered the adverse effects of rapid industrialisation at the time when the pursuance of her traditional economic activities would have yielded their highest return. Argentina chose to ignore one of the fundamental facts of industrialisation, namely that in the short-term at least, import substitution requires that the level of importation should flow at a

[19] *The Review of the River Plate*, 10 July 1970, 148, pp. 50-1.

faster rate, or be maintained. Moreover, the type of industrialisation/ import substitution that Argentina successfully attempted was one that necessitated a continued flow of imports for an even greater period. Industrialisation in Argentina although eminently successful in reducing the need for certain products could not support a policy of autarky. Nor could Argentine industrialisation sustain itself. Despite efforts to the contrary, industrialisation was essentially confined to the consumer goods sector. Fostered behind a protective barrier Argentine industry operated within a relatively small market: it was high cost and unable to compete in the world market, even when supported by differential exchange rates.

While total Argentine exports averaged $1,255 million a year between 1960 and 1965, 'miscellaneous items', amongst which were included Argentina's secondary exports, averaged but $66 million.[20] The meaning of this equation is clear. In more ways than one, Argentine agriculture had to pay the price of industrialisation. Argentina lacked several factors which were essential to the process of industrialisation. She could not supply all her power requirements domestically, neither could the local economy generate the flow of capital necessary to sustain the continued process of industrialisation. Local industry was unable to gain the foreign exchange needed to guarantee the supply of these factors. Consequently the onus fell upon the traditional export sector which, when its earnings were most needed, and at a time when its products were most valuable, found its strength and vitality sapped by the very process of industrialisation.

Argentine industrialisation, as we have seen, had several adverse effects upon trade. Not only did industry compete with agriculture for resources, but, as a result of industrialisation, domestic consumption was increased at the expense of the exportable surplus. Increased real incomes and higher expectations led to a steady rise in local demand. This trend affected foodstuffs, particularly meat, and also 'industrial' primary produce such as linseed and wool. Until the outbreak of the Second World War Argentina had been an important source of linseed. During the 1920s and 1930s she had accounted for approximately 50 per cent of total world production, and had supplied an even greater proportion of the total world exportable surplus. Yet Argentine exports of linseed and linseed oil declined drastically in the early 1950s.[21] In part, this decline was due to the pressure placed on agriculture at the time — linseed production was labour intensive — but also to an increase in domestic consumption.

[20] *ibid.*
[21] U.N., *A Study of Trade between Latin America and Europe*, p. 85.

Initially the bulk of the annual harvest had been exported for processing, but, with the development of a local industry, began to be processed at home. At the same time local industrialisation led to an increased domestic consumption of linseed oil. Consequently, when linseed harvests began to improve after 1956, exports reacted more slowly, and when exports registered an increase, the product exported consisted of processed and not raw linseed.

These were the inevitable indirect effects of industrialisation upon trade. But import substitution was bound to affect directly the consumption of foreign produce in Argentina. Textiles, one of the first commodities liable to import substitution, provide a suitable case study. Since the early 1930s the Argentine textile industry has exhibited a pattern of strong, sustained growth. For many years it was Argentina's fastest developing industry. The rate of increase in textile production was invariably greater than the general level of the increase in total manufacturing production. Only during the 1960s was its progress rivalled by that of the domestic food processing industries, and petroleum refining. The result was a decline in imports as domestic output increased.

Table 5.10 Argentine consumption of cotton textiles (thousand tons)[22]

	Domestic output	Imports		Domestic output	Imports		Domestic output	Imports
1945	62	10	1952	80	11	1959	88	1
1946	64	7	1953	74	2	1960	96	1
1947	66	28	1954	83	-	1961	95	1
1948	70	18	1955	92	2	1962	76	-
1949	70	19	1956	101	1			
1950	76	11	1957	98	1			
1951	92	10	1958	100	2			

The above presents an example of Anglo-Argentine trade in a microcosm. International trade between Great Britain and Argentina was more than a mere exchange of a secondary good for a primary product; of textiles for meat. Nor were the two countries operating in a vacuum as were the countries in the economist's model. Yet the processes which occasioned a reduction in the trade of these two products were to effect the whole spectrum of Anglo-Argentine trade.

This process was unique neither to Argentina, nor peculiar to her trade with Great Britain. In general, after 1948, Latin America as a

[22] Díaz Alejandro, *op. cit.*, pp. 451-2.

whole played a comparatively less important role in world trade. Indeed, for some of the commodities in which Latin America traded the decline was both relative and absolute. In part this decline was due to structural changes in world trade, but was also accounted for by local factors.

Table 5.11 Latin America's share of world trade[23]

	1938 %	1948 %	1950 %	1951 %	1952 %	1953 %	1954 %	1955 %	1956 %	1957 %	1958 %	1959 %	1960 %
Wheat	13	18	13	14	13	19	23	25	26	14	10	25	15
Maize	64	51	17	7	14	21	39	7	18	11	19	26	22
Meat	40	34	27	24	20	18	18	17	24	25	25	20	17
Wool	17	21	19	11	15	21	15	14	16	11	13	14	14
Linseed	44	58	75	77	34	60	54	50	32	55	74	84	76

In the case of most of these temperate products Argentina was the main Latin American supplier, and as she maintained, or marginally improved her share of the total Latin American export during this period, the above percentages in reality indicate Argentina's share of world trade for the product concerned: her share of the Latin American exports ranged from an average of 69 per cent for wool to 97 per cent for wheat. Thus it is possible to trace Argentina's history as an exporting nation during this period in the wider world context. As can be seen, the decline in Argentine exports is greatest in the case of meat, one of her most valuable commodities. Britain had previously been the most important customer for this, her most important product. Before the Second World War Argentina had supplied some 43 per cent of total British meat imports, in 1950 this percentage declined to 28, and the following year, admittedly a bad one, Argentina provided only 17 per cent of total British imports.[24]

It seems clear that Argentina's trading performance during the period was adversely influenced by a number of factors associated with the process of import substitution. The redistribution of national income which occurred during the late 1940s and early 1950s initially encouraged domestic consumption of the exportable surplus, but might, given the marked propensity to import exhibited by Argentine consumers, have been expected to stimulate the demand for foreign products in the long term. The prospect of an improvement in the volume of trade was, however, prevented by

[23] U.N., *The Economic Development of Latin America in the Post-War Period*, pp. 140-1.

[24] U.N., *A Study of Trade between Latin America and Europe*, p. 99.

government policy which not only sought to discourage certain types of trade, but may also be held largely responsible for the stagnation that existed in Argentina during much of the fifties.

Table 5.12 Rate of growth of gross product and real income[25]

	Total		Per capita	
	Gross product	Real income	Gross product	Real income
	%	%	%	%
1945/50	4.6	5.6	2.5	3.5
1950/5	2.4	2.1	0.3	Nil
1955/61	2.0	2.2	Nil	Nil

The above figures relate to Argentina, Bolivia, Chile, Paraguay and Uruguay, but, due to her weighting, they are essentially an indication of Argentina's economic performance during the period. Indeed, the overall trend was produced, despite real improvements in the case of Bolivia, Paraguay and Uruguay, as the result of Argentine stagnation.

Because real per capita incomes failed to grow there was little scope for an increase in trade. Moreover, when the situation eased after the early 1960s the release of pent-up demand tended to produce balance of payments crises which further frustrated a real improvement in foreign trade. Changes in national income distribution increased the domestic consumption of exports, the output of which was adversely affected by official policies. Consequently, when the possibility of expanding the volume of foreign trade occurred as the domestic situation improved, the country's capacity to import was substantially reduced.

4. Trade and foreign investment

Nor was the government's attitude with regard to foreign investment designed to encourage the growth of trade. After the war the state adopted at best an equivocal policy towards foreign capital. The repatriation of foreign investment, and the restraints placed upon further foreign involvement in Argentina's economy served to cramp economic development when expansion was most needed, and the yield would have been most remunerative.

The vacillations in government policy and the dilemma of the foreign investor are appropriately indicated by the predicament in which the British-owned Argentine railway companies found themselves. At the end of the war the railways required a massive

[25] U.N., *The Economic Development of Latin America in the Post-War Period*, p. 6.

recapitalisation. Operating economies, introduced as short-term measures during the depression had been maintained through the war years. Yet cannibalisation of equipment and a frugal husbandry of resources had resulted in a gradual run-down of the network. By the end of the forties the railway system needed an infusion of new capital to make good the deficiencies of over a decade of inadequate provision for depreciation. Nationalisation was regarded as an inevitable, though not necessarily as an immediate, solution. Such an objective had been officially enshrined as national policy during the pre-war Justo administration, which had actually effected the purchase of minor British-owned lines. The companies recognised the Argentine government's position and were prepared to co-operate in negotiating an equitable settlement.

With the expiry of the Mitre Law an opportunity presented itself for a radical revision of the structure of the transport industry in Argentina. Unfortunately, at this juncture, the future ownership of the railways became inexorably intertwined with the vexatious question of Argentina's blocked sterling balances. As the result of war-time sales of foodstuffs to Britain, Argentina had accumulated large reserves of sterling. The method and timing of the liquidation of these balances posed a conundrum to which no ready solution could be found. That these balances continued to be augmented during the immediate post-war period did not facilitate a settlement. Argentina required a speedy liquidation of her sterling account, or failing this the payment of a reasonable interest upon her balances and the provision of adequate safeguards against the likely possibility of a British devaluation. Britain, for her part, preferred that the liquidation of Argentina's account be achieved over a longer period that would take cognizance of the international position of sterling. Also, she was not prepared to sanction the payment of more than a moderate rate of interest upon the account.

Purchase of the British-owned Argentine railways with these blocked funds presented a facile solution to the *impasse*. Yet, on reflection, it is possible to speculate upon the desirability of such a move. Subsequently, Argentina lacked the capital to reorganise her railway network. Moreover, the manner in which nationalisation was effected could hardly be calculated to encourage further foreign investment. Negotiations between the state and the railway companies for the formation of a mixed corporation that would ultimately become wholly nationally owned had reached an advanced stage. Such an arrangement could have offered benefits to both parties: the realisation of the government's policy would have been achieved without the severe sacrifices that were consequently imposed upon the Argentine economy; the much needed flow of foreign capital could have been maintained; Argentina's sterling might have been employed to better advantage. The abandonment of the concept of a mixed corporation appeared to indicate a determination on the part of the Argentine government to discourage foreign investment in the country. Finally, the cavalier fashion in which the government honoured its undertakings, and the whole course of the private negotiations with the railway companies did little to redound to the credit of the state at precisely that time when the government was becoming more directly involved in the economy and was attempting to regulate international trade by means of contractual arrangements negotiated through organisations of the state.

For Britain the liquidation of her investments in Argentina, of which by 1946 the railways were the major part, had a depressing effect upon trade. Although the British-owned companies operating in Argentina had not exclusively bought British, there had been a tendency for them to do so. As the chairman of one of the railways stated, his company purchased virtually nothing in the country within which it operated, merely quebracho sleepers — a legal obligation which the railway companies undertook upon accession to the Mitre Law.[26] Between 1924 and 1934, the great inter-war period of railway renewal and expansion, the British-owned companies expended approximately £70 million upon stores and equipment, virtually the whole of which represented orders placed in Britain.[27]

5. British factors

At this juncture, when most of her traditional trading links with Argentina were being severed, Britain faced increased competition from her European and North American rivals. During the war years, in particular, North America exporters obtained substantial markets in Latin America as a whole. This often created a preference for U.S. produce that was subsequently difficult to overcome. When further supplies of goods were required, or replacements sought, the tendency was to look to the U.S.A. This trend was most discernible in the trading patterns which began to appear immediately prior to the outbreak of war. Once again the textile industry provides a useful model. The rapid expansion of the Argentine textile industry which occurred at the end of the 1930s resulted in large orders for machinery being placed in the U.S.A. Accustomed to North

[26] P[ublic] R[ecord] O[ffice], F[oreign] O[ffice Papers], 371-13460, Sir E.F. Crowe to R.L. Craigie, 23 May, 1929, enclosed memorandum.
[27] P.R.O., F.O. 371-18633, Sir H. Chilton to Sir S. Hoare, 11 June, 1935, enclosed memorandum.

American suppliers Latin American producers considered U.S. machinery as better suited to local requirements: it was regarded as more economical in its use of labour; had a higher productive capacity and was more 'modern' than that produced in Europe. In reality, however, the best North American machines were no better than European high quality products, nor were they any cheaper. Nevertheless, this prejudice in favour of North American equipment persisted after the war and remained strong even after devaluation had reduced the cost of British machines, and increasing costs of production in the U.S.A. drove up the price of American models.

Table 5.13 Argentine imports of textile machinery (thousand dollars)[28]

	From U.S.A.	From U.K.
1938	1,039	900
1949	7,284	5,114
1950	1,581	2,995
1951	1,159	2,548

The difficulties experienced by the British economy during the immediate post-war era are well-known, and they too served to influence the already declining pattern of Anglo-Argentine trade. The balance of payments crisis, and the need to re-equip basic industry in Britain, were hardly conducive to a rapid expansion of trade. During the years after the war when it appeared that Argentine markets were likely to be restricted, or slow to expand, Britain directed her attention to more accessible markets in Europe or the Commonwealth. By the time that British interest in Latin American markets in general, and Argentina in particular, had been re-kindled during the early 1960s, her European and Japanese competitors had built a strong position and secured a substantial share of the limited market.

Moreover, the general uncertainties of trading in Argentina, certainly during the earlier period, also served to discourage British businessmen. Exchange difficulties and the problems of obtaining payment added to those which were experienced by British enterprise in obtaining credits at home.

Given the dollar shortage experienced by most countries during that period, it might have been anticipated that Anglo-Argentine commerce would have expanded after the mid-1950s. But this development was unlikely in view of the tendency prevalent amongst Latin American nations in general to demand, when possible, dollar payments for their exports. In the face of a dollar shortage all countries were liable to attempt to obtain that currency from trade

[28] U.N. *A Study of Trade between Latin America and Europe,* p. 105.

with third parties. Indeed, this was partly the reasoning behind the multiple exchange rates adopted by Argentina at this time. Advantageous rates were only granted to those commodities unlikely to find a market without such support.

Conclusions

In retrospect the decline in Anglo-Argentine trade appears inevitable. The changes in the commercial relationship of the two countries which occurred after the Second World War is, in effect, a reflection of the changes which have taken place in their respective domestic economies and their relative trading position. Argentina, in pursuing after the war a policy of increased industrialisation, set in motion trends which would inevitably alter her traditional commercial position. It was, however, her misfortune to neglect in the process those sectors of her economy which although 'traditional' still had a vital function to play in furthering the country's progress along the new paths which she chose to tread. Whether Britain alone could have exerted more effort to maintain the old relationship is debatable. The answer is probably in the negative. After the war it is unlikely that British industry could have sustained unaided the flow of capital which Argentine industrialisation required, even if that had been desired.

Subsequent events appear to confirm the continuance of this decline. Despite renewed interest, Anglo-Argentine trade seems doomed never to regain its pre-war significance. The stagnation which has occurred in Argentina since 1968, and Britain's sustained interest in Europe through the 1960s made any vast improvement unlikely. Yet the concern expressed in Argentina at the possible consequences of British entry into the Common Market indicates that for Argentina at least, Anglo-Argentine trade is still important.

6

Perón's Policies for Agricultural Exports 1946-1948: Dogmatism or Commonsense?

JORGE FODOR

For more than twenty years Argentina has been in an almost continuous state of economic crisis. Although many different economic policies have been tried out, they have all failed. But instead of searching for a structural explanation for this state of affairs, many of the economists who have analysed the postwar performance of Argentina have been satisfied with blaming a particular government for most of the country's economic difficulties: the government of General J.D. Perón, that lasted from 1946 to 1955. As 1955 becomes more and more distant, this explanation becomes progressively less convincing; not only have the problems remained unsolved, but their complexity seems to increase.

An analysis of the main accusations against Perón's economic policies may be valuable and contribute to a better understanding of some of the key problems of Argentine economic history. If these accusations can be shown to be unjustified, the need for a major revaluation of the causes of Argentina's economic problems will become apparent.

Some of the most serious criticisms of the economic policies undertaken by Perón's Government have been directed against those aspects connected with the international economy. The following points have been singled out:

1. the 'dissipation' of the foreign exchange accumulated during and immediately after the war;
2. the nationalisation of the foreign-owned railways and the repatriation of the external debt; and
3. the tendency to increase the degree of autarky of the economy by encouraging industry and relatively neglecting agriculture, especially during 1946-8, when external demand for Argentine foodstuffs was high.

Unable to find any economic rationale for these crucial actions, critics have sought explanations either in terms of the political features of the Peronist movement, in short-sighted nationalism and demagogy, or in a mistaken evaluation by the Peronist leadership of the opportunities offered to Argentina by international economic conditions. In this essay I shall concentrate on the third of these criticisms, the question of international economic conditions, and explore briefly the reasons why agriculture did not receive more encouragement between 1946 and 1948.[1] It is hoped to show that these aspects of its policies can be explained by the international economic situation. It should be borne in mind, however, that even if these aspects are the ones that have concentrated the attention of orthodox liberal economists, they are only a part of the general picture, and are not sufficient for an overall evaluation of the Peronist Government.

The 1946-8 period and current views on Peronist economic policies

The period 1946-8 is seen by most commentators as a decisive stage in Argentine economic history. The end of the war found Argentina almost free from foreign debt, with substantial reserves, a growing industry and an apparent choice of economic strategies open to her.

With high European demand for foodstuffs, and high prices prevailing, this period has been seen by recent historians as the age of golden but lost opportunities.

Both the Peronists and the anti-Peronists have helped to create the impression that the international economic situation during 1946-8 was extremely favourable for Argentina. The Peronists used it to stress the favourable conditions in which the country lived under Perón, while their opponents used it later to lament his failure to use these alleged favourable conditions to strengthen permanently the economic structure.

To commentators writing in the sixties, in what they believed was a world tending towards free trade, the specific difficulties of the early postwar period seemed relatively unimportant and the end of the war came to be seen as the beginning of the era of freer trade. The following picture of the period therefore emerges: high demand for Argentine goods, favourable terms of trade and easy access to supplies that were not available during the war.

Because after 1948 the situation changed for the worse and the terms of trade deteriorated, the impression has gained ground that by

---

[1] Forthcoming articles will deal with the nationalisation of the railways and the decline of foreign exchange holdings.

then Argentina had 'missed the boat'. Had she used the favourable 1946-8 years to export even more, and establish the conditions for a modernized economy, her economic vulnerability would have diminished.

This view of the period is well exemplified in an otherwise penetrating article by E. Eshag and R. Thorp.[2] In the section entitled 'Opportunities Lost under Favourable Conditions 1946-8' they provide a good summary of the accepted view of the opportunities open in this period to Argentina. 'With the end of the Second World War, shortages of foreign exchange and of supplies of equipment were no longer an obstacle to renewing and enlarging the capital stock of the country.'[3] They blame the Government for the 'major mistake' of not using its foreign exchange to correct structural weaknesses in the economy, such as creating an efficient import-saving oil and steel industry, and for spending it on nationalising the railways and repatriating what was left of the foreign debt. Since they regarded the immediate postwar period as offering an easy opportunity for obtaining valuable foreign exchange and necessary goods, they argued that agricultural exports should have been encouraged at the expense of internal consumption:

> Although there was a relatively strong case for diverting export products to domestic consumption during the Depression and the Second World War, this did not hold in the immediate post war period. At this time, owing to the strong foreign demand for food, any rise in domestic consumption implied a corresponding reduction in foreign exchange earnings.[4]

Other attacks on Perón's policies are easy to find, but as they tend to reflect existing academic consensus, they have rarely been questioned. Comments like the following are representative of this consensus:

> The second period when the contract between Argentina and Australia has been striking is that of 1943-64. As Professor Smithies convincingly tells the story, it is all a matter of the economic consequences of Mr Perón.[5]

---

[2] 'Economic and Social Consequences of Orthodox Economic Policies in Argentina in the Post-war Years', *Bulletin of the Oxford University Institute of Economics and Statistics*, February 1965, pp. 3-44.

[3] *ibid.*, p. 7.

[4] *ibid.*, p. 8.

[5] W.M. Corden, discussing a paper by A. Smithies in *American Economic Review, Papers and Proceedings*, 1965, p. 40.

However there are very few systematic discussions of the subject. Because of this it is especially valuable to analyse Díaz Alejandro's section on the Perón period in his 'An Interpretation of Argentine Economic Growth since 1930'.[6] The second part of this article is divided into two sections, whose subtitles are significant: 'Delayed Responses to the Great Depression (1943-55)' and 'Towards the Elimination of the Foreign Exchange Bottleneck (1955 to the present)'. This indicates the line of reasoning followed. The economic policies of 1943-55 are seen as a response not to the economic environment of that time, but to memories of the past; and as affected by misjudgment of present (1946-8) and future possibilities. It is also worth noting that to choose to take 1943-55 as one period in which to study foreign economic policies has tacit but immediate political implications. 1943 was the year that saw the downfall of a conservative government and the rise to power of the group from which Perón later emerged as leader. 1955 was the year of his fall. So far as economic policies in the light of external conditions are concerned, 1943 does not represent any significant break with the past. If anything, the new government took in 1943 measures that pre-supposed a more optimistic view of the future of the world economy, such as its action lifting restrictions on areas to be sown with some cereals. 1955 does not provide any landmark in economic policies towards the outside world either. The main characteristics of the post-1955 policies, such as better relative prices for agriculture in order to encourage exports, and the granting of attractive conditions to foreign capital, were already present by 1953.

On the other hand, to view the post-1955 period as the beginning of the tendency towards the elimination of the foreign exchange bottleneck seems unrealistically optimistic.[7]

In Díaz Alejandro's argument, the existence of economic policy options is crucial. He contends that the postwar world did offer to Argentina the opportunity of increasing its exports as much as it needed. Because Argentina did not take advantage of this he condemns the Peronist government:

Public policy had an option which was not present during the

---

[6] Carlos F. Díaz Alejandro, 'An Interpretation of Argentine Economic Growth since 1930', *Journal of Development Studies*, Part 1, pp. 14-41, October 1966; Part 2, pp. 155-77, January 1967.

[7] A more satisfactory periodisation has been proposed by Eshag and Thorp. They see 1946-8 as one period; 1949-55 is seen as an 'early resort to orthodox economic measures', and 1959-63 as 'the culmination of orthodox economic measures in the IMF stabilisation policies'.

great depression: to guide the growth of the economy on an expanding level of exports of both rural and manufactured goods.[8]

He assumes that the export option existed because the world was starved for food, and this created what he calls the 'extraordinarily favourable external conditions of 1946-8'.[9]

In this key period between 1946 and 1948 the decisions to nationalise the railways, to erase the foreign debt and to continue the process of industrialisation were taken. But instead of trying to discover the characteristics of this period which help to explain the decisions which were taken, Díaz Alejandro looks for explanations in terms of political opportunism and psychology. This is how he arrives at his original and curious idea of explaining these decisions as a delayed response to the Great Depression:

> The policies followed during 1943-55 are in many ways more extreme forms of those followed during 1930-43, and continued trends in allocation of resources which, while justified in the great depression, were out of line with the more favourable conditions of 1943-55.[10]

He stresses the 'continuity of pre- and post-1943 economic policies, with the latter becoming crude caricatures of the former'[11] and the fact that the postwar world offered the kind of opportunities that made these decisions unnecessary:

> Once again we have the Perón regime applying policies which, although they had a low opportunity cost in earlier depression and war years, had become less desirable on economic grounds as a result of changing external conditions after the Second World War. Unfortunately for Argentina, she went for extreme nationalism when its price was highest.[12]

Explanations such as 'Argentine pride had been hurt'[13] are briefly mentioned. However, he stresses, wrongly in my view, the political necessities of the Peronist movement and its dislike for the

[8]   Díaz Alejandro, *op. cit.*, p. 155. This option is also implied by Corden (*op. cit.*, p. 40): 'No doubt the comparison with Australia is instructive for students of Argentina; it shows "what might have been" if politics had been stable and economic policies reasonably sensible.'
[9]   Díaz Alejandro, *op. cit.*, p. 167.
[10]   *ibid.*, p. 162.
[11]   *ibid.*, p. 164.
[12]   *ibid.*, p. 165.
[13]   *ibid.*, p. 156.

landowning interests. (They were associated with foreign trade and the production of exportable goods,[14] while industrialisation helped to give employment to the urban working class whose support the government needed.)[15]

Díaz Alejandro's summary is clear:

> These policies taken together present a picture of a government not so much interested in industrialisation as in a nationalistic and 'populistic' policy of increasing the real consumption and the employment and economic security of the masses and of the 'kept' entrepreneurs even at the expense of capital formation and the capacity to transform the economy.[16]

The analysis of the period ends with a significant reference to memories.

> Bitter memories of the great depression, as well as dimmer memories of the period immediately after the First World War, led the Argentine economic authorities to neglect the long run economics of growth for the sake of short run economic security.[17]

Forecasts on the future of the world economy and its implications for Argentina

The approach used here will give as little importance as possible to such aspects as psychology and even politics. Instead the international economic environment will be explored, and an attempt will be made to find in it the causes for the actions that have to be explained. The aim is to show that external conditions explain to a very large extent the policies which were followed.

However, before analysing these it will be useful to describe what was believed during and immediately after the war about the future of the world economy and its possible consequences for Argentine agriculture.

The problem facing the Argentine government was to evaluate what role Argentina could play in the international economy. For this, the central factor was whether the thirties had been a temporary aberration or whether they had marked the end of the era in which Free Trade had played a very important role. If the trend towards protectionism was about to be reversed in the United States and

[14] *ibid.*, p. 156.
[15] *ibid.*, p. 158.
[16] *ibid.*, p. 167.
[17] *ibid.*, p. 167.

Europe, if these countries were to grow quickly and if their income elasticity of demand for food remained high, this offered the possibility of returning to the traditional organisation of the Argentine economy: that is, growing agricultural exports, a high level of imports, and little protection for industry. The fact that under certain conditions this option might have been possible should not, however, be taken to imply that it would have been considered desirable. The disparities in regional development, the maldistribution of income, and the vulnerability of the whole economy to such factors as weather conditions or increased agricultural production abroad, reduced the general attractiveness of a return to the traditional economy.

On the other hand, if the multilateral system was not going to be restored, if agricultural protectionism was going to continue in Europe and the U.S.A, and if the external demand for Argentine products was unlikely to grow substantially through time, a new path of growth had to be sought.

The most complete interpretation of what was happening in the world economy from the point of view of Argentina was the one elaborated by Raúl Prebisch. He had had an important influence on the shaping of Argentina's economic policies during the thirties. His key role in the Central Bank had become even more important with the outbreak of the war. The most important aspects of Anglo-Argentine payments were settled between the two Central Banks, with very little interference from anybody else. Besides being very influential Prebisch was also extremely well-informed. His main ideas that are of relevance for the present essay are easily accessible in two United Nations publications, written when he was already working at E.C.L.A.[18] It should not however be thought that he developed his ideas in Chile after leaving Argentina; in a course of lectures delivered in Buenos Aires in 1944 he had already clearly arrived at the main conclusions which later became well known.[19]

Prebisch begins by dividing the world into an economic centre and its periphery. The engine of growth for the latter is provided by its exports, which mainly go to the centre; therefore the behaviour of the import requirements of the centre for goods from the periphery determines in great part the rate of growth of the underdeveloped

[18] *The Economic Development of Latin America and its Principal Problems*, which Prebisch had already finished in 1949, and *The Economic Survey of Latin America 1949*. Its Part 1 was written by him.
[19] I am indebted to Mr A. O'Connell for drawing my attention to a two volume mimeographed copy of his lecture notes corrected by Prebisch himself. They are entitled *La moneda y los ciclos económicos en la Argentina* and a copy is deposited in the library of the Argentine Central Bank.

countries. The import requirements of the centre are determined by the rate of growth of the centre and its import coefficient. If the import coefficient changes neither at the centre nor at the periphery, and the direction of world trade remains constant, the rate of growth of the periphery will be equal to the rate of growth of the centre. If the centre reduces its import coefficient and a country of the periphery maintains its own, the underdeveloped country will have a rate of growth lower than that of the centre, because its supply of foreign exchange will increase at a lower rate than the rate of growth of the centre. The low or negative rate of growth of the main Argentine markets during the thirties, coupled with a shrinking import coefficient from countries other than their colonies, showed that the only way to avoid stagnation or a reduction in income was to reduce Argentina's import coefficient. This was successfully done during the thirties and during the War.

While Great Britain had remained the economic centre of the world, its development had brought in its train the economic transformation of other regions, mainly those of temperate climate. The United Kingdom, by specialising in industry and coal, and by maintaining free trade, had allowed imports to flow freely. The fact that its agricultural interests were no longer very powerful made it possible for agricultural imports to increase rapidly without creating too many problems for its economy. The excess of imports over exports provided the rest of the world with the necessary sterling to pay for debt services and profit repatriation that resulted from Britain's loans and investments abroad. This had been the era that had provided the opportunity for Argentina's export-led growth.

However, with the First World War and British balance of payments problems, the situation changed. Loans from London lost importance, and finally Protection, Imperial Preference and Bilateralism became the main elements of the new period.

The import coefficient of the United Kingdom had fallen from above 30 per cent from 1870 to 1913 (in this period only six years had a coefficient lower than 30 per cent, of which five were above 29 per cent and the remaining one 28.90), to around 18-19 per cent in the late thirties and 13.23 in 1945. This situation was no better as far as Latin America was concerned. The United Kingdom's import coefficient from this region collapsed from over 3 per cent in 1928-9 to 1.61 in 1938 and for 1945 and 1946 it was 1.26 and 1.85 respectively.[20]

Meanwhile, the United Kingdom had lost its position at the centre of the world economy, and was being replaced by the United

[20] U.N., E.C.L.A., *Economic Survey 1949*, p. 30.

States. Prebisch believed that the United States was not adequately prepared for its new role, and that it acted, especially in times of crisis, as if it were still a peripheral country, that is, without regard for the consequences of its acts upon the rest of the world economy and finally upon itself. Its increased protectionism at the beginning of the Depression had made life much more difficult for the other countries, which were in desperate need of dollars:

> In synthesis, I believe that the attitude of the US since the crisis was simply that of a dog in the manger that neither eats nor allows other people to eat; the US did not trade nor allowed other countries to trade.[21]

By this, he meant that the US restricted its imports and 'fought rudely'[22] against discriminatory trade. But this (discriminating against dollar imports) was the only way open to the other countries to keep international trade at a relatively undepressed level.

These words, written in 1944, are highly significant. They clearly show the spirit with which Argentina viewed the opportunities that the post-war world offered her.

Analysing post-war international monetary plans, Prebisch insisted that unless the US drastically changed its behaviour, even the granting of loans would not solve the problems of the countries that suffered from a dollar shortage. Loans would simply postpone the issues, but in the end they could not avoid a return to 'monetary and economic autarky'.[23]

The early post-war dollar shortage, the return to sterling inconvertibility in August 1947 after the American Loan to Britain had been almost totally exhausted, and the continuation of United States agricultural protectionism, did not make Prebisch change his mind.

The import coefficient of the United States in 1945-8 averaged 2.7, compared with more than 3.5 during the thirties and over 5 in the twenties.[24] In part this was certainly due to the lack of imports from devastated Europe. But this certainly does not apply to Argentina, which had the necessary goods to export and was trying desperately to gain access to the U.S. market for many of its products. They were kept out through quotas and other restrictions.

Given this situation, industrialisation was the only way out. The way to avoid having a smaller rate of growth than the stagnant countries of Europe that were reducing their import coefficient, was

---

[21] *La moneda y los ciclos*, vol. 2, p. 234.
[22] *ibid.*, vol. 2, p. 245.
[23] *ibid.*, vol. 2, p. 245.
[24] U.N., *The Economic Development of Latin America*, p. 24.

to reduce Argentina's import coefficient, and to grow as the famous expression put it, *hacia adentro* (inwards).

Prebisch was not alone in thinking in terms of economic growth on the basis of relatively stagnant exports. The pattern of inter-national economic relations that had lasted with some difficulty until the late twenties was seen by most economists and politicians as definitely gone.

To understand attitudes towards the future, it is especially illuminating to analyse an explicit attempt at forecast written during the war.[25] Colin Clark had acquired a high reputation in some influential Argentine circles, and his predictions for the world economy and its implications for Argentine policies were absorbed by the group of people linked to the *Revistà de Economía Argentina*.

He assumed extremely favourable conditions for agricultural ex-ports, assumptions that were to be disproved by subsequent events. His premises were:

a) that the U.S. would become a substantial importer of farm products;
b) that the terms of trade between primary and industrial products would improve in favour of the former by 90 per cent. by 1960 over the 1925-34 level; and
c) that free trade or similar conditions would·prevail.[26]

Even under these extraordinarily optimistic conditions, Clark's predictions for Argentine exports were definitely not encouraging:

> Among the exporting countries, the great expansion of pro-duction will come in certain parts of Asia, Africa, Latin America (other than Argentina and Uruguay) and the Balkans. Among the exporting countries of the present day, it appears that exports from the Argentine and Uruguay will expand only slightly, while in Australia, New Zealand and Denmark they will actually fall.[27]

Quantifying, he assumed that world trade in primary products would increase by 1960 by 329 per cent over the 1934-8 average, while over the same period he thought that exports from Argentina and Uruguay would only increase 16 per cent. Argentina's and Uruguay's share in the world trade of primary produce, he believed, would fall from 12.65 per cent in 1934-8 to 4.47 per cent in 1960. However,

[25] Colin Clark, *The Economics of 1960*, London, 1942.
[26] *ibid.*, pp. 49-63.
[27] *ibid.*, p. 63.

with stagnant agricultural exports and a possible decline in primary production due to migration to the cities, his forecast for Argentine per capita income is extremely illuminating. Argentina and Uruguay would have a per capita income of 754 in his units of measurement, the second in the world, with the U.S. leading with 879 and Europe lagging far behind.[28]

Stagnant exports were seen as perfectly compatible with a far above average rate of growth. The era where agricultural exports had been the engine of growth was regarded as gone forever. This was not to be regretted, since the opportunities that the future seemed to offer looked much more exciting.

This was not only the idea of selected economists. Many thought that Argentina, like some other countries, could easily transform itself from a rich agricultural country into a modern industrial one. In the United Nations Economic Report for 1945-7[29] the point is made that the 'formerly sharp distinction' between 'industrialised' countries and those producing primary products tends to become more and more blurred', and that 'in the long run these tendencies, especially if supported by deliberate action to promote development schemes, could prove more significant than the present prominence of the United States in world production, which was perhaps to be expected immediately after a period of war devastation in the rest of the industrialised world'.[30]

The prospects ahead seemed to point unambiguously towards industrialisation as the only long run solution for Argentina's problems. As will be seen in the following section, the international economic conditions during 1946-8 tended to confirm rather than invalidate this view.

Foreign trade conditions, 1946-8

(a) Direction of trade

Most of the problems that Argentina faced during this period arose from the breakdown of the international economy, as the trade triangle that had characterised the twenties and the thirties, with a trade surplus with the U.K. and Continental Europe, and a trade deficit with the U.S., became even more pronounced.

The devastation of Europe created a huge demand for Argentine foodstuffs, but weakened drastically the capacity to export of

[28] France for instance was expected to have 429, Sweden 527; *ibid.*, p. 70.
[29] *Salient Features of the World Economic Situation, 1945-47*, New York, January 1948.
[30] *ibid.*, p. 10.

Argentina's traditional European trading partners, increasing thereby Argentina's favourable trade balance. As a logical counterpart of this, Argentina's usual deficit with the United States became even worse, as she had to buy there the goods she used to buy in Europe. Most European currencies however, were now inconvertible, and Argentina could no longer compensate her deficit with the U.S. with her surplus with Europe. She needed dollars or gold, but could receive instead only inconvertible currency, such as sterling, French francs or lire. Because of this, figures of total exports and imports do not give an adequate picture. The fact that exports were much higher than imports may give the impression that the situation presented few problems. In fact, however, as the value of total reserves expressed in pesos grew, her dollar and gold situation was becoming unbearable.

Table 6.1 Argentina. Exports, imports and trade balances with main trading areas, 1945-8, in million pesos

	£ Area			Western Europe			U.S.			All Countries		
	E	I	B	E	I	B	E	I	B	E	I	B
1945	749	187	+562	455	146	+309	553	136	+417	2469	1008	+1461
1946	1157	367	+790	1302	335	+967	595	556	+39	3947	1980	+1967
1947	2006	529	+1477	1812	863	+949	544	2010	-1466	5421	4507	+914
1948	1877	783	+1094	1933	1154	+779	535	2028	-1493	5465	5341	+124

E = Exports   *I* = Imports   *B* = Balance

Source: B.C.R.A. Annual Report, 1949, pp. 13 and 16. Western
Europe does not include Switzerland.

The trade situation with the United Kingdom was particularly serious, as sterling's collapse in August 1947 destroyed the whole of Argentina's international economic strategy. In September 1946, Argentina had signed an agreement with Britain which dealt with the main economic difficulties between the two countries. Argentina granted extremely favourable conditions to the British railways, a relatively low price for meat and earmarked a high percentage of its exportable meat quota for Britain. On the other hand, Britain allowed that the sterling earned from then on by Argentine exports would be· convertible, while most of the old sterling balances remained blocked. Although, owing to the provisions of the Anglo-American Loan Agreement, Britain had to grant convertibility of sterling earned on current account in any case, this seemed to restore the conditions that had enabled Argentina to develop before the Great Depression; its trade surplus with the U.K. could be used to finance its deficit with the U.S. Unfortunately, sterling remained convertible for only six weeks after the relevant provisions of the Anglo-American Loan Agreement became operative, as countries that had a trade surplus with the U.K. started to demand dollars.

The collapse of sterling convertibility had profound effects; it proved to the world that the necessary conditions for multilateral trade and full convertibility were still far away, and that the early hopes of the Americans of establishing multilateralism and full convertibility in most of the world had been wildly optimistic.

Argentina's economic strategy towards Britain had been based on two premises: sterling convertibility, as promised by Britain in 1946, and the resurgence of Britain as an important exporter of the goods that Argentina needed. It was hoped to balance in this way the economic and political influence of the United States, which during and after the war had imposed embargoes — for political reasons — on many of its exports to Argentina. The fear that British exporters would profit from this situation had been one of the main elements of pressure on the American State Department, and had helped Perón to play a complex Anglo-American game. 1947 proved that both premises had been mistaken; the decision to suspend sterling convertibility in August destroyed one, while the coal crisis in Britain, which had reached alarming proportions at the beginning of the year, with no electricity for industrial consumers in such areas as the Midlands, London, the South East and the North West, showed that Britain would continue with huge export problems for a long time.

Industrial, agricultural and financial reconstruction suffered a powerful and unexpected blow in 1947, not only in Britain but in the whole of Europe, making Argentina's position more and more difficult. The possibility of financing the dollar deficit with a sterling surplus had disappeared, and the prospects of receiving the necessary goods from Europe, and from Britain in particular, were far from encouraging.

However, even if the United Kingdom was unable to pay in convertible currency or provide the necessary goods, it still remained a key buyer for many products. Analysing the export figures by country and product that were available to the Argentine authorities at the time of the British decision to end the convertibility of the pound, it is easy to see the difficult position in which they were placed (see Table 6.2).

The United Kingdom was by far the most important importer of salt ox hides, frozen beef quarters, frozen mutton carcases, frozen lamb carcases and canned meat. In fact, it was the only substantial importer of these goods.

After the painful adjustment during the war from agriculture to livestock to meet external demand, Argentina discovered that its only important buyer of meat was unable to pay. It could not deliver

Table 6.2 Quantities and destinations of principal exports from Argentina, January 1 to July 31, 1947 and a comparison with the first seven months of previous years

Destinations	Wheat Tons	Maize Tons	Linseed Tons	Oats Tons	Barley Tons	Other Wheat Products Tons	Queb-bracho Extract Tons	Canned Meat Tons	Calf Skins No.	Dry Ox hides No.	Salt Ox hides No.	Wool Tons	Frozen Beef Quarters	Frozen Mutton Carcases	Frozen Lamb Carcases
United Kingdom	303,091	157,387	—	—	10,438	32,010	17,610	71,712	353,426	46,409	1,197,242	2,130	2,020,382	325,400	2,610,491
United States	—	—	—	19,485	39,016	—	54,738	597	14,998	2,000	25,278	41,910	202,531	97,627	307,961
France	7,532	72,188	—	3,309	29,212	5,125	10,844	283	2,000	10,177	34,977	5,806	138,484	15,724	255,287
Belgium	20,301	36,890	—	—	663	368	5,946	5,126	59,200	—	110,659	8,871	108,728	—	—
Italy	162,594	12,000	—	2,544	—	2,032	—	675	118,199	170,324	112,743	2,874	18,959	13,205	19,335
Holland	25,002	41,492	—	—	32,922	4,373	1,770	520	193,804	17,865	149,888	3,831	—	—	—
Norway	—	21,658	—	9,500	406	—	1,620	—	6,750	—	49,610	40	—	—	12
Sweden	24,520	15,845	—	—	5,055	88,429	3,117	350	404	2,000	50,972	2,460	195,977	—	—
Spain	216,051	10,999	—	—	—	2,143	2,947	1	5,337	46,000	5,000	3,399	27,682	—	—
Switzerland	69,445	29,290	—	8,080	19,397	17,660	630	124	10,471	2,093	24,162	1,930	98,110	—	—
Rest of Europe	20,000	12,752	—	—	739	36,334	1,378	—	18,470	—	5,500	—	—	—	—
Brazil	234,302	—	—	—	—	—	2,640	—	—	—	—	254	—	—	—
Other S. Am. Reps.	180,928	5,000	—	10,798	450	17,088	5,559	1,019	513	—	16,445	1,383	26,084	14,302	—
Other Countries	43,400	243,167	—	115	9,919	13,252	9,052	5,618	89,711	34,005	54,608	12,176	84,537	12,038	70,514
Totals	1,307,166	658,618	—	53,831	148,217	218,814	117,851[1]	86,025	873,283	330,463	1,837,084	87,536	2,921,474	478,296	3,263,600
7 Months 1946	983,124	1,160,833	38,954	176,436	421,931	125,635	162,714	71,231	515,801	154,883	1,313,614	134,852	1,833,657	361,882	3,053,032
7 Months 1945	1,585,777	308,082	38,083	15,505	105,604	20,130	114,478	65,421	469,511	109,884	1,669,488	47,457	1,233,483	276,597	2,669,427
7 Months 1944	1,343,753	187,147	244,526	51,756	118,272	5,861	99,822	153,300	529,910	176,489	2,884,510	76,786	2,748,717	387,971	3,261,197
7 Months 1943	887,475	98,718	285,416	36,257	25,363	7,794	98,232	79,199	816,279	800,137	2,397,332	51,678	2,940,807	163,815	2,770,143
7 Months 1942	1,322,977	101,370	266,547	15,159	72,437	6,782	112,874	93,116	955,763	411,760	2,378,438	161,131[2]	3,093,317	345,619	1,973,571

[1] Includes 7,055 tons of quebracho extract from Paraguay shipped through Argentine ports.

Source: *The Review of the River Plate*, 29 August, 1947.

enough of the goods which were needed in exchange nor could it pay in convertible currency.

In this situation, the idea of exporting to the U.K. and accumulating more and more sterling balances that paid at most half per cent interest was certainly not attractive. The old slogan *Comprar a quien nos compra* ('buy from those who buy from us') reflected Argentina's lack of markets during the late twenties and the thirties. As a consequence, the slogan was used in favour of Britain, which was seen as the only relatively secure market for Argentine products. The slogan *Vender a quien nos vende* ('sell to those who sell to us'), instead, accurately showed the change which had occurred. During and immediately after the war, everybody was willing to buy essential goods, but not able to pay for them in either convertible currency or in other necessary goods. This new slogan was used against Britain as she could supply only very few goods in return.

The alternatives open to Argentina were equally unattractive: it could either let its agricultural production rot, or grant credits to the impoverished European nations. During the First World War Argentina had granted credits to the U.K. and France to help them purchase Argentine exports. The situation after the Second World War was much worse, and Argentina had to give substantial credits to its most important trading partners. In 1946 Spain was authorised to issue a loan in Buenos Aires for 400 million pesos[31] plus a credit of 350 million pesos; Chile was given a credit of 100 million pesos, and Belgium a credit of 110 million pesos. In 1947 France had its 150 million pesos credit granted in October 1945 increased to 600 million pesos. By the end of the year, 70 per cent of the 600 million pesos had already been spent. Italy received a 350 million pesos credit in October. By the end of the year, more than half had already been used. Rumania received a credit of 25 million U.S. dollars to be spent in Argentina; Finland 75 million pesos.

In 1948 a further credit was granted to the Netherlands for 235 million pesos. The credit to Spain was increased from 350 million pesos to 1750 million, to be used over five years at the rate of 350 million a year, another 75 million pesos was granted to Finland and others.[32]

The conditions under which these credits were granted were extremely favourable to the recipient countries, making it clear that

[31] To appreciate the magnitudes involved it is necessary to remember that the U.S. dollar was quoted at 3.50 pesos.
[32] See H.B. Carnes, *Notes on Argentina's Bilateral Compensatory Trade Agreements*, New Orleans, 1949, and Annual Reports of the Argentine Central Bank.

Argentina did not enjoy a strong bargaining position. While it is obvious that there were many countries that were anxious to buy Argentine exports, it is equally obvious that these countries could not pay. It was very easy for Argentina to sell, but very difficult to get anything in return. Whether these countries would recover at all was very much an open question, and the setback that reconstruction had suffered in Europe in 1947 made the outlook grim.

The only major country that could provide the necessary goods was the United States. But this was not a potential stable market for Argentina. The Agricultural Adjustment Act (A.A.A.) of 1933 had been aimed at raising the prices of agricultural products in the United States above world levels. In order to make exports possible and in order to prevent imports from taking advantage of this situation, in August 1935 Congress amended the 1933 Act by adding Section 22, which established the very general principle that imports should not 'render ineffective, tend to render ineffective, or materially interfere' with A.A.A. In addition, Section 32 provided that 30 per cent of the annual customs revenue could be used to subsidise exports of farm products.[33] This system by which production in the United States was artificially encouraged, and the surplus dumped on world markets, not only continued after the depression, but has become a characteristic of United States agricultural policy that continues to this day. After the war, it became clear that agricultural protectionism in the United States was about to increase. From 1941 and 'culminating' in 1948, measures were taken by Congress to increase support for farm prices. The Agricultural Act of 1948 continued in the postwar period the wartime measures in support of agriculture, and in addition provided larger funds for export subsidies.

The position for Argentine exports between 1946 and 1948 was not similar to that in the thirties; it was worse. Europe could not pay; the United States would not buy. The prospects for the fifties were not better. All the European nations were rebuilding their agricultural sectors as fast as possible, thereby indicating that the free trade era for agricultural products would not return. There was little hope for a change in the United States' attitude.

In addition most experts believed that overproduction of farm products in the medium run was almost certain. At the end of the war shortage of food was expected, but after a few years, chronic surpluses were expected to appear:

> After a relatively short relief period, which may still be

---

[33] John M. Leddy, 'United States Commercial Policy and the Domestic Farm Program', in William B. Kelly (ed.), *Studies in United States Commercial Policy*, Chapel Hill, North Carolina, 1963, p. 192.

interspersed with shortages of some food commodities, the chief agricultural countries of the world are likely to face a serious commodity-surpluses problem. They may need to re-adjust production capacity after its overexpansion during and immediately after the war.[34]

The first paragraph of the preamble of the 1948 International Wheat Agreement shows that three years later the same opinion was widely held by the governments concerned:

> The Governments on whose behalf this Agreement has been signed, recognising that there is now a serious shortage of wheat, and that later there may be a serious surplus . . .[35]

The alternative faced by the Argentine Government was clear; either to transfer more resources to agriculture in order to meet a high but transitory demand for exports for which few goods could be obtained in return, or try to industrialise.

(b) Terms of trade
The other factor that has been influential in shaping the image of the years 1946-8 as very favourable for Argentina's foreign trade has been the relatively high terms of trade enjoyed by the country.

Table 6.3 (1937 = 100)

Year	Terms of trade
1945	69.2
1946	107.4
1947	106.8
1948	116.0

Source: E.C.L.A., *Economic Survey of Latin America 1949*, p. 98.

High demand for Argentina's products, coupled with favourable terms of trade, has been interpreted retrospectively as sufficient conditions for encouraging exports. However high demand without capacity to pay was not very helpful for trade. It has already been

---

[34] Karl Brandt, *The Reconstruction of World Agriculture*, New York, 1945, pp. 311-12.

[35] Minimum agreed prices for wheat for the next years were determined in the Agreement. It is interesting to note that the minimum price agreed for 1948-9 was U.S. $1.50, falling continuously through time and arriving to U.S. $1.10 for 1952-3, making it very clear that the governments of the producing countries expected overproduction of wheat with the consequent drastic fall in its price. See *Foreign Agriculture*, May 1948, p. 106.

seen how misleading it is to draw conclusions about the payments position of a country, when there is no convertibility among different currencies, from total import and export figures (even leaving invisibles aside). The situation is similar for global terms of trade. Argentina did sell its goods relatively expensively to some countries, and a unit of its exports could buy more imports than before the war. But the countries that paid high prices were mainly those that could send very little in return. Thus, even if their exports were relatively cheap, since their amount was extremely limited, favourable terms of trade with them had little significance. It did not mean that more goods could be imported from them; the only practical consequence for Argentina was that those countries exhausted sooner the credits granted to them by Argentina. When these credits were repaid, the terms of trade had already worsened drastically for Argentina, and world inflation and the devaluation of the currencies which Argentina had been obliged to accumulate had deeply eroded their value.

With the United Kingdom the terms of trade were not so favourable. From available evidence it is clear that meat, for instance, was sold relatively much more cheaply than the price of British imports. With the United States, fragmentary evidence suggests that the terms of trade probably worsened. In his estimates of Argentina's external terms of trade, Díaz Alejandro dismisses the available Argentina data for import prices, merely because their evolution gives a different picture from that of Canadian and Australian import prices and that of U.S. wholesale prices. He then proceeds to calculate Argentina's terms of trade on the basis of Argentine export prices and Canadian import prices, which he thinks give a more 'realistic picture' of Argentina's trade position after 1946. This index is most probably very biased, because Argentina had to buy many essential goods in the United States at what Miranda, the 'economic czar' of the period, himself called black market prices,[37] that is, much higher prices than those paid by other countries. This situation was due to Argentina's political problems with the United States which were not shared by other countries who could import American goods more easily.

The agricultural sector

We can now, in the light of these considerations, deal with the

[36] Carlos F. Díaz Alejandro, *Essays on the Economic History of the Argentine Republic*, New Haven, 1970, p. 88.
[37] As for instance petrol: *La Nación*, 16 November, 1947.

position in agriculture itself. The main characteristic of this period was the drastic fall in area sown with the agricultural crops which were Argentina's traditional exports.

Table 6.4 Area sown with wheat, linseed and maize, selected years 1929-48

	1929	1939	1945	1946	1947	1948
Thousands of hectares	16,817	16,628	12,245	11,578	12,190	10,396

Source: U.N., E.C.L.A., *Economic Survey 1949*, p.128.

This fact was constantly mentioned by the anti-Peronist press, and used as an example of how the prices for agricultural goods which were fixed by the Government were leading to a drastic fall in the production and the abandonment of land. They urged that the government agency's huge profits should go to the agricultural producers themselves; that without this additional income agricultural production had become unprofitable; and that the fall in cereal production was the natural consequence of government policies that led to chaos and poverty. Attempts were also made to show that figures like these were the inevitable consequences of state intervention in the economic sphere.[38]

These figures give a very distorted picture of the situation. The growth of the Argentine economy and its international trade problems strongly influenced the structure of agricultural production. Areas sown with rye, barley, oats and sunflower expanded rapidly increasing by 3,975,000 hectares between 1925-9 and 1945-8.[39] With the development of the edible oil industry in Argentina, sunflower increased from zero in 1933 to 1.5 million hectares in 1948. The area cultivated with industrial crops (sugar cane, wine, peanuts, tobacco, yerba mate and cotton), expanded from a yearly average of 439,000 hectares for 1925-9 to 1,061,000 hectares in 1945-8. Production had increased for those products for which there was internal demand.

There remains, however, an important fall in total area sown which has to be explained. It was not true that land was being

[38] For one of many examples of a distorted use of these figures, see *La Nación*, 26 September 1947, *Memoria de la Cámara de Exportadores*. International academic journals also gave these dramatic figures without the necessary clarifications.

[39] U.N., E.C.L.A., *Economic Survey 1949*, p. 128.

abandoned.[40] What had happened was simply that beef production had increased. Beef production increased by 24 per cent between 1937 and 1947, while mutton increased during the same period by 16 per cent.[41]

During 1946 meat seemed to have good possibilities of gaining access to the United States market and becoming a dollar earner. A campaign began in the United States press in favour of Argentine beef. Sanitary restrictions against it were regarded as a trick to protect American producers. The United States Army was more than willing to have Argentine beef; everything seemed to confirm 'the charge that the real trouble with Argentine beef is that it competes with American beef'.[42] The Mayor of New York, O'Dwyer, asked for Argentine meat to be allowed into the U.S.,[43] while the ex-Mayor, Fiorello La Guardia, used his weekly radio programme on two occasions to argue that the way to combat United States meat shortages was by importing Argentine beef.[44]

In addition, between 1938 and 1944 grain production had to be subsidised.

The excellent maize harvests at the beginning of the war had been a financial burden of enormous magnitude. The Grain Regulating Board made a loss on maize alone of 397.1 million pesos between 1939 and 1942. Taking as a whole wheat, maize, barley, linseed and sunflower, between 1938 and 1944, the Grain Regulating Board and the Agricultural Production Regulating Board, made a total loss of 376.7 million pesos, including the profits made on linseed and sunflower.[45]

Due to the lack of markets, cereals had to rot or be used as fuel. It was estimated that in 1943 alone, 1.7 million tons of wheat and 1.5 million tons of linseed had been burnt.[46]

Exports of cereals had varied‧ enormously. Maize exports had fallen from a yearly average of 6.1 million tons during 1935-9 to a yearly average of less than 0.4 million tons during 1941-4. In 1941 the Board was paying maize producers 4.75 pesos per *quintal* and

[40] These rumours were widely believed by sections of the middle and upper classes. The government had to deny explicitly that the land was being abandoned. See Miranda's speech, *La Nación*, 16 November, 1947.

[41] U.N., E.C.L.A., *Economic Survey 1949*, p. 133.

[42] Leader in *Christian Science Monitor*, 28 October, 1946.

[43] *New York Times*, 7 October, 1946.

[44] *New York Times*, 7 and 14 October, 1946.

[45] Harry Woltman, 'The Decline of Argentina's Agricultural Trade: Problems and Policies' (unpublished Ph.D. dissertation, Food Research Institute, Stanford University, 1959), p. 166.

[46] U.N., E.C.L.A., *Economic Survey 1949*, p. 132.

selling some of it for 0.40 pesos. This was not enough to use the maize surplus and the Board was authorized in July 1941 to destroy the 1940 crop. Even though, for instance, the Argentine Electric Company planned to burn as fuel 508,000 tons of maize (20 million bushels), maize was still overabundant and had to be destroyed.[47]

Meat exports had, on the contrary, remained comparatively stable. These relatively favourable conditions for livestock explain why cattle increased at the expense of cereals. This shift also explains what had happened with the land. The total decline in cultivated area in Buenos Aires, Córdoba, Santa Fé, La Pampa and Entre Ríos between 1936-7 and 1946-7 had been 7.2 million hectares. Between 1937 and 1947 cattle had increased in these same provinces by 7.4 million heads, an addition in land terms of slightly over 8 million additional hectares.[48]

I.A.P.I. and pricing policies

We have seen that the price policies of the Argentine Government did not lead to the abandonment of the land, but the impression persists that Perón ruthlessly exploited the countryside. The reason for this lies in the internal and international pricing policies of Argentina.

In the international field she tried to obtain as high prices as possible, especially when there were few prospects of obtaining needed goods in return. During the war, the Allies had established the Combined Food Board, to buy agricultural products at low prices, thus avoiding a situation by which each country had to bid against each other; this body continued operating after the war under a new name. To counter this monopsony, Argentina decided to establish a State selling agency called I.A.P.I. (*Instituto Argentino para la Promoción del Intercambio*: the Argentine Institute for the Promotion of Trade). The situation had thus changed from one where a monopsony faced unorganised producers, to one of bilateral monopoly. This gave the Argentine Government the means of protecting the country from existing world conditions.

To speak of 'high international prices for food' in the immediate postwar period is misleading, insofar as it gives the impression that they were established by impersonal market forces. A world market did not exist. There were only bilateral and a few international agreements. The forces that determined the international price were not as impersonal as may be believed: Miranda was quite happy to toss

[47] For details on the corn situation, see Pavel Egoroff, *Argentina's Agricultural Exports during World War II*, Stanford, 1945, p. 9-14.
[48] U.N., E.C.L.A., *Economic Survey 1949*, p. 133.

a coin to bridge a gap of one million pounds in a discussion on future prices of meat.[49]

The international prices obtained for cereals were high if compared with prewar levels, and had risen much more than internal production costs in Argentina. This gave huge profits to I.A.P.I., which were not transferred to rural producers but used to promote essential imports at subsidized prices. I.A.P.I. was selling maize at 22 pesos per quintal to the U.K. while paying 10 pesos to the Argentine farmer. Wheat was bought at £1 6s 4d or less and sold at £4 15s 6d per quarter.[50]

By stressing the profits made by the Argentine Government, the British Press gave its readers the impression that the prices Argentina was obtaining amounted to highway robbery.[51] This was not the case, as can be seen by comparing the prices received for the same products by different countries in agreements with the United Kingdom.[52]

For frozen beef fore quarters, the United Kingdom paid in 1946 £6 per cwt. to the United States, £3.40 to the Argentine and £2.20 to Australia. In 1947 the prices were £6.40 to the United States, £3.80 to Argentina and £2.40 to Australia. For hind quarters the 1946 prices were to the United States £6.10, to Argentina £3.70 and to Australia £3.00. For chilled or frozen mutton, the 1946 prices were to the U.S. £4.64, to Argentina £3.10 and to Australia £2.61. For wheat the 1946 prices were: to the U.S. £1.35, to Argentina £0.90 and to Canada £0.94, while the corresponding 1947 prices were £1.35, £1.74, and £0.98. In 1947 Argentina obtained a higher price for wheat, but the Canadian farmers had refused to sell their wheat at that price. In addition, it should be noted that while the U.S. and Canada received dollars, Argentina received sterling.

From these figures we can see not only that no international price existed, but also that the price obtained by each country depended mainly on its bargaining strength. Argentina had to sell its meat cheaply because it had been warned by the United Kingdom that unless it did so, no refrigerated ships would be sent to collect meat for transport to other countries.[53]

[49] Sir John Lomax, *The Diplomatic Smuggler*, London, 1965, pp. 256-7.

[50] *Daily Telegraph*, 14 May 1947.

[51] See for example *Daily Telegraph*, 17 February 1947, where a £15 million wheat sale from Argentina is said in the headlines to contain £7.5 million of profit for the Argentine Government.

[52] Data from *Annual Statements of Trade*. United Kingdom prices have been decimalised.

[53] Argentina's commercial relations with the United Kingdom will be the subject of another article.

Argentina had used all its bargaining power, but not having the position of strength of the United States, it could not obtain similar prices. It is highly unlikely that any other Argentine government would have obtained similar prices. These prices, however, did not mean an increased supply of necessary imports.

In their protests, the Argentine farmers concentrated on the prices obtained abroad, claiming that they were being exploited by the State. If by this it is meant that the Government made profits on its agricultural transactions, this is undoubtedly true. If however, it is intended to mean that the farmers' income had been squeezed, this cannot be supported by facts.

Table 6.5 Relative prices of wholesale rural goods and overall wholesale price level (1939-48)

Year	Overall level	Rural goods
1939	100	100
1940	107	97
1941	117	95
1942	147	106
1943	161	115
1944	175	119
1945	190	139
1946	220	221
1947	228	220
1948	263	246

Source: Díaz Alejandro, *Essays on the Economic History of the Argentine Republic*, p. 459.

This should dispose of arguments like the following:

> Domestic farm prices were forced down to a level that destroyed incentive, and while sales abroad during the boom period yielded handsome profits, these were in large part wasted or misappropriated. The most disastrous result was the crippling of agriculture. One indication was the reduction of the area under cultivation from an average of 21.5 million hectares in 1934-44 to a little less than 19 million hectares in 1949 although population was increasing rapidly.[54]

The 1946-8 period saw a dramatic rise in the internal terms of trade for rural goods, thereby increasing the income of the producers. Although this increase in internal agricultural prices was not as high

[54] Arthur P. Whitaker, *Argentina*, Englewood Cliffs, N.J., 1964, p. 125.

as the one obtained by the government in its sales abroad, it was still considerable.

There is a further key point here, that has not received attention: that many of the goods exported were sold only because of the credit conditions given by I.A.P.I. to customers abroad. This had far-reaching implications. Had I.A.P.I. not granted credits on very favourable terms, the prices that the European nations would have been able to pay would have been lower, had they been able to buy at all.[55]

The huge and highly publicised profits that I.A.P.I. made on some of its transactions existed because of its own credits. These credits were clearly inflationary. Very schematically the reason for this is the following. Normally, the Argentine producer sold its exportable produce to an exporter who paid him in pesos. The exporter sold this produce abroad, receiving foreign exchange which he sold to the Argentine Central Bank in order to obtain pesos to pay for his expenses. This foreign exchange would then be sold by the Central Bank to an importer that needed it to pay for goods abroad which he would sell inside the country for pesos. In this way the purchasing power received by the agricultural producer had its counterpart in the additional (imported) commodities that were available.

This was not the case with the agricultural produce sold abroad on credit. The producer did receive pesos for it, but the country as a whole did not receive more goods in return for these exports. The increased amount of money in circulation did not imply a corresponding increase in available commodities, but this additional purchasing power given to the agricultural producers was at the expense of the purchasing power of the rest of the community.

Under these circumstances, it was quite natural that the purely book-keeping profits made by I.A.P.I. were not transferred to agricultural producers, whose long run export propects were dim.

Argentina would have been willing to sell at lower prices had she been guaranteed supplies:

> . . . The Government might well be found disposed to accept the world level of prices for its surplus corn, or even something lower, provided there was some guarantee of being able to buy what it requires in the United States.[56]

An example of this, that confirms what has been said above about the significance of global terms of trade figures for such a chaotic

---

[55] In this sense, sales to Great Britain can also be seen as credits, because Argentina was forced to accumulate sterling.

[56] *Christian Science Monitor*, 14 Oct. 1947.

time as the early postwar period, can be seen from the different relative maize-coal prices that Argentina was willing to accept from South Africa according to the amount of coal she would receive:

(a) 400,000 tons of maize at 135 pesos against
400,000 tons of coal at 80 pesos.
(b) 400,000 tons of maize at 145 pesos against
320,000 tons of coal at 70 pesos.
(c) 400,000 tons of maize at 130 pesos against
600,000 tons of coal at 80 pesos.[57]

On 1 October 1947, the United States imposed an export permit system rationing the export of 'tinplate, pig-iron, steel bars and plates, piping, motor vehicles, petroleum, coal and general machinery — everything in fact that this country (Argentina) wants for its Five Year Plan'.[58]

The situation before had not been better and Argentina had to put the utmost pressure on its trading partners to obtain essential supplies. The Brazilian Ambassador was reported to have said: 'Every time I asked General Perón for wheat he retorted with a request for rubber. 'We want iron and steel,' virtually shouts President Perón, and that goes for all those who want Argentine grain and meat.'[59]

But essential goods were very difficult to obtain. The opportunity of buying freely in the United States only began in April 1946. Then Argentina was removed from the List E where it had been in the company of Spain, Hungary, Austria and the possessions of Germany and Japan. But by October 1947 United States export licences were again needed.

As has been mentioned before, Perón has been accused of failing to use Argentina's accumulated reserves of foreign exchange to purchase the capital goods required to build heavy industries such as oil and steel. Given an international situation in which there was even a world wide shortage of raw materials such as coal and oil, it is extremely unlikely that he would have been able to find these capital goods for sale. In addition, during some of this period, the United States was not very helpful to Argentina, as the following quotation indicates from the (U.S.) Acting Secretary of State to the U.S. Chargé in Argentina: 'Export policy I. Export of capital goods should be kept at present minimum — it is essential not to permit the

[57] Public Record Office, Foreign Office Series 371, Volume 44729, AS 5750/189/2; telegram from Foreign Office to Buenos Aires No. 562, 31 October 1945.
[58] *Christian Science Monitor*, 14 October 1947.
[59] *Christian Science Monitor*, 29 August 1946.

expansion of Argentine heavy industry . . .'[60]

As Europe could clearly provide very little, the suggestion that if Argentina had exported more agricultural goods during 1946-48 she would have been able to import more essential goods, can be easily dismissed. This, plus the grim long term outlook for agricultural exports, were convincing enough reasons for anybody taking decisions in that period to dismiss the possibility of long run growth being based on agricultural exports.

Conclusion

A British M.P. gave a clear explanation of the situation:

> If, as Sir John Orr prophesies, the world scarcity is ended by 1950, may not the Argentine be left with few friends and stocks of meat, corn, and feeding stuffs that she is unable to dispose of?
>
> President Péron and Señor Miranda are no fools. If what would be the worst for them happens, and the world is no longer hungry, they will at least have succeeded in financing their Five Year Plan and will have gone a long way towards making their country self-sufficient on the German model.
>
> That will have been accomplished at proportionately less cost to the Argentine taxpayer. Also if, as a result of cereal glut, the Argentine is compelled to lower her prices, it will be no hardship to the Argentine farmer, who has never in the time of world scarcity received any benefit from the Government's high selling prices. Looked at in this light, Señor Miranda's high profit margin is seen as an economic cushion.[61]

It is also convenient to quote the 1949 E.C.L.A. report. Stressing the need for Argentina to reduce her import coefficient, to increase imports from where she can sell, and for closer contacts with neighbouring nations, all necessities of the thirties, it notes that 'the problems of economic development have reappeared in a way which does not differ substantially from that of the 1930s, in spite of the intensive growth of the country'.[62]

This view by the experts of the period is the key explanation of the continuity between the economic policies of the thirties and of the early post war period. The continuity was not due to the

[60] Telegram 141, 3 Feb. 1945. In *Foreign Relations of the United States, 1945*, vol. 9, p. 527, Washington, D.C., 1969. The marks of omission are those of the editors; it would be very interesting to know what else the sentence said.

[61] R.H. Turton, *Yorkshire Post*, 15 April, 1947.

[62] U.N., E.C.L.A., *Economic Survey 1949*, p. 190.

nationalistic designs of the Peronist leadership nor to their memories of the Great Depression. It occurred because many problems were remarkably similar, and this explains why agriculture was not encouraged more during 1946-8. The conditions were not at all favourable. The golden opportunity did not exist.

Given this fact, it is easy to understand why agriculture was not encouraged even more. Exports had been possible only by granting credits to nations whose prospects of recovery looked extremely dubious. Increased exports would not have meant increased imports but only more inconvertible balances and more inflation. In addition, constant U.S. hostility made it impossible for Argentina to develop a heavy industry.

Relative prices for agricultural goods were higher in the immediate postwar period than during the war, when it was considered that the agricultural sector as a whole was not doing badly. It would not have made much better sense to improve even more the internal terms of trade for rural goods.

When the conditions of the world economy improved and Europe was again able to export the necessary goods, the Perón Government had no inhibition whatsoever about giving more economic incentives to agricultural production. But to have done so in the earlier period would have been to ignore the economic reality surrounding Argentina.

7

The Popular Origins of Peronism

WALTER LITTLE

Introduction

Although the popular support which the Peronist regime enjoyed was largely working-class in character, its leaders showed little more than rhetorical enthusiasm for the pursuit of strictly working-class interests. On the contrary, they repeatedly subordinated them to what they believed to be the interests of the nation as a whole. There is nothing very surprising about this. It is a reflection of the fact that they were drawn for the most part from amongst middle-class stratae, never became declassé, and remained dependent throughout their exercise of power upon the tacit acquiescence of important business and military interests. Their subjective preference for poly-clasist outcomes was thus reinforced by the objective weakness of their position within the Argentine political system.

However, it is more difficult to account for the ease with which they were able to impose their views upon the Peronist Movement as a whole and yet retain the support of the rank and file. In particular, since the latter were always of solidly working-class status their support for so polyclasist a leadership seems paradoxical.[1] This apparent contradiction between the potentially radical social structure of Peronism and its actual reformist behaviour is commonly resolved by denying both that its leaders enjoyed the support of the entire working class and that the working class as a whole constituted a class in the proper meaning of the term. These denials have

[1] This view is at odds with that of P.H. Smith, 'The Social Base of Peronism', *Hispanic American Historical Review*, vol. 52, no. 1, February 1972, pp. 55-73. For a discussion of popular support for Peronism see W. Little, 'Electoral Aspects of Peronism', forthcoming, *Journal of Interamerican Studies*, August 1973.

generally been expressed in terms of the notion of working-class dualism.

Working-class dualism

Dualist explanations of working-class reactions to Peronism argue that by 1943 the urban working class had become divided into sharply contrasting traditional and non-traditional sectors. The non-traditional sector consisted primarily of recent migrants from the interior who had been attracted to the towns by the new industries which had developed after 1930. They were ill-educated, ill-organised, and socially atomised within the urban milieu. Their lack of class consciousness and a traditionally affective outlook on politics predisposed them towards the acceptance of charismatic authority and they later became the principal source of working-class support for Peronism. In contrast, the traditional urban working class which was largely of European immigrant origin was well integrated, relatively well organised, and highly instrumental in its political attitudes. It was fully conscious of its class position and later became the main source of working-class opposition to Peronism. In this way the paradox is resolved by declaring that that sector which was conscious of its class position opposed Peronism, but that that sector which did support it did not constitute a manifest class.

This dualist interpretation is premised upon five general assumptions about the way in which the social character of the working class increasingly became divided into traditional and non-traditional sectors between 1930 and 1943 and the different ways in which these sectors reacted to the challenge of Peronism after 1943. These have become widely accepted in both the academic and polemical historiographies of Peronism, but it is the contention of this essay that they are the result of ex-hypothesi reasoning and inaccurate empirical observation.[2] It concludes that the working class was dualist neither in structure nor in behaviour but was relatively homogeneous and that explanations of popular support for Peronism

[2] Documented views are discussed in the footnotes which follow but for a variety of purely assertive expressions of the same basic idea of dualism see: Mario Amadeo, *Ayer, hoy, mañana*, Buenos Aires, 1956; Eugenio Moreno, *El fenómeno social del peronismo*, Buenos Aires, 1966; Rodolfo Puiggrós, *El proletariado en la revolución*, Buenos Aires, 1958, and *El peronismo: las causas*, Buenos Aires, 1969; Alberto Belloni, *Peronismo y socialismo nacional*, Buenos Aires, 1962; Robert J. Alexander, *The Perón Era*, New York, 1952; and Tomás Fillol, *Social Factors in Economic Development: The Argentine Case*, Cambridge, Mass., 1961.

must be derived not from transitory phenomena such as migratory movements but from the course of Argentine history as a whole.

The first dualist assumption involves four subordinate beliefs concerning the social character of the internal migration from which the non-traditional sector is believed to have developed. In general it is assumed that the migration was on a massive scale, that it involved movement from traditional rural areas to Greater Buenos Aires, that it was predominantly masculine, and that most of it occurred in the late 1930s and early 1940s. The first of these views is justified by available information[3] but there are strong grounds for modifying the monolithic social character ascribed to the migration by the others.

In the first place, as Table 7.1 indicates, it appears that a majority of the migrants were from the relatively developed Littoral provinces rather than from the more traditional western and north-western areas of the country. Moreover, it is probable that most of this in-migration was from the medium and large towns of the Littoral.[5] This is of some importance since the presumed traditionalism of the migrants is generally seen as a function of the traditional environment from which they moved. Clearly, the social and cultural structures of the highly integrated towns of the Littoral cannot be equated with those of the rural communities in the economically more backward provinces, a much lower percentage of whose population was of European immigrant origin.

Moreover, a high proportion of the migrants were probably women. In 1936, for example, of a total of 359,245 in-migrants in the Federal Capital 213,755 were women. Although the demand for industrial labour increased after this date (especially in Greater

---

[3] By 1947 some 1,368,800 people had moved from the interior of the country to Greater Buenos Aires and the proportion of such migrants in relation to the population of the metropolitan area as a whole had risen from 12 per cent in 1936 to 29 per cent in 1947. For more details of this see Gino Germani, *Política y sociedad en una época de transción*, Buenos Aires, 1968, p. 307, and *Estructura social de la Argentina: análisis estadístico*, Buenos Aires, 1955, pp. 74-8.

[5] In one survey which was made on this question in two *villas miserias*, it was found that only 15 per cent of the migrant inhabitants were from centres of less than 2,000 people, more than 33 per cent had been born in centres of 2,000-20,000 people, while the remainder were from large centres. See Germani and J. Graciarena, *Investigación sobre los efectos sociales de la urbanización* . . . Universidad de Buenos Aires, Facultad de Filosofía, Publicación Interna no. 5, 1958. Available information does not cover the possibility of step-migration from the poorer provinces to the Littoral but even if such step-migration was of significant proportions its social impact would have become progressively attenuated.

Table 7.1 Migration to Greater Buenos Aires by 1947

Source of migrants	Numbers in 000's	% of total migration to Greater Buenos Aires
Littoral total	*1016*	*59.6*
Prov. Buenos Aires	672	39.5
Santa Fe	109	6.4
Entre Rios	106	6.2
Corrientes	46	2.7
Córdoba	83	4.8
North-west total	*117*	*6.8*
Catamarca	14	0.8
Tucumán	37	2.2
Sgo. del Estero	42	2.4
La Rioja	12	0.7
Salta	9	0.5
Jujuy	3	0.2
Centre-west total	*61*	*3.5*
San Luis	26	1.5
San Juan	11	0.6
Mendoza	24	1.4
North-east total	*17*	*0.9*
Chaco	8	0.4
Formosa	2	0.1
Misiones	7	0.4
South total	*53*	*3.1*
La Pampa	37	2.2
Neuquén	3	0.2
Comodoro Rivadavia	—	—
Rio Negro	6	0.3
Chubut	5	0.3
Santa Cruz	2	0.1
Tierra del Fuego	—	—
Unspecified	*439*	*25.8*
Total	*1703*	*99.7*

Buenos Aires), there is no evidence to suggest that it was predominantly male directed, or that it dramatically modified the high female contribution to the process of in-migration.[6] Furthermore, although these female migrants were of undoubted electoral advan-

4   Source: Calculated from República Argentina, Ministerio de Hacienda, Dirección Nacional de Estadística y Censos, *Hechos demográficos*, 1944-54, Buenos Aires, 1956. Percentages accurate only to 0.3 owing to rounding.

6   The reasons for this high female migration are obscure but it is possible that the fairly buoyant demand for domestic servants and poor employment possibilities in the interior may account for part of it.

tage to the Peronists in later years, they remained largely unorganised and were not even enfranchised until after the regime was in power. They therefore cannot account in any significant sense for its initial evolution.

Finally, it is worth noting that well over one third of the migrants in Greater Buenos Aires by 1947 had been there for at least eleven years.[7] If social integration is related to the time spent in a particular environment (and there is every indication that this is so) then it is reasonable to assume that the cultural disorientation of these migrants had long since diminished. Thus it seems that far from being recently-arrived men from backward areas, the migrants tended to be from developed areas, as often as not to be women, and in many cases to have been relatively well integrated within the urban milieu.[8]

The second dualist assumption involves the idea that the migrants and non-migrants worked in different sectors of the urban occupational structure. Thus it is generally accepted by proponents of the dualist thesis that the migrants tended to enter the newer, manufacturing industries rather than the service sector of the economy where the more privileged traditional sector of the working class was concentrated.[9] This belief is then used to relate the widespread support which Perón later received from the industrial unions with

[7]   See República Argentina, Municipalidad de la Ciudad de Buenos Aires, *Cuarto censo general, 1936*, vol. 2, Buenos Aires, 1939, passim. This calculation is based upon Germani's estimate that by 1947 some 1,368,800 in-migrants were living in Greater Buenos Aires.

[8]   Germani's estimate that 29 per cent of the inhabitants of Greater Buenos Aires were in-migrants by 1947 is widely cited as an instance of the extent to which the migrants had altered the social structure of the urban working class. But if this figure were to include only working class migrants it might reasonably be reduced to 27 per cent. If women were eliminated it would fall to around 14 per cent. If migrants long-resident in Greater Buenos Aires were then excluded, the percentage of 'ideal type' migrants would fall to about 9 per cent.

[9]   The reason for this view's persistence is its ideological attraction. Thus: 'A whole army of labourers with a very important characteristic was concentrated in the new factories. They were of purely native stock and were uninvolved with the inglorious past ... of 'leftist' parties. They were men from the backward zones, provincials who had been on the fringe of production and who now entered the national scene. They were to be the great (mass) ... who were to fill the Plaza de Mayo on the 1st of May and the 17th of October.' Alberto Belloni, *Del anarquismo al peronismo*, Buenos Aires, 1960, p. 59. (All quotations given in this essay have been translated by its author.) For expressions of similar views see also Roberto Carri, *Sindicatos y poder en la Argentina*, Buenos Aires, 1967, pp. 25-8, and Jorge Aberlardo Ramos, *Revolución y contrarrevolución en la Argentina*, vol. 2, Buenos Aires, 1965, pp. 523-4.

the fact that the new industries were areas of migrant concentration where an authoritarian type of political culture prevailed.

The idea that migrants entered different occupational sectors is derived from changes that occurred in the economy and society of Argentina after 1930. These are generally identified as the development of import-substitutive domestic industry and the decline in the agricultural sector which followed upon the slump between 1929 and 1933, and which were further consolidated by the depressed 1930s and the Second World War. This reorientation of the economy led to a decreased demand for agricultural labour and an increased demand for industrial labour. Along with the decrease in the supply of immigrant labour that followed more stringent immigration laws, this led in turn to the mass migration of workers from the agricultural to the industrial sector and ultimately to the emergence of the non-traditional sector of the working class.

However, it is more accurate to maintain that the reorientation of the economy led to a transfer of labour from the rural to the urban areas rather than from the agricultural to the industrial sector. It is true that employment in manufacturing increased disproportionately during the 1930s, from 890,000 in 1925-29 to 1,310,000 in 1940-44, but there is no evidence to suggest that this increase of 420,000 was predominantly composed of migrants from the interior. Without surveys of the personnel records of individual firms there is no way of determining which occupational categories attracted migrant labour.

It is often implied that since the industrial development of these years was labour intensive it required low skills and was therefore attractive to the presumably less skilled migrant workers. Even if this view of the industrial development is accurate it may be inferred that since most migrants appear to have come from more developed areas, (presumably with more skills available), and since the non-migrant sector itself included large reserves of unskilled labour, increased demand for industrial labour was met at least equally by the inter-sectorial transfer of labour from within the urban areas.[10] This is not to deny that industrial growth indirectly stimulated the movement of population into the towns by creating a secondary demand for unskilled labour, or that some migrants became employed in the newer industries, but it does suggest that industrial

[10] In the same period employment in the transport, communications, power and construction sectors increased by only 55,000. This is a disproportionately low increase and may reflect the displacement of urban labour to the industrial sector. See C.E.P.A.L., *El desarrollo económico, argentino*, Santiago, 1958, passim, and Guido Di Tella and Manuel Zymelman, *Las etapas de desarrollo económico argentino* (Buenos Aires, 1967).

workers were not of predominantly migrant origin. This is of some importance since it weakens those explanations of support for Peronism amongst industrial workers which attribute it to the authoritarian political culture of migrant workers and suggests that their enthusiasm for Peronism may be explained in less exotic ways.

The third dualist assumption consists of the belief that there was further division within the urban working class at the organizational level.[11] The traditional sector is seen as consisting principally of workers of European origin employed in the printing and publishing trades, in the foreign-owned transportation sector, and in the public sector. They are regarded as having been relatively well organised, having enjoyed privileged wage rates, working conditions and fringe benefits, and having been represented by socialist and syndicalist unions of reformist outlook. In contrast, the non-traditional sector consisted especially of *criollo* workers from the interior employed in the expanding metal, food-processing, clothing and manufacturing industries. They were ill-organised, correspondingly badly paid and underprotected, and insofar as they were represented at all, were represented by militant communist unions. Finally, the fact of this organisational differentiation is seen as further confirmed by the fact that the General Labour Confederation (C.G.T.) was itself divided on similarly ideological lines throughout the 1930s.

This assumption is not supported by the information available on union organisation prior to the coup d'etat of 1943. Table 7.2 illustrates that the most important characteristic of the working class as a whole at this time was its generally low level of organisation. Not only were the majority of workers not organised, but most unions were small and fragmented. The only significant exception to this was the transportation sector. This apart, there was no clear distinction within the working class between privileged and non-privileged sectors. For example, both in 1936 and 1941, the reputedly well-organised printing industry had a lower percentage of its labour force unionised than the reputedly ill-organised clothing industry. Of course, different standards of living obtained within the working class according to occupational skills and particular circumstances, but this was not related in any clearly discernible way with the notion of traditional and non-traditional sectors. Far from being divided the urban working class seems to have been relatively

[11] For general expressions of this assumption see Angel Perelman, *Como hicimos el 17 de Octubre*, Buenos Aires, 1961, pp. 27-8, and Alberto Belloni, *Del anarquismo al peronismo*, pp. 41-4. For factual accounts of events of these years see Jacinto Oddone, *Gremialismo proletario argentino*, Buenos Aires, 1949, passim, and, in more personal vein, José Peter, *Crónicas proletarias*, Buenos Aires, 1969, passim.

Table 7.2 Union organisation, 1935-41

Activity	1935-6			1941		
	Total No. Occupied	No. of Unions	No. of Members	Total No. Occupied	No. of Unions	No. of Members
1. Agropecuarian	807,087	1	–	–	10	4,287
2. Extractive Industries	17,354	2	2,100	23,847	2	842
3. Good, drink and tobacco	120,233	18	10,688	172,640	39	29,171
4. Textiles	52,576	2	5,550	81,397	2	12,504
5. Clothing	30,875	7	9,428	42,953	10	12,906
6. Wood	32,395	5	8,827	57,382	10	6,304
7. Paper & printing	36,087	4	3,700	46,008	2	5,045
8. Chemicals	15,441	2	166	27,184	2	250
9. Rubber	3,584	–	–	4,765	–	–
10. Leather	19,575	–	–	9,110	–	–
11. Construction	51,239	14	32,588	–	34	74,283
12. Metals	92,856	3	1,975	228,356	4	4,459
13. Electricity & gas	16,509	–	600	21,387	4	650
14. Non-land transport	–	28	10,272	–	14	14,306
15. Land transport	–	23	141,562	–	30	140,601
16. Communications	–	3	4,779	–	2	3,200
17. Commerce & finance	–	80	64,876	–	69	60,841
18. Services	–	26	16,907	–	50	–
19. Various	–	57	10,576	–	57	23,566
State	302,250	14	44,655	368,700	15	31,480

12 Source: Calculated from República Argentina, Ministerio de Hacienda, *Censo industrial de 1935*, Buenos Aires, 1938; *ibid.*, Dirección General de Estadística y Censos, *Estadística industrial de 1941*, Buenos Aires, 1944; Departamento Nacional del Trabajo. *Boletín informativo*, Año 17, Epoca 6, Septiembre-Octubre 1936, pp. 4728-63; *Organización sindical* . . Buenos Aires, 1941.

homogenous in both its lack of privilege and its poor organisation.

In sum, the belief that migrants were concentrated in the industrial sector, that they were more militant in outlook than the traditional sector, and that the success of the communist unions in this sector was specifically due to the support of migrants seems at best debatable. It is significant in this respect that all attempts to relate levels and kinds of organisation to the presence or absence of migrants have been of the retrospective kind. No contemporary observer, (and there were many), came to any such conclusion and in the absence of any confirmatory evidence it cannot be assumed that any such clear relationship existed.

The fourth dualist assumption consists of the idea that urban and rural environments in the 1930s were thoroughly differentiated and that they inclined their populations to different modes of evaluation, expectation and action. Thus, in the rural environment familial and employment relations are seen as having been structured around semi-rational systems of authority in which social sanctions were personalised and moral values uncomplex. This inhibited the development of autonomous evaluation and action in the migrant worker and predisposed him towards the adoption of an authoritarian personality. In sharp contrast the pre-war working class milieu of Greater Buenos Aires is regarded as having had a greater degree of rationality, anonymity and moral complexity, and a greater level of independence, self-awareness and competence is consequently attributed to the more traditional urban worker.[13] This distinction was further reflected in the inability of the migrant to adapt to the urban political system and in his isolation from channels of self-expression and advancement. Finally, this led to considerable· tension between the traditional and nón-traditional sectors and ultimately to the creation of ideal conditions for a mass-based demagogic movement.[14]

It has already been noted that the rural environments from which migrants came were less culturally differentiated from the towns than has commonly been supposed and that the level of consciousness of the urban working class, (at least insofar as it is reflected in union organisation), was not so great as has generally been assumed.

---

[13] For example, their maintenance of a complex and interacting system of voluntary associations in seen as a sign of their maturity. See Torcuato Di Tella, *El sistema político argentino y la clase obrera*, Buenos Aires, 1964.

[14] For statements of this idea see S.L. Baily, *Labor, Nationalism and Politics in Argentina*, Rutgers University Press, New Brunswick, New Jersey, 1967, p. 82, and, in journalistic vein, J. Sebrelli, *Buenos Aires, vida cotidiana y alienación*, Buenos Aires, 1966, p. 170. See also G. Germani, *Política y sociedad* . . . p. 308, and T.R. Fillol, *op. cit.*, passim.

Although the notion that migrants were unable to manipulate the urban political system has some plausibility, it can equally be maintained that the same was true of a majority of the traditional working class. Moreover, the thesis of conflict between sectors of the working class cannot be verified. Available primary literature of the period contains virtually no reference to any such conflict and it is unlikely that it would not have attracted some press attention if it had been as significant as has generally been believed.

The final dualist assumption argues that the idea of a dualist working class is confirmed by the way in which organised labour reacted to Peronism after 1943, it being generally asserted that the labour unions — and, by extension, the working class as a whole — tended to either oppose or support the Peronist cause.[15] In particular it is accepted that opposition to Peronism was strongest amongst the privileged sector and amongst the more established unions and that support for it was strongest amongst the least privileged sector and amongst the less well established unions. This assumption is partly a reflection of the pre-electoral polarisation that occurred in 1945 and partly a reflection of later Peronist demands for ideological conformity, both of which tended to give the impression that organised labour was divided into either Peronist or anti-Peronist camps. However it is clear that far from reacting in a divided fashion on these lines, the labour unions acted in a wide variety of different ways and that there was no clear relationship between the extent to which they were traditional or non-traditional and their reactions to Peronism.

This can be illustrated by an examination of the reaction of organised labour to Peronism between 1943 and 1946 and between 1946 and 1955. In the period 1943-6 the unions reacted in three ways to Peronism: they fought it, they supported it, and they tried to take advantage of it without committing themselves. Most of the unions which fought the *de facto* Peronist regime were either led by communists, as in the case of the construction and meat workers, or by socialists and syndicalists, as in the smaller craft unions of shoe workers, tailors and the like. Their anti-Peronist stance was only partly of their own choosing for even before Perón had become particularly influential within the revolutionary *junta,* the *junta* had already ordered their intervention. But they were in any event resolutely opposed to the paternal interventionism in union affairs for which Perón stood.

Those unions which supported Perón and the newly created *Secretaría de Trabajo y Previsión* consisted partly of unions that

[15] About the only exception to this approach is that of S.L. Baily, *op. cit.*

sprang up in the textile, construction and food processing industries in.the place of those who had been intervened by the regime, partly of small unions in the interior of the country that had never previously enjoyed State patronage, and partly of new unions in the towns such as the power workers who enjoyed the support of the State in disputes with their employers for the first time.

The majority of unions, however, did not adopt such clear positions. For example, the railroad workers, commercial employees, public service workers, maritime workers and printers, all adopted a variety of positions varying from total disengagement in the syndicalist tradition to unashamed opportunism in the case of the socialist-led railroad workers. The particular stance adopted by these unions depended for the most part upon the particular ideologies of their leadership and the extent to which they were divided amongst themselves. In most cases the objective of their policies was to extract maximum advantage from the revolutionary regime along with minimum commitment towards it.[16] But there was an entire spectrum of behaviour open before them. This only became defined temporarily at the time of the October 1945 crisis and finally during the second Peronist government between 1951 and 1955.

The multiple rather than the dualist reaction of the organised working class is further confirmed by the fact that in the period 1946-55 six clear reactions can be identified.[17] In order of the conflict reached with the regime and the time span occupied these may be categorised as oppositionism, labourism, liberalism, independent Peronism, opportunism, and loyalism. Oppositionism consisted of the adoption by a number of union leaders of rigid and doctrinaire opposition to Peronism. This was strongest in the period 1943-6 amongst certain craft unions such as the shoe workers and by sectors of other unions such as the printers, textile workers and public employees. It was particularly characterised by the sacrifices — imprisonment, exile, and severe harassment — which their leaders endured rather than compromise with Peronism. But with the increasing pressure towards conformism as the regime progressed,

---

[16] The case of both the railroad unions illustrates this position. Although the policy of rapprochement with the regime had begun under the auspices of government interventors in 1943 it was enthusiastically continued by the socialist leaderships of these unions. Nevertheless when the time came to support Perón in the crucial days of October 1945 he received only the mild support of one and the total opposition of the other.

[17] For more details on this see W. Little, *Political Integration in Peronist Argentina*, unpublished Ph.D. dissertation, Cambridge University, 1971, pp. 55-69.

they diminished in importance and had disappeared as a practical political force by 1948.

Labourism may be identified as the ideological position adopted by a wide variety of unions such as the metal and meat workers and sections of the railwaymen and other major groups between 1945 and 1948. It combined qualified support for the regime with a belief in the need for powerful, independent, critical and highly politicised unions. Perón of course needed unions that were powerful and politicised but that were also dependent, and from 1946 onwards the incompatibility between these objectives became even clearer. By 1948 most *laboristas* has either collided with Perón and lost, or had quietly succumbed to the changing terms of the Peronist alliance.

The liberalist category consisted of the attitude of those unions which cooperated with the Peronists until they reached the point that a clear conflict of principle had arisen which they were unable to ignore. In such cases the increasing pressure from the State led to conflict between differing groups within the union, to the emergence of open conflict between them, and to the eclipse of the liberalist group. It is interesting however that only among the highly politicized printers and locomotive engineers can such an attitude be said to have existed.

The reaction which has been categorised as independent Peronism fell between labourism and loyalism. It comprised the willing acceptance of most of the demands of the Peronist State and emphatic support for it, but it also retained a capacity for independent action in extreme cases of conflict such as wage negotiations. In particular, loyalist leaderships often found themselves in a position of independence as a result of rank and file pressure over wages as occurred in the strikes of the bank workers, meat and metal workers in the late 1940s.

Opportunism was of course common to all unions, but it is particularly useful to describe the evolution in the attitude of certain kinds of unions such as the commercial travellers and other small unions with a strong voluntarist tradition, who accepted and formally adhered to the changing demands of the Peronist State, but, which made little attempt to communicate their position to their members. The mere formalism of their support was made possible by the fact that they were seldom of sufficient numerical importance to make it worthwhile for the State to openly collide with them.

Lastly, in the closing years of Peronist rule the increasingly monolithic and authoritarian nature of the labour union/State relationship found expression in loyalism in which the unions occupied a completely subordinate, consensual position *vis à vis* the State. Some groups adopted this position from the early days of

Peronism, and all came to it gradually as the demands made upon the unions increased in the course of the development of Peronism as a whole. But it is clear that before this stage was reached organised labour had reacted in a wide variety of ways and not merely in a dualistic fashion.

Finally, the adoption by any union of an ideological position was not in any way a reflection of the social character of its rank and file members. On the contrary it was a reflection firstly of the ideology of its leadership and the extent to which they were united in their opinions but more importantly of the attitude which the State adopted towards it. For example, in the period 1943-46 the three major reactions of the unions were in a sense forced upon them by the triple policy which Perón adopted, of coercion and supplantation of militant unions, of fairly widespread concession to the less militant, and of minor concessions to those recently organised groups which had little alternative but to support him. Once in power *de jure* any constraints that he might have had during his *de facto* tenure of office vanished and it is clear that the power of initiative lay with him and that the unions were forced merely to react to the ever-changing dicta of the Peronist State.

Conclusion

Although it has been shown that the dualist notion finds little confirmation in available information and that some other sort of explanation must be adduced to account for working class reactions to Peronism, the reasons for the popularity of dualist explanations will bear some examination. Apart from the superficial plausibility of the statistical arguments it seems that one reason for the attraction they have had lies in their theoretical provenance. For example it is interesting that they were promoted by social theorists in the 1950s, just at the time when the functionalist approach to the study of social modernisation was strongest. In particular, the widespread use of ideal-types (folk-urban, Gemeinschaft-Gesellschaft, sacred-secular etc.), to contrast contemporary with historical societies seems to have been the basis for the distinctions drawn between the traditional and non-traditional sectors. In the process of transposition, however, the caveats surrounding the use of such ideal-types were lost and they were applied in the simple and descriptive sense which has been the object of criticism in this essay. Thus it cannot be maintained that factual criticism fails to diminish the explicative value of the dualist notion since its very exponents have been the first to abuse it by regarding it as literally as well as metaphorically true.[18]

But there is another reason for the wide currency of the dualist notion. This is the appeal which it has for all shades of Argentine nationalism. In its own heady language, popular support for Peronism can be regarded as the culmination of a movement for national redemption. Thus the internal migrations symbolized a nativist reaction to the exploitation of the Littoral with European capital and labour that had characterised the development of Argentina since the latter half of the nineteenth century. When this is combined with the belief that is also represented the emergence of the common people as a major force it makes for extremely appealing political rhetoric.[19] Lastly, the notion of dualism has also appealed to many observers of liberal persuasion who have regarded Peronism as an essentially populistic and in some way deviant phenomenon and who are relieved to be able to ascribe deviant causes to it. As a result internal migration has been seized upon as the sole abnormal social development of major proportions that occurred immediately prior to the *coup* of 1943 and has been used to explain both the initial Peronist success as well as its later excess.

The contrary notion posited in this essay is that far from being divided the working class was remarkably homogeneous and that explanations of popular support for Peronism must be developed on this basis. In the first place the evidence for structural and behavioural differentiation within the working class is in no way significant. This has been demonstrated in the proceding section and is further confirmed by a variety of lesser observations. For example there is no evidence at all to suggest that there was any significant opposition

[18] A good instance of this has been the use of the term 'European' to distinguish the traditional from the non-traditional sector. This has a slight value insofar as certain union leaders and their ideologies are concerned but the term becomes meaningless when it is extended to the mass level. For example, according to the 1947 Census data, with an average of 25.7 per cent foreigners in secondary activities, the construction and wood industries (both militantly Peronist) had 31.7 per cent and 34.0 per cent respectively.

[19] For example, it is commonly maintained that the split within the working class was in part a reflection of its dependence upon British imperialism prior to 1943. Thus Perelman, an active unionist at the time and later a convinced Peronist, says of the unions in the traditional sector that they 'were formed by the great imperialist companies of British capital. The bureaucrats who directed these great (union) organisations were not only reformist and collaborationist to the utmost of their power but (also) politically spineless and in one way or other agents of the companies whose personnel they represented. Imperialism had tended to divide the working class into distinct social groups. This social differentiation produced a political differentiation and a differentiation in the degree of combativity' (Perelman, *op. cit.*, p. 9).

to Peronism from the working class as a whole. Thus it is notable that whatever they might have meant to their leaders, the strikes in the railway, banking, printing and sugar industries in the late 1940s were not regarded by the strikers as an attack against Perón but against their employers and their previous leaderships.[20] Moreover, it is significant that in none of the internal schisms that characterised the unions were any of the competing parties able to mobilise the rank and file against each other or against the regime. Throughout they remained resolutely indifferent to appeals of this sort. Finally, it is clear from the variety of unions which took up similar stances and from the rapid way in which these were altered under government pressure that their ideological position bore little relationship to the social character of their rank and file memBership.

In the second place variations in relative privilege within the organised working class were of slight significance compared to the fact that such groups were but a fraction of the urban working class as a whole which remained thoroughly underprivileged and ill-organised. The recognition by the working class of this status is confirmed by the enthusiasm with which it greeted the modest reforms introduced after 1943. For example it is particularly noticeable that little general legislation was enacted and that such legislation as was passed was normally of minor significance and frequently merely regulatory in character. For example, the recently founded Secretariat of Labour would lend a union the necessary land on which to build a clinic, it would reassess a particular labour classification, apply existing statutes to new situations, help initiate and finance pension funds, medical services and so on. The overwhelming character of this legislation was calculatedly narrow in extent and it is clear that no juridical revolution took place.

Moreover, the support of the Secretariat was accorded on a variable basis and, contrary to common belief, benefits were largely limited to the well-established and powerful unions. Improvements on behalf of the newer and weaker group of labour unions was in general limited to exhortation and encouragement, legal recognition, and help in wage negotiations and disputes. It is sufficient to compare the relative treatment of certain more established unions with the treatment received by some of more recent origin. In the

[20] The metallurgical strike in 1953 is often cited as evidence of the growing dissatisfaction of the working class with the Peronist system as a result of the austerity demands in its later years. Nevertheless it was the only instance of its sort and disenchantment with Peronism was reflected in absenteeism and apathy rather than in hostility towards Perón himself. As the 1954 election results indicated, the workers and unions realised that no political alternative to Peronism existed for them.

case of the prestigious railway unions for example. Perón was prepared, indeed eager, to make repeated concessions in the field of social and economic benefits. His aim was not even necessarily to win the railway unions over to the Peronist cause but rather to involve them with the Secretariat to such an extent as to either win their neutrality or at least create groups within them prepared to co-operate with the Secretariat. In the case of more recent unions such as the meat or power workers, he was able to bind them completely to the Secretariat merely by intervening on their behalf in wage bargaining. There was no need for complex legislative activity by the Secretariat in the case of the newer unions for he was aware of the differences not only between the amount of good and harm that they could do him but also between the amount of effort needed to win them over to his cause.

It is also apparent that although the working class responded enthusiastically to the benefits offered by the Peronists because it was aware of its underprivileged position, it was not fully conscious of its class position. Tactical considerations aside, such a consciousness would have inhibited the acceptance of the Peronist benefits but it is significant that the only unions to do this were small craft unions with no mass following at all and a few leaders of industrial unions who were unable to carry their membership along with them. Moreover, the ease with which unions switched ideological positions and the inability of competing groups to mobilise members against each other or against the regime would suggest that the working class as a whole was distinguished in this respect more by its lack of political understanding than by dualism.

Finally, it is evident that the notion of dualism has become something of a red herring which distracts attention from the fact that most traditional urban workers were less sophisticated and less differentiated from their rural counterparts than has generally been maintained and that the working class as a whole had long been prevented from occupying the role in Argentine politics to which its social position entitled it. The imbalance between its socio-economic integration and its political representation developed after the First World War when overseas immigration began to decline but when the working class failed to win access to institutional power. This was reserved for middle class radicals and it is noticeable that the elite that had been displaced in the 1916 election made no attempt to recruit working-class support. Had this occurred the rudiments of a two party system might have appeared but it did not, and the working class remained largely outside the political system.

It makes more sense to see the popular support for Peronism as another phase in a well-established pattern of social conflict, followed by integration and consolidation that was, in its turn, subjected to further social conflict. The unitarians in the middle of the last century, the modernising oligarchy at the turn of the century, and the emergence of middle class groups with Radicalism early in this century, were all manifestations of the same pressure towards growth and consolidation within the country as a whole. With regard to the working class, it is clear that although it was relatively well integrated into the social fabric of Argentina by 1920 the liberal political system proved resistant to its exercising a corresponding political influence. Indeed it is arguable that had the Army High Command that overthrew Yrigoyen in 1930 thought similarly to their 1943 counterparts then the whole Peronist saga could well have begun a decade before it actually did. It is clear that Peronism was supported not by marginal groups but by the overwhelming majority of the common people who had been systematically excluded from the exercise of the political rights to which their social importance entitled them by the resistance of those middle and upper-class groups that had already become powerful in Argentine society.

8

The Survival and Restoration of Peronism

DAVID ROCK

Since 1943 Peronism has been Argentina's strongest political party. On numerous occasions it has demonstrated an unassailable popular support based principally on the urban working class and the trade unions. At the same time it has subsisted as a class alliance between working-class and non-working-class groups. It is among the best known of the populist movements outside the developed countries.

The success and continuing durability of this movement has most frequently been argued in personal terms, as reflecting the political skills of General Perón himself, and later the good fortune of his longevity. Certainly this is important, as quickly became apparent after his death in June, 1974; his presence and the characteristics of his leadership were a vital unifying force holding together the fissiparous and heterogeneous elements of the movement.

Yet at the same time political genius is a quality strongly conditioned by opportunity. Although it is important to keep Perón's personal role in mind, particularly when assessing the subtle qualities of Peronism, it would also be useful to examine the conditions and forces which prevented other parties and political leaders in Argentina from usurping his position after 1955. Between 1955 and 1973 Perón was in exile in different parts of Latin America or Spain. Given the length of his exile, and his obvious difficulties in maintaining communication with events in Argentina, his continuing prominence seems remarkable. Even stranger is that in two presidential elections held in 1973 the great bulk of popular support should go to a veteran politician not far short of eighty years old.

The picture becomes even more intriguing when one remembers the tremendous antipathies to Perón among a large number of key power groups in Argentina. In many cases the very groups and political figures which conspired his fall in 1955, and afterwards hysterically opposed his return from exile, were to be found eighteen years later during the confused events of 1973 almost encouraging his candidature for the presidency. At late as 1968 General Alejandro Lanusse, who as President between 1971 and 1973 organised the elections which swept the Peronists back to power, declared:

> I am not opposed to putting Juan Perón's bust in Government House. But if that man . . . should set foot on this land again, one of us, he or I, will leave it feet first, because I shall not let my sons suffer what I have.[1]

There can be few cases of so dramatic a change of attitude, and so spectacular a revival of personal fortune and reputation.

In this essay my intention is to judge the survival and restoration of Peronism against some of the salient developments of Argentina's recent history. It contains a summary review of Perón's administrations between 1946 and 1955, and seeks to explore some of the social and economic conditions which led alternatively to the growth and decline of a class alliance structure of politics between 1943 and 1973. It considers the failure of anti-Peronist and rival parties to supplant Perón's influence since 1955. Also it seeks to explore the main reasons why Peronism finally escaped proscription in the early 1970s and was permitted to win control over the national government.

Partly for reasons of space, and partly because research remains fragmentary in certain crucial areas, this analysis and its conclusions are incomplete and to some extent schematic. Some important issues and events can be dealt with only summarily. No attempt has been made to assess Peronist ideology, nor to present any formal study of Argentina's class structure or of the changes in the country's international position. Since the analysis is in these respects incomplete, the synthesis can only be regarded as exploratory.

In some ways the failure of what might loosely be called anti-Peronist neo-populism after 1955 is surprising. If Peronism always remained a factor to be reckoned with during this period, it was not always as strong as it finally appeared in 1973. At the time of the military rebellion led by General Eduardo Lonardi in September, 1955, Peronism was on the verge of bankruptcy. It was violently opposed by key power groups like the armed forces and the Church. It was held in odium by the traditional political elites, the commercial bourgeoisie of Buenos Aires, the pampas farming interests, and also by the newer and increasingly powerful industrial interests. Among the middle classes only a small number of groups tied to Perón by

---

[1]   Quoted in *Primera Plana,* 10 September 1968.

the umbilical cord of state patronage lamented his downfall. Also its key area of support among the urban working class had been palpably sagging for some time. The main instrument of communication between Perón and the workers, the General Confederation of Labour (C.G.T.), had degenerated some time previously into little more than a coercive and manipulative bureaucracy. Once Perón had left the country many formerly fervent Peronists seemed willing to abandon their old allegiances in favour of a new bargain with Lonardi.[2]

A penchant for negotiation and proclivity for seeking favours from its apparent enemies remained a characteristic of the union movement long after the crises of 1955 had passed. This is not meant to imply any particular moral turpitude on the part of union leaders. Their role and loyalties were of necessity always highly ambiguous. They were both the main local agents of Perón, and simultaneously responsible to their clientele for wage negotiations and collective bargaining. This latter role led them into contact with their political enemies among employers and government. However, in performing this task they helped to foster a favourable climate for attempts to be made to construct a neo-populist class alliance.

This was also evident, for example, during the administration of Arturo Frondizi between 1958 and 1962. Here certain prominent Peronist union leaders were observed working in favour of 'Integrationism', Frondizi's philosophy of alliance with the trade unions. There were similar developments under the Onganía regime between 1966 and 1970. Again certain union leaders lent their support to the government's policy of 'Participationism', or joined in what fleetingly became known as 'the New Current of Opinion'.

Thus the search for *détente,* if not *entente,* with a non-Peronist state was never completely abandoned. It was paralleled by an often equal willingness to negotiate by different governments. Each administration after 1955, at some stage or other, flirted with the Peronist unions in the hope of harnessing their support. Each was impelled to do so by the need to improve its general political bargaining position by winning working-class support. Indeed much of what has been called 'anti-Peronism' was directed against the former president and his immediate retinue only. It did not mark a consistent attempt to exclude the working class and the unions from the political bargaining process. Thus in spite of the recurrently polarised and collisive character of Argentine politics, it conserved

---

[2] For accounts of this relationship see Gabriel Varas Durán, 'Porqué se dividen los peronistas', *Cuarto Poder,* 2 June 1972; Santiago Senén González, *El sindicalismo después de Perón,* Buenos Aires, 1972.

certain pronounced transactional features.

This was also apparent in many of the abortive 'returns to democracy' during the past two decades. The army, as the main direct arbiter over the political process and the institutional structure, periodically allowed the reintroduction of an electoral system in the hope that one or another of the non-Peronist parties could successfully take over the unions. As one recent commentator graphically puts it, the army frequently set up a game for the different non-Peronist factions, the prime objective being the articulation of working-class support. The political conurdrum this produced stemmed from the fact that any attempt to supplant Perón's influence implied first the need to negotiate with him. However, such negotiation was explicitly prohibited by the army. Whenever concessions were made to the Peronists before 1971, the army invariably called the game to a halt by means of a coup d'etat. Thus in effect the 'game' had been played according to 'rules' which made it impossible to 'win'.[3]

But this does show that all the political factors at play, the unions, the parties and the major power groups, have often tried to create something approaching a 'Peronism without Perón', in the sense of a new populist alliance embracing working-class support. Additionally the Peronist movement has often been split, sometimes on a class or regional basis, or on tactical and strategic grounds between the supporters and opponents of a new alliance. There have also been many challenges against Peronist control of the unions. These began after the 1955 coup with an assortment of challenges from Communists and Social Democrats. In the late 1960s another major threat was posed by New Left groups, led by the Third World Catholic movement and by internationalist revolutionary guerrilla groups. Finally in the early 1970s a new militant wing emerged within Peronism, the Peronist Youth, and this led to further outbreaks of factional tension within the movement.

Against this general context the continuing importance of Peronism becomes even more remarkable. It was not the case that Peronism remained a monolithic majoritarian movement throughout the whole period from 1955. Its survival after the overthrow of Perón can only be treated ultimately as reflecting the weakness and inconsistencies of the challenge to it. The reasons for this lie in the broader currents of Argentina's development since the 1940s.

---

[3] Guillermo O'Donnell, 'El "juego imposible". Competición y coaliciones entre partidos políticos en la Argentina, 1955-1966', Instituto Torcuato Di Tella, C.I.A.P., July, 1972.

The Perón period 1943-55

The apparent rigidity of the Argentine political structure, and the failure of neo-populism since 1955, can best be approached by briefly enumerating the main factors which allowed for the growth of Peronism itself after 1943. The framework around which a populist class alliance was constructed in the 1940s began with a period of astute political engineering by Perón after the military coup of 1943, which brought him into the government. He became Secretary of Labour and used this position to develop wide contacts with union leaders, and in some cases to make spectacular gestures of support to the urban working class in Buenos Aires. A union leader at the time recalled his activities in the following way:

> He began working with the union leaders because he had no other support. I remember one day, after one of many disagreements we had with this gentleman, telling him that we in the union movement were not there for ever, that we were men of principles . . . And he, very ironically, told me that the union movement at that moment was an orchestra, and that if some violin was playing out of tune, he realised it but had to make do because he had nothing to replace it. He was a man who made cold calculations. He knew well enough what he wanted.[4]

This was to some extent a revival of President Yrigoyen's practices during the First World War. But it was carried out this time in a much more organised and determined fashion. There was a vigorous attempt to prompt unionisation and to bring the workers into a unified structure of control. Perón would only confer his favours on unions with legal status (*personería gremial*) which his department could control.

In comparison with his *yrigoyenista* predecessors Perón enjoyed a much greater freedom from the interference of the traditional anti-working-class opposition among groups like foreign capital, the army and the exporting landed and commercial elite groups. During the Second World War a major restructuring of political forces occurred in Argentina. The power of traditional elite groups linked to the primary exporting economy was undermined by the vigorous growth of industrial groups, which evolved in conjunction with a process of import substitution. Also industrialisation came to be seen

[4] Lucio Bonilla, Oral History Project, Instituto Torcuato Di Tella. Interview of 2 March 1971 p. 78. See also Samuel L. Baily, *Labor and Nationalism in Argentina*, Rutgers University Press, 1967; Walter Little, 'Political Integration in Peronist Argentina', Ph.D. dissertation, Cambridge, 1972.

by important power groups, most notably the army, as a new way forward for the country's economic development. [5]

In this way the pre-1930 'liberal' consensus gradually came under challenge in a wave of pro-industrial economic nationalism. Peronism was in many respects a product of this rising conflict. After 1943 the liberal traditionalists and the new nationalists began to compete for wider political support in the hope of establishing a hegemonic position. Perón's politicisation of the unions, and his creation of a pool of working-class support, were in great part aspects of this struggle between competing elite groups.[6]

The period between 1943 and 1946 was thus mainly significant in that it engendered a new *vertical* structure of political allegiances, which apparently joined the classes together under upper class control within two broad bands. At this point the antithesis between Peronism and anti-Peronism began. It ended the *horizontal* system, which had emerged with the depression of 1930, based on the divisions between the liberal exporting elite groups, the 'dependent' tertiary-dominated middle-class groups, and the urban working class.

[5]   This transition can be followed in Marta Panaia and Ricardo Lesser, 'Las estrategías militares frente al proceso de industrialización (1943-47)', in Miguel Murmis and Juan Carlos Portantiero (eds.), *Estudios sobre los orígines del peronismo*, Vol. 2, Siglo XXI, 1973, pp. 83-164.

[6]   For an interesting general assessment of this phenomenon in the light of the comparative development of 'nationalist populism' in Latin America see Francisco Weffort, 'Clases populares y desarrollo social', *Revista Paraguaya de Sociología*, 5, No. 13, December 1968, pp. 62-159. One of Weffort's most suggestive observations is that populism emerged during the period 1935-50 in various parts of Latin America as a response to a state of political stalemate between the 'liberal' upholders of the traditional primary exporting structure, and a new group of import-substituting industrialists. The question is more complex than this because the two groups were subtly intermixed between one another: some of the 'liberals' supported industrialisation, and some of the 'industrialists' opposed an integral programme of industrialisation. But since in Weffort's view, clearly supported in the case of Peronism, mass politicisation is stimulated from above, as an aspect of a competitive struggle for hegemonic political control, this helps to explain some of the peculiar stylistic traits of 'nationalist populism': the personalisation and concentration of power, the partly manipulative relationship between leadership and base, and an often pseudo-radical ideological component with its ambiguous commitments to 'democracy', 'participation' and 'national development'. This description might be thought somewhat unfair to Peronism in view of its achievements in developing an industrial economy and in providing a much more positive distribution of income. It is meant only to refer to the subordinate role of the working class under Perón and to the much more pragmatic view taken towards foreign investment than would seem to be indicated by the Peronist nationalist ideology. In general Peronism had much greater affinities with social democracy than with fascism.

This change had been clearly foreshadowed in the late 1930s, when influential members of the traditional elite — Federico Pinedo is the most quoted example — began to support import substitution as a means to alleviate the problems posed by a chronic weakness in the balance of payments.[7] Perón was the immediate heir of this new attitude. He became one of the chief proponents of the new development model after 1943, and he mobilised working-class support to give him the power base to carry it out.

This indicates an important element of continuity between Peronism and reformist elements within the traditional elite in the 1930s. It can be argued that rather than marking a revolutionary hiatus in the country's development, Peronism was more a further stage in the process of structural readjustment which had begun in 1930. Equally only in a limited sense did it mark the emergence of a new class-based challenge against the traditional power groups. In spite of its working-class support, its nationalist ideology and its orientations towards social reform, it was a 'movement' pivoting upon a vertical axis, rather than a 'party' with a horizontal class-based structure. Perón's appeal to the working class during the wartime period was more moral and symbolic than materially based. He exploited the latent desire of union leaders and workers alike for recognition by the state and for political participation. During this period before 1946 there was little redistribution of income in favour of wages. Instead, as one Peronist union leader has written:

[7] See Miguel Murmis and Juan Carlos Portantiero, 'Crecimiento industrial y alianza de clases en la Argentina, 1930-1940', in *Estudios sobre los orígines del peronismo*, Vol. I, Siglo XXI, Buenos Aires, 1971. This masterly account unfortunately leaves one vital aspect of the matter unaccounted for. Individuals within the elite like Pinedo who supported a measure of import substitution during the 1930s were not supporters of the Peronists in the 1940s. Although Peronism is held to be a vertical structure with support from elite sectors, in purely empirical terms it has never been shown (to my knowledge) who exactly its elite supporters were. The assumption must be that they were mainly in the army. At the same time there were important splits in a number of key elite institutions, such as the Industrial Union (*Unión Industrial Argentina*). The general position taken up by entrepreneurs during the critical period between 1940 and 1946 was probably determined basically by how they stood to gain or lose from Perón's contacts with the unions. Some employers could conceivably benefit from increased wages through the opportunity it afforded them of broadening their market; others, faced with a situation of more inelastic demand, would oppose this on the grounds of its dislocating effect on costs and profits. These aspects deserve much wider study and ought to be related to a reinterpretation of the 1943 revolution. The process of industrial growth in the 1930s and 1940s is analysed in Eduardo F. Jorge, *Industria y concentración económica en la Argentina*, Siglo XXI, Buenos Aires, 1971, pp. 107-90.

Perón gave the worker dignity, laws to protect him, he gave him rights that historically had been denied to him. He led him towards social justice along a road where the man began to feel the satisfaction of wholly realising himself.[8]

With massive working-class support, and with the endorsement of key groups in the Army and renegade segments of the traditional parties, Perón won the presidency in the elections of 1946. His opponents had by this time also grouped themselves into a coalition, which was also a vertical class alliance similar to Peronism. The Democratic Union (*Unión Democrática*) of 1946 was made up of a whole spectrum of parties and interest groups. Its main unifying feature was a common support for the Allies during the War and a shared distaste for Peron's 'fascism' and 'demagogy'. On the whole the coalition represented the groups which had benefited most during the pre-depression primary exporting period, the pampas-exporting interests and the professional and bureaucratic middle classes. It selected its candidates, and received most of its support from the Radical Party, though it also embraced the Conservative Party, the Socialist Party, the Communist Party, the leading landowners' association, the *Sociedad Rural Argentina,* and the bulk of the Industrial Union. It also had very strong support from the United States government. Insinuations over American interference became on of the keystones of Perón's election campaign.[9]

The consolidation of Peronism took place between 1946 and 1949. This was also the most vital phase in the light of the country's later political development. The key to this period was a highly favourable situation for Argentina's traditional exports. For a time this permitted a very high rate of economic growth, which Perón exploited both to promote further industrialisation, and to augment his control over the urban working-class groups.

In the immediate post-war period the prices of Argentina's traditional exports increased rapidly on the international market. During these years the export quantum remained roughly the same, but between 1945 and 1948 its value rose from 700 million to 1500 million dollars.[10] This gave a tremendous boost to the domestic

---

[8] Miguel Gazzera and Norberto Ceresole, *Peronismo: autocrítica y perspectivas,* Buenos Aires, 1970, p. 36.

[9] It has been suggested by contrast, with some evidence, that the British supported Perón in 1946 in the hope of forestalling American influence. Cf. Milcíades Peña, *Masas, caudillos y elites: La dependencia argentina de Yrigoyen a Perón,* Buenos Aires, 1971, p. 85.

[10] These figures, and any later figures given without a reference, are taken from Eprime Eshag and Rosemary Thorp, 'Las políticas ortodoxas de Perón a Guido, (1953-1963)', in Aldo Ferrer *et al., Los planes de estabilización en la Argentina,* Buenos Aires, 1969, p.75.

economy. During the War GNP had risen by an annual average of 3%; between 1945 and 1948 this increased to around 10%.

In political terms a rapid rate of growth had the effect of loosening class tensions and strengthening the vertical-alliance populist structure which had emerged during the War. It allowed the Peronists to buttress their earlier symbolic appeal to the urban working class with a vastly heightened flow of material benefits. It gave large groups a vested interest in the fate of the government, as their support was attached by means of state patronage.[11]

Success in the export sector created new supplies of foreign exchange and thus helped to increase the rate of import substitution. There was a broadening of the industrial base and a dramatic spurt in the volume of industrial production. This increased by one third between 1945 and 1948. Growth was mainly marked in light industry, particularly in areas using labour-intensive techniques of production. In turn this provoked a swift acceleration in internal migration and urbanisation, as former agricultural workers became incorporated into the industrial sector. By virtue of its size and importance in the economy, the industrial working class increased in significance as a political force.

These two conditions — a rapid growth rate and the diversification of industrial production — came to underpin Perón's political strategy. Between 1945 and 1948 real wages of industrial workers increased by 20%. The share of wages in national income increased from 40.1% in 1946 to 49% in 1949. The share of profits declined from 59.9% to 51%, the bulk of the shift occurring in 1948 and 1949.[12] This allowed personal consumption to rise on average annually by about 7½%.[13]

Perón used this to consolidate further his grasp on the unions. The revolution in working-class standards of living was presented as an act of grace by the regime and became an integral component of its populist style. Perón's wife, Eva Duarte, emerged as the chief political broker between the trade unions and the state. She allocated

---

[11] Attempts were made after Perón's fall to quantify the amount of 'unproductive' expenditure of this sort. Like many of his predecessors and his successors Perón tended to respond to structural employment among the urban middle-class groups by increasing the size of the state bureaucracy. But some have also included in such 'unproductive' spending the nationalisation of foreign-owned public utilities in Argentina and the repatriation of external debts. This is not altogether an impartial evaluation. See E.C.L.A., *El desarrollo económico de la Argentina*, Mexico, 1959.

[12] E.C.L.A. *Economic Development and Income Distribution in Argentina*, New York, 1969, pp. 122 ff.

[13] Eshag and Thorp, *op. cit.*, p. 3.

many of the benefits, helped to select key personnel, and gradually established a firm communications and control structure between Perón and the working class. But as Milcíades Peña points out, Peron did not entirely deserve all the credit he claimed from this process. Both rising real wages and the redistribution of income could in some part at least be regarded as a spontaneous response to the process of economic growth:

> It is evident that if Perón had not made concessions, the proletariat would have itself fought successfully to obtain them. Full employment and increasing demand for labour made an improvement in working-class conditions inevitable.[14]

Even so the fact that the Peronist government supported these major improvements makes it evident that its relationship with the working class was not manipulative and exploitative. The opportunity for political participation which Perón had first offered to the working class during his period as Secretary for Labour was now complemented by something much more tangible and significant. Perón was no longer merely the source of a newly found 'dignity' within the working class. His position now also rested on the transformation of its material position. This contributed tremendously to the strength of *peronista* populism.

However, the impact of these changes on other groups was not so dramatic as it might first appear. The key to this period is the rate of growth. This allowed a redistribution of income to the working class without in most cases resulting in any absolute deterioration in the income position of other groups. If their share of the total fell, the rate of growth allowed for the maintenance of profit margins and in most cases of standards of living among non-working-class groups. This upheld the vertical structure of politics which had emerged since 1943, maintaining Peronism as a class alliance. All the evidence indicates that on the whole the industrial entrepreneurs benefited greatly during this period from the vigorous growth of industrial production and the rapid increase in the size of the domestic market. They were also helped by changes in the price ratio between industrial and rural products.[15] In effect both workers and employers were benefiting in part at the cost of the agricultural sector, perhaps the former more than the latter, but the latter nevertheless. Precisely how much active support Perón obtained from the industrialists is difficult to document. Vital factors in determining

---

[14] Peña, *op. cit.*, p. 71.

[15] E.C.L.A., *Economic Development and Income Distribution in Argentina*, p. 241.

their political loyalties were the degree of tariff protection they enjoyed, their access to credit, foreign exchange and import licences, and the type of industrial relations they enjoyed with the unions. Perón used all these as levers of political control in a manner parallel to his dealings with the unions.[16]

Although recently the matter has become the subject of some controversy, the weight of the evidence suggests that the sector mainly penalised by this policy was the agricultural producers.[17] E.C.L.A.'s figures suggest a 27% decline in agricultural incomes between 1946 and 1949. Some part of this may be accounted for merely through the shift of manpower from the rural to the industrial sector. No specific information has been brought forward to illustrate the income position of the larger pampas farmers during this period. It should also be remembered that Peronist supervision of agricultural prices, which allegedly operated as the main instrument of income redistribution, merely brought to fruition ideas which had been developing since the depression of 1930. I.A.P.I., the state board which controlled agricultural profits, had been among the proposals of the conservative Pinedo Plan of 1940. But of course, as the farming interests pointed out, if Perón claimed the credit for increasing real wages and dynamising the industrial sector, it would only be consistent to blame him for the shrinking of agricultural incomes.[18]

Finally Perón's control over government patronage gave him the means to attract an important contingent of non-entrepreneurial white-collar groups, the sectors which had traditionally supported the Radical Party. Under Eva Perón's influence voting rights were granted to women and much of their support articulated to the regime. In this fashion the lines of the class alliance were strengthened and broadened. Peronism was opposed increasingly bitterly by the farming interests and other less adaptable elements in the traditional conservative elite. They continued to find some support from middle-class groups debarred by their previous party affiliations from access to state patronage. The opposition remained in a

[16] 'Nationalist financial and moral backing also came from certain light industrial interests which stood to profit from Perón's policy of subsidising import-substitutive domestic industry', Walter Little, 'Party and State in Peronist Argentina, 1945-55', *Hispanic American Historical Review*, Vol. 53, No. 4, November 1973.

[17] For further more detailed discussion of this aspect see Jorge Fodor, 'Perón's policies for agricultural exports: dogmatism or commonsense?' This volume, Chapter 6.

[18] Cf. José Alfredo Martínez de Hoz, *La agricultura y la ganadería argentina en el período 1930-1960*, Buenos Aires, 1967.

minority both in popular and in power-group terms. The Army, until a few years before the guardian of the export interests, was now fully committed to industrial development. This gave the industrialists a decisive role in the patterning of political power and influence.

The general conditions under which Peronism had first emerged in the 1940s began to change fundamentally after 1948. This reflected the abrupt end of the post-war boom in Argentina's traditional farm exports. After a slight recovery in 1950-1 during the Korean War, the economy plunged into a deep recession in 1952 following major harvest losses through drought.

The period beginning in 1949, and continuing in the early 1950s, marked the first signs of a long-term economic crisis in Argentina. The country's traditional export markets in Europe came under challenge first from heavily subsidised American farm products, then from the 'Green Revolution', which vastly expanded agricultural output in the developed countries, and finally in the 1960s from the farm policies adopted by the European Common Market. These changes, and others in the world economy, manifested themselves through a deterioration in the international terms of trade between agricultural goods and industrial and capital goods.

In Argentina after 1949 an increasingly unfavourable balance of payments, and an acute shortage of foreign exchange, began to undermine the earlier pattern of import-substitutive industrialisation. By 1952 industrial production had slumped almost back to the level of 1946. In the same year the volume of both exports and imports had dropped to under half the average between 1946 and 1948. The terms of trade between farm and industrial goods, taking a base of 100 for 1950, had been 117.6 in 1948; by 1952 the ratio had fallen to 73.1.[19] As a result product per capita in Argentina declined by over 7% between 1948 and 1953. There was also a 5% drop in per capita incomes. Although by 1955 there were signs of a modest, though temporary, recovery, per capita GNP was still considerably less than in 1948.

These dramatic changes underlay the subsequent decline of Peronist populism in the early 1950s. Perón's response to the crisis was the Economic Plan of 1952, which introduced further controls on imports, and by means of a wage freeze sought to increase exports of food goods by restrictions on domestic consumption. In the hope of increasing the export quantum, the agricultural producers were given new price incentives in the form of subsidies by I.A.P.I.

---

[19] Guido Di Tella and Manuel Zymelman, *Las etapas del desarrollo económico argentino*, Buenos Aires, 1967, pp. 492 ff.

However, because of climatic difficulties, and because of the high cost of agricultural capital goods, the farm sector was unable to profit very much from this major reversal in state policy. According to E.C.L.A.'s figures, all the major groups — the farmers, the industrialists, the urban middle class and the industrial working class — suffered an absolute fall in their incomes during the crisis of the early 1950s. For example, in 1952/3 real wages were 20% less than in 1949.[20]

On the other hand, in spite of the wage freeze and falling absolute income levels, there was no major redistribution of income away from the working class during this period. What in relative terms the farm interests gained came not so much from the workers, but from the urban self-employed. Many of these, one may safely assume, were industrial entrepreneurs.[21] Of all groups they suffered the most. Later, during the partial recovery of 1954-5, there were attempts to reverse this situation by again manipulating the internal terms of trade between agriculture and industry in favour of the latter. Once more, however, this did not affect adversely in any degree the position of the industrial working class.[22]

This point deserves some emphasis. In many ways Peronism had evolved as a system of external control over the working class, with the workers occupying a subordinate and dependent role in the movement. On the other hand, because in turn the regime depended on their support, they received relatively greater consideration than other groups during a period of economic crisis. The crisis thus raised important and fundamental questions. Which of the three main groups should carry the burdens of economic contraction? Was it politically feasible to defend working-class interests at the cost of the industrialists, when the latter enjoyed the support of the army? Finally what were the implications in political terms of a situation where the further growth of industry was perceived to depend on the performance of the agricultural export sector? Was it possible to uphold a vertical cross-class political structure in these circumstances?

It was fully evident after 1952 that the whole question of incomes policy had far-reaching political implications. The state's adjudicatory role in the economy ceased to be a matter of allocating relatively higher rates of return to one group or another in the midst of an expanding surplus. Economic recession meant that its role became more coercively redistributive.

[20] Eshag and Thorp, *op. cit.*, p. 82.
[21] E.C.L.A., *Economic Development and Income Distribution in Argentina*, p. 169.
[22] *ibid.*, p. 251.

The tensions to which all this gave rise led eventually to the emergence of a new system of political alliances out of which eventually came the military rebellion of 1955 when Perón was overthrown. The industrial interests, as opposed to the 1940s when they had acceded to an arrangement which penalised the agricultural sector and helped themselves and the urban working class, now moved towards an alliance with the farmers against the workers. In the context of the early 1950s this was a logical step. They themselves wanted to be in a position to force down wages to relieve the pressure on their production costs. The economic crisis with its effects on the terms of trade had increased the costs of imported capital inputs. At the same time they could support to some extent a redistribution of income from the workers to the agricultural sector. By reducing domestic consumption of food goods, it would be possible to export more, and thus hopefully resume the industrialisation programme by allowing for increased imports of vital capital goods. Although cuts in working class standards of living threatened the domestic market, this might be compensated for by higher agricultural production and higher exports to relieve the balance of payments. Whichever way the problem was posed it added up to a rupturing of the links between the industrialists and the workers. In political terms these links were exemplified by Peronism, and it was therefore necessary to overthrow Perón.

The main thrust of the industrialists after 1952 was against the increasingly bureaucratic and *étatiste* structure of the Peronist government which operated the mechanisms controlling the distribution of income. They began to support a return to an open market economy, which, as they knew, in depression conditions could be used as a lever to force down wages.[23] What further encouraged this were the first signs of a major qualitative shift in the pattern of industrial development. Under the stress of depression, and in a desperate attempt to revive the industrial sector, in 1953 and 1954 Perón began to seek agreements abroad which would allow for significant foreign investment in Argentine industry.[24] The new line

[23] This became apparent during a Congress of Productivity between unions and employers in March, 1954. For a brief account see Roberto Carri, *Sindicatos y poder en la Argentina*, Buenos Aires, 1967, p. 52; also Peña, *op. cit.*, p. 113. By this time there was also mounting resentment against the state's control over domestic savings through agencies like I.A.P.I. Increasingly savings were allegedly being used to pad the bureaucracy. See Ernesto Laclau, 'The Argentinian Contest', *New Left Review*, 62, July-August, 1970, p. 4.

[24] In the 1940s, during Perón's aggressively nationalist phase, foreign investments in Argentina declined by over 50%. However, in 1953 a Law of

adopted by the government also had to recommend it the promise of new sources of investment without the need to cut working-class consumption any further to mobilise domestic savings. However, recourse to foreign investment meant the introduction of new labour-saving technology, which contrasted with the labour-intensive techniques employed during the expansive phase of the 1940s.[25] This had extremely significant implications for the labour market. It added a further motive to the industrialists' opposition to Perón's system of a controlled blanket-wage structure and contributed to their growing support for a new regime of open wage bargaining.

The 1955 revolution thus marked an abrupt return to the horizontal, class-based structure of politics which had prevailed during analogous depression conditions in the 1930s. The industrial and farming sectors now united, and were finally able to carry the army and the Church along with them.[26] By this time Peronist support among the working class had also perceptibly weakened. After 1948 the fall in real wages meant that Perón's system of union control was sustained less by material benefits than by fringe allowances and social legislation. This marked in part a return to the techniques of ideological and moral appeal which had been first employed after 1943. Evidence that this was not always sufficient came in the form of occasional outbreaks of industrial unrest and in the increasingly monolithic rigidity of both the Peronist Party and the C.G.T. From 1954 onwards one of the main roles of the C.G.T. was to quash wildcat strikes and incipient shop-steward movements.[27]

Foreign Investments was introduced which allowed for concessions to Standard Oil in partnership with the State to develop the oil industry. Later a loan of $60 million was secured from the United States for the development of the steel and car industries.

[25] Cf. Jorge M. Katz, 'Características estructurales del crecimiento industrial argentino, 1946-1961', *Desarrollo económico*, 7, 26, July-September, 1967, pp. 59-76.

[26] 'Until the economic recession of the late 1940s and early 1950s, the Peronists had the moral and financial capital with which to reconcile these interests [ie. workers and employers]'. Under the austerity that followed, the coalition was rapidly eroded, increasingly being held together by state coercion of *golpistas*, of union leaders who pressed inflationary wage claims, and of recalcitrant clerics' (Little, *op. cit.*, p. 66).

[27] 'The organisation the state introduced for the working class, the CGT, was like a giant trap. While the superprofits of the capitalists were high enough ... to allow for improvements to the working class, the trap remained open; inside it the workers won one improvement after another. But when the superprofits disappeared and it was necessary to reduce working class standards of living to maintain normal profits, the trap shut tight on the proletariat and paralysed it' (Peña, *op. cit.*, p. 71).

The economic crisis of the early 1950s therefore brought about a reverse shift of the conditions prevailing during the boom period. In the 1940s the main opposition groups to Peronism could be kept either isolated or neutral; this became impossible in the 1950s. In the earlier period the urban working class supported Peronism with enthusiasm and spontaneity; afterwards their relationship with the state was upheld more by cajolery and coercion. The crisis of the 1950s underlay the transformation of Peronism from participatory populism into something approaching a bureaucratic dictatorship. If before 1950 the government had displayed certain authoritarian features, mainly because of its need to regiment the working class and its fear of a right-wing military coup, afterwards these became more pronounced. They were further exaggerated, paradoxically, by the need to mete out relatively equal sacrifices to each of the major groups during a period of economic contraction. When the government found itself unable to rule by a consensual majority of class and interest groups, it attempted to do so by force, and sometimes by terror.

In 1955 Peronism fell not so much because it took the side of the workers, but because its policies of state-controlled 'class harmony' sought unavailingly to erase a dynamic situation of intensifying class conflict. Its main deficiency, common to all populist movements, was a lack of structural flexibility. There was a rising conviction, apparently shared even among certain sections of the working class, that class and group interests could best be furthered by freeing social interrelationships from the cumbersome control of an interventionist state. But perhaps the most significant lesson of the Peronist period was that rhetoric and the binding force of ideology ultimately proved less of a constraint on political loyalties than the question of the allocation of the economic surplus. To survive intact as a functionally cohesive force, the populist class alliance needed to be backed up with rapid economic growth. Only in this way could a pluralist transactional structure of politics be upheld.

The post-1955 period: the survival of Peronism

The main feature of the period after Peron's fall was the persistence of the extremely slow growth rate which had first become marked in 1949. Yet 'stagnation' is a term more illustrative of long-run tendencies after 1955 than an accurate description of year to year developments. The main short-term characteristic of the Argentine economy during this period was its chronic susceptibility to violent cyclical oscillations. Essentially this was caused by recurrent balance of payments difficulties, the so-called 'external bottleneck'. The problem of the falling international terms of trade between agrarian and industrial goods created an inherent excess demand in Argentina for imports for the domestic industrial sector as against the capacity of the primary agricultural export sector to generate sufficient reserves of foreign exchange. This both determined the main characteristics of the economic cycle and imposed the incubus of stagnation.

Thus there were some years of rapid growth, but they were always followed by a period of crippling depression, when GNP dropped back almost to the level at the beginning of the cycle. For example, comparing 1965 with 1958, both of which were peak years, per capita production had increased only by .5%. Average family incomes did not exceed the post-war peak of 1949 until the mid-1960s. According to the Central Bank's figures, between 1956 and 1966 annual growth rates of real GNP at factor cost were positive only during six years, and negative during four.[28] There were similar major fluctuations in private consumption. Between 1959 and 1963, only in one year, 1961, did private consumption exceed the level of 1953. It was also a period of acute inflation. Between 1958 and 1967 retail prices increased by an annual average of 27.7%.[29]

The period also brought significant fluctuations in the distribution of income. The main impact of this, as opposed to the early 1950s, fell on the urban working class. Between 1950 and 1955 wage income accounted for an average 41.8% of GNP. In 1956-8 this dropped to 39.6%, and in 1959-61 to 35.8%. These figures were not representative of a permanent trend, but they illustrate the extent of short-term fluctuations. Such major changes in income distribution, combined with stagnation and stop-go syndromes, and with recurrent bouts of hyper-inflation, spawned a Hobbesian world of strife and competition, as different groups struggled to maintain their real incomes.[30]

[28] Carlos F. Díaz Alejandro, *Essays in the Economic History of the Argentine Republic,* Yale, 1970, p. 351.

[29] Mario Brodersohn, 'Estrategías de estabilización y expansión en la Argentina: 1958-67', in Ferrer *et al., op. cit.,* p. 33.

[30] 'The changes which occurred in the distribution of income were particularly felt. They meant not only changes in relative income positions, but also that the losing group was likely to suffer a decrease, often of a substantial nature, in its absolute income as well. The struggle for relative shares was also a struggle to maintain absolute positions, and in any given year there were always important groups which could point to a deterioration in their real income level. In such circumstances the conflict is likely to be a bitter one' (E.C.L.A., *Economic Development and Income Distribution in Argentina,* p. 136).

Such conditions had important political implications. Since government policy was the single most powerful factor determining income allocation, the economic struggle became radically politicised. Similarly stagnation underlay the maintenance of the horizontal class-based political associations, which had developed immediately prior to Perón's fall. Under these circumstances it is hardly surprising that neo-populism should fail after 1955. The main structural precondition of a populist system lay in the objective possibility of rewarding different class groups simultaneously, and thus creating a cross-class coalition. This was impossible under the zero-sum conditions imposed by protracted stagnation; what was accorded to one group necessarily came at the expense of another.

Stagnation, however, and its corollary of heightened conflict over rival development policies between different socio-economic interests, also gives further insight into an important paradox. If during this period the objective preconditions for a class alliance had disappeared, in certain aspects Argentine politics retained some of its inter-class transactional elements.[31] At the fall of Perón the stage was set for a simple Marxian class confrontation with the bourgeoisie unitedly exploiting its coercive powers to put pressure on the working class. This is, of course, a central thread during the whole period after 1955. But such united pressure was not sustained over the longer term in any consistent or systematic fashion. It was more a short-term feature of certain stages of each economic cycle, and it was generally followed by a reverse policy which aimed at class conciliation. Such fluctuations of policy largely explain the frequent short-term oscillations in working-class incomes. Draconian attempts to cut working-class consumption were usually followed after short intervals by periods when real incomes were again allowed to rise. Although during this period there were massive variations in the distribution of income, most of the extant statistics suggest that over the long term the share of wages in national income did not decline markedly.

What tended to undermine the simple trend towards class confrontation was in the first instance the power of the trade unions and their ability to resist exogenous pressure by varying forms of industrial action. However, their bargaining position was greatly assisted by virtue of the fact that economic stagnation and its ancillary pressures not only divided society along horizontal class lines, but provided a radical impulse for the division of the classes within themselves. If the revolution of 1955 marked a reassertion of the horizontal elements in Argentine politics, in later years political

[31] See introduction, pp. 180-2.

structures assumed an atomised and segmentary guise as both vertical and horizontal orientations struggled against each other for supremacy.

Rather than being able to maintain a united front against the workers after the rebellion of 1955, the Argentine bourgeoisie quickly fell into a state of internal disunity. The alliance between agrarian and industrial interests soon showed signs of foundering on issues like taxation, the timing and extent of devaluations, access to credit and state subsidies and so forth. The alliance had been originally held together by the recognition on the part of the industrialists that to achieve further industrial growth it was necessary to increase agrarian production and exports, and thus escape the balance of payments constraint on capital goods imports. But during the latter 1950s and the 1960s the terms of trade problem showed few signs of improving significantly. At the same time agrarian production failed to respond adequately to price incentives. As a result this development strategy increasingly lost adherents.

A second major division of this period, which became critical in the late 1960s, was between the two major segments of the industrial groups. In some ways this marked a continuation of the disputes of the war period between the import-substituting light industrial groups, and the liberal elements, which had traditionally controlled the Argentine Industrial Union. It was provoked by the latter's success in pushing for a new development strategy in the 1960s. This resumed on a much larger and more ambitious scale one of Perón's later policies of seeking to attract foreign capital investment.[32] Essentially this development model aimed to skirt balance of payments contraints on industrial growth by permitting the introduction in Argentina of subsidiaries of major foreign companies. In this way, it was hoped, it would be possible to develop certain basic capital and consumer industries and give the country the benefits of the most modern techniques of production. It was also perceived as a means to escape economic stagnation.

The types of difficulties this gave rise to are well known. The volume of investment from abroad was never sufficient to create a sustained dynamic impulse in the economy to outweigh its destructive effects on the old structure. Foreign companies, aided by a new banking system, tended to establish a stranglehold over domestic savings at the cost of other groups. Periodic devaluations, by reducing the dollar cost of locally-owned firms, led to takeovers

---

[32] Guillermo Martorell, *Las inversiones extranjeras en la Argentina*, Buenos Aìres, 1969, pp. 91-5.

in its most competitive branches. The repatriation of profits by foreign companies became a further substantial negative addition to the balance of payments, and led, it has been contended, to a net outflow of capital. Foreign firms extorted monopoly rents for the transfer of technology and the granting of local licences. The old labour-intensive structure of Argentine industry was undermined, and contributed to the emergence of a 'marginal' proletariat.

The bulk of foreign investment came in the early 1960s under Frondizi. Between 1958 and 1963 an average of $86 million was invested annually. Between 1964 and 1966 this dropped to an average of $40 million, and to $38 million between 1967 and 1970. 70% came from the United States, and was invested in extractive and manufacturing activities. Figures on industrial concentration suggest a growing importance of foreign firms at the apex of local industry. In 1948 half the production of the manufacturing sector was controlled by .83% of the total number of firms. In 1964 this had dropped to .69%. Of the latter fraction 41% came from firms where foreign capital had a majority holding. Of the hundred companies in Argentina with the highest value turnovers in 1956, 75 were Argentine. In 1966 the figure was 50, and in 1970, only 39. At the end of 1967 only 20 of the 50 largest companies in Argentina were owned domestically, and of these 5 were state-operated.[33]

In party polemics this was represented as a 'takeover' of 'national industry' by 'foreign monopolies'. There can be no doubt that it did bring about a sizeable appropriation of national resources by foreign firms, and it curtailed local control in many key areas of economic decision-making. Yet its most significant aspect was its dislocative effect on the structure and composition of Argentine industry. This underlay a growing division between the neo-liberal supporters of foreign capital and its opponents among the so-called national entrepreneurs.

The expansion of foreign investment and the concomitant process of industrial concentration swept aside some of the old independent local businesses of the past, and paved the way for the rapid proliferation of others in an ancillary satellite status under the umbrella of foreign companies.[34] Resentments among domestic

---

[33] Figures taken from Mauricio T. Arcángelo and H. Carlos Quaglio, 'El imperialismo: el caso argentino', *Los Libros* 26, May 1972, pp. 10-14; Pedro Skupch, 'Concentración industrial en la Argentina', *Desarrollo económica*, 11, 41, April-June, 1971, pp. 3-15; Julián Delgado, 'Industria: el desafío a la Argentina', *Primera Plana*, 3 September 1968.

[34] Discussions of this question invariably stress the simple polarisation between 'national' and 'foreign' industry. However the process of partial dissolution and the satellitisation of the domestic groups suggests the presence of at least

entrepreneurs stemmed from two directions. The first was their growing subordination and client status. The second was the violence of the transition and the demoralising impact of the threatened liquidation of the old structure.

The coteries of interest in Argentina which were committed to this programme of development were first confronted with the need to create a favourable environment for the fulfilment of their objectives. In the late 1950s and early 1960s, under the promptings of the International Monetary Fund, vigorous attempts were made to deal with the problem of inflation in order to provide the foreign companies with stable conditions for their costing and market evaluation projects. As a result came a series of 'stabilisation plans', which aimed to reduce inflation by monetary controls.[35] But these, in company with pressures arising from the economic cycle, invariably provoked serious deflationary spirals, which culminated in massive unemployment and in a spate of business failures. Such cataclysmic experiences contributed to the increasingly atomised and fragmented character of Argentine politics during the first decade after Perón's fall.

The final major feature of this process, and the one documented the least, was its effect on the workers and the trade unions. The growth of a marginal working-class population had regressive effects on the distribution of income. After 1955 the system of fixing blanket wages gave way to more open bargaining procedures. Reflecting the emergence of wage differentials was the appearance of a new aristocracy of labour in areas dominated by foreign firms.[36] The increasing differentiation and stratification of the working class may prove crucial variables in the analysis of the trade union behaviour during this period. If some of this may be attributed to the power manoeuvrings of union bosses, in all probability it also mirrored important objective conditions.

---

three groups: the old import substitutors of the Perón period, the oligopolistic foreign sector and its neo-liberal backers, and the satellite domestic groups made up mainly of component producers. Although the industrial sector assumed a top-heavy appearance during this period, according to the E.C.L.A.'s figures the total number of families with incomes from self-employment actually rose during the 1960s. The important issue would seem to be not the proletarianisation of former independent producers, but their increasing subordination to the foreign sector.

[35] Eshag and Thorp, *op. cit.*

[36] Increasing income disparities within the working class make class comparisons in the distribution of income increasingly difficult for this period. The presence of a marginal population made average wages less representative of income levels.

Such intra-class divisions underlay the persistence of transactional 'vertical' features in Argentine politics after 1955. Efforts by the army, the main arbiter over the political process, or different political parties to protect specific groups from the effects of stagnation, or to implement particular development programmes favouring others, led to attempts to win working-class support. But for a long period there was little chance of their having any success. The various pressures making for a horizontal structure of politics were too strong.

The matter was further complicated by the proscription of Peronism by the army after 1966. This gave further emphasis to the 'game' features of Argentine politics. To win the presidency and an overall majority in Congress it was necessary to win working-class support. To do this it was necessary to negotiate with Perón. But any such negotiations which accorded any substantial concession to the Peronists immediately provoked the army's political intervention. Between 1955 and 1973 Argentina had eleven different governments. Over the same period there were six military coups d'etat. By 1963 there were over a hundred active political parties.

It is also important to point out that the stagnation-growth interpretative model used here is only a primary indicator of events of the political level. It largely governed the growth and decline of populism, and shaped the linear structures of Argentine politics. But its explanatory powers cannot be abused. At the side of these structuring influences were important secondary variables emerging from anterior historical processes, and which were largely unconnected to the process of economic development.

Many of these points can be documented and developed further by outlining in brief the main course of each administration after Perón's downfall. Perón's immediate successor, General Lonardi, was the first of several presidents who attempted to supplant Perón's control over the unions. Apparently his aim was to hold fresh elections in seven months. Peronism was expected to win, but after a purge had taken the place of its more intransigent elements. The intention was that Lonardi, or one of his immediate supporters, should become President with working-class support and continue to discharge, with superficial modifications, Perón's role.[37]

This plan foundered against the opposition of more extreme groups in the revolutionary coalition. Their aim was clearly to pave the way for an attack on wages and for a complete purge of the

[37] Juan Carlos Torre and Santiago Senén González, *Ejército y sindicatos: los sesenta días de Lonardi,* Buenos Aires, 1969.

Peronists. In November 1955 Lonardi was ejected from power by the Army and replaced by General Pedro Aramburu. This second coup in 1955 was strongly supported both by industry and by agriculture, which, it was apparent, were determined to appropriate the spoils of their victory against Perón. The pattern of subsequent events in 1956 and 1957 was the most vital factor in ensuring the survival of Peronism after 1955.

Once in power the Aramburu government began a major political and economic offensive against the unions and against the working class. There was first an attempt to revive agricultural exports by granting price incentives and devaluations in favour of the farming sector. This was accompanied by restrictions on private consumption and attempted wage freezes. Collective wage contracts agreed under Perón were prorogued. The government also dismantled the main organs of the Peronist state's control over the economy, in line with the demands of both industry and agriculture. In returning to a more laissez-faire system, one of Perón's more significant fringe benefits from the early 1950s, the state subsidy to basic foodstuffs, was abolished. This brought about the first major redistribution of income against the working class. Between 1954 and 1957 the share of wages in national income oscillated between a high of 45.6% to a low of 41.4%. Much of this was done on the instance of Raúl Prebisch, representing E.C.L.A., whose services the Aramburu government had sought.

In part the earlier Lonardi government's rather timid dealings with the unions was dictated by the fear that any excessive pressure would provoke a working-class rebellion and a Peronist counter-revolution. But after an abortive general strike in November, 1955, the weakness of the Peronist apparatus became apparent. The Aramburu administration therefore moved into a full-scale attack on the Peronist unions. Control over the C.G.T. was vested in the government, and the privileged legal status of the unions annulled. There were also mass arrests of Peronist union leaders.[38] Accompanying this came a series of clumsy attempts by anti-Peronist union leaders, Communists and Social Democrats, to take over the unions.

But instead of securing their desired effects of extirpating Peronism, eliminating the political role of the unions, and paving the way for a permanent shift in the distribution of income against the working class, these measures served to unite the workers in a spirit of solidarity and to rehabilitate Peronism as the focus of working-class allegiance. The Communists and the rest came to be regarded as the traitorous collaborators of a reactionary government. All that the

[38] Carri, *op. cit.*, pp. 66-8.

purges achieved was the freeing of the union structure from its cumbersome bureaucratic contraints, and the re-establishment of a vigorous chain of communication between union leaders and the rank and file. Peronist union leaders were able to point back to the 'golden age' of the 1940s, and to the glories of the famous march on Buenos Aires by Peronist militants in October, 1945. The depression period of the early 1950s they were now able to represent as also comparing favourably with the present, when the workers had been protected by a benevolent government. A Peronist shop-stewards' movement spontaneously developed, which the Peronists subsequently dubbed 'The Resistance'.

All this made evident the underlying strength of the trade union movement, its institutional maturity and its ability to withstand the shock of a direct assault by the state. In comparison with much of the rest of Latin America, the urban working class in Argentina had the benefit of homogeneity and a high degree of organisation. It was geared to relatively high standards of consumption, and it had acquired a consciousness of its pivotal political importance. The Aramburu government was unable to offer it anything substantial to coax it away from its established loyalties, and under these circumstances its allegiance to Peronism proved insuperable.[39]

As a result of this Peronism itself underwent certain important changes. Its populist class-alliance features became less marked. It became instead the doctrine of working-class struggle. Between 1956 and 1958 there was a wave of strikes. Days lost through strikes were 144,000 in 1955, over 5 million in 1956, over three million in 1957, and over six million in 1958.[40] Overall these were successful. The paradox of the Aramburu period was that when the government ceded control in May, 1958, real wages were 14% higher than in 1955.

Attempts to purge the Peronists from the unions failed completely. In 1957 the autonomy of the C.G.T. from government control was restored. An attempt was made to elect delegations from the unions. It failed in the face of disputes between the Peronists and their rivals on the question of representation and credentials. From

[39] Carri comments: 'The annullment of laws regulating the unions, such as the Law of Professional Associations, laws introduced and upheld during the Peronist administration; the freezing of wages after a tiny increase in January, 1956, . . . the other repressive measures . . . All this strengthened the awareness of the workers of the striking differences between the Peronist administration and the new government . . . [Peronism] now became a militant ideology, and every single one of the workers felt a commitment to the movement' (*ibid.*, pp. 66-76).

[40] *ibid.*, p. 76.

the ensuing split two wings of the union movement emerged, the majority '62 Organisations', which were Peronist, and the non-Peronist rump, the '32 Democratic' unions. There were also clear signs that the Peronists had conserved much of their electoral support. When a preliminary election was held in 1957 to set up a constitutional convention, a massive blank vote indicated the continuing strength of Perón's popular following.

Aramburu's successor was Arturo Frondizi, who ruled from 1958 until he was overthrown in a military coup in March, 1962. During this period the strength and durability of Peronism became even more evident. To win the presidential elections of 1958, Frondizi and his chief adviser, Rogelio Frigerio, made a secret deal with Perón, which arranged for concessions to the Peronists in return for their voting support. However, Frondizi's real aim, enunciated in the doctrine of Integralism, was another class alliance where the urban working class and unions would be drawn into supporting the capitalist-developmentalist orientation of Frondizi's party, the *Unión Cívica Radical Intransigente* (U.C.R.I.).

To cement this relationship in the second half of 1958 Frondizi increased monetary wages by 60%, an amount significantly above the rate of increase in the retail price index.[43] But this gesture was immediately undermined by problems directly emerging from economic stagnation and the economic cycle. In the absence of significant growth an inflationary spiral developed. It was accompanied by a major deficit in the balance of payments. Frondizi's development objectives, and his pressing need for external financial assistance to alleviate the crisis, proved more powerful commitments than the political calculations stemming from his links with the unions. On the instance of the International Monetary Fund, which laid this down as a condition for its financial support, a stabilisation programme was introduced. In an effort to end inflation it called for an end of price controls distorting market conditions, the elimination of the budget deficit, and severe restrictions on credit.

But instead of ending inflation the markedly depressive impact of these measures merely served to accelerate it and to induce a minor economic catastrophe. In 1959 the retail price index increased by a monumental 133.5%, as against an increase of 31.2% in 1958. GNP fell in 1959 by 7.5%, which triggered unemployment and cut significantly into real wages.[42] Private consumption fell by around

[41] This favoured the weaker working-class groups more than the unions, since the increases were based on wage levels at the beginning of the year. In the intervening period many of the stronger unions had won increases.

[42] Eshag and Thorp, *op. cit.*, pp. 83 ff., and Brodersohn, *op. cit.*, p. 33.

15%. The group most affected was the industrial working class, where the Peronists were strongest. The crisis of 1959 resulted in a return to the pre-Second World War pattern of income distribution. with wages making up only about 38% of domestic income. In 1959 only the rural sector was any better off then 10 years before. Urban real wages were 20% less than in 1949.[43]

The situation was only relieved to some extent in 1960 and 1961 with the recovery of the export sector and with the inflow of foreign capital.[44] It was not long, however, before opposition to foreign investment began to mount. Already in the early 1960s there were discussions of the 'denationalisation' of domestic industry, and campaigns were waged against the 'foreign monopolies'. Although foreign investment was partly responsible for the recovery in income levels in 1960 and 1961, and patterns in the distribution of income became more progressive, considerable unemployment continued. The great bulk of foreign investment went into capital intensive sectors, oil, consumer durables and petro-chemicals. Recovery in the non-durable, more labour-intensive industries was much less marked. Thus while there was an expansion in production, there was no significant rise in urban employment.

Frondizi's initial attempt at conciliation with the unions was predicated on his confidence in the dynamic, politically integrative potential of a boom in foreign investment. He failed to assess accurately both the economic effects and the political cost of achieving the preconditions for this. In the shock of events of 1959 both his alliance with the Peronists, and his planned rapprochement with the unions, swiftly disintegrated. 'Integrationism' only found any substantial support among the new industrial working-class sectors controlled by foreign capital. Most of the union leaders who supported the government were swiftly overturned in a further spate of shop-stewards' movements. In 1959 there were more strikes than ever before. The number of days lost through strikes exceeded 10 million, almost double the worst year of the Aramburu government.[45]

In the hope of curbing rank and file militancy the government sought to bolster the position of the C.G.T., weakly copying the techniques Perón had used in the early 1950s. The Law of Professional Associations, one of the great symbols of the Peronist regime, was restored. But this expansion in the C.G.T.'s prerogatives

[43] E.C.L.A. *op. cit.*, p. 10.
[44] Between 1955 and 1961-2 American investments in Argentina increased from $81 million to $300 million (Laclau, *op. cit.*, p. 6).
[45] Carri, *op. cit.*, pp. 87-106.

did little more than consolidate further Perón's position. From 1960 onwards, with the aim of reviving its electoral support, the government was forced into an increasing number of concessions to the Peronists, while being compelled to uphold a programme of austerity on the economic front. Again this made evident the impossibility of implementing a class alliance with piecemeal concessions and without a distributable material largesse to sustain it. Eventually Frondizi fell foul of this contradiction. In gubernatorial elections in the province of Buenos Aires in February, 1962, he was forced to accede to a Peronist victory. This proved the signal for a military coup d'etat.

The next period up to the middle of 1963 was taken up with internecine disputes in the army over what step to take next. There was a division of opinion between those preferring to continue with a veiled military dictatorship under the puppet president, José María Guido, or to attempt elections once more in hope that Peronism could be destroyed. The other point at issue was which institutional structure would provide optimal conditions for further foreign investment. One of the reasons why the coup against Frondizi had come so quickly was to forestall a flight of capital at the prospect of a Peronist restoration. Eventually, after a series of army mutinies, the faction supporting a return to elections, the Blues (*azules*) triumphed over the Reds (*colorados*).

The Guido interregnum also coincided with another bleak depression. In 1963 GNP again dropped by 5% to a figure below that of 1958. Private consumption was also down by 10% in comparison with 1958, and in per capita terms it approached 15%. Again the workers were most affected, and as before this helped to uphold their Peronist loyalties. In 1963 real wages were 15% below 1958, and unemployment, which was mainly marked in textiles and metallurgical production, reached 8%. It had been an unpleasant five years. The cost of living had risen in monetary terms by 400%.

The next stage brought few significant variations to this central pattern. Under the impact of depression the Peronists remained in as entrenched a position as any time since 1955. It was now even more difficult to envisage electing a majority government without their support. The Peronists were again proscribed from the elections, and the army had forbidden any negotiations with them. The result was that the anti-Peronist Popular Radical Party, led by Arturo Illía, won the elections but on the basis of less than 25% of the popular vote. The new government's unrepresentative character was again to prove a fatal weakness.

The Illía administration's strategy was to seek to consolidate its support among the anti-Peronist urban middle classes and the rural sector by pursuing a vigorous trade policy and a pragmatic position towards foreign investment, mediated by the expansion of state control over vital sectors of the economy.[46] It sought to escape balance of payments constraints on growth by developing new markets for Argentina's farm exports. As a counterweight to its unwillingness and inability to reach any agreement with the Peronists, the government made some attempt to foster divisions among the unions. Its attitude towards the working class was based on avuncular neutrality and tempered favouritism, reminiscent of the position taken up under Yrigoyen over forty years before. But these manoeuvrings triggered increasing opposition from the Peronists. There was a series of general strikes and factory occupations, which the government proved unable to curb.

During its first two years of power the government benefited from an improvement in the economic situation. In 1964 and 1965 both consumption and real wages increased. But rather than redounding to the government's credit, the gains made by the workers came to be seen as a sign of its weakness.

In military circles the government lost favour because of its alleged tolerance for the profiteering activities of its followers in public administration. Although its economic policies proved the most successful to date, the absence of a clearly perceptible *Wirtschafts-wunder* reduced many of its former supporters to apathy. By 1965 the government was struggling against a crisis of legitimacy. It enjoyed neither positive popular support nor the backing of the major power groups.

In 1966 there was another recession, less severe than its immediate predecessors but accompanied by the familiar socio-political tensions. Unlike previous governments the Illía administration used its police powers sparingly, and made no attempt to place the burdens of contraction on the working class. The uncharacteristic result of this was that wages did not decline as fast as profits. This rapidly lost the government the support of the entrepreneurial classes. There was also at the same time the prospect of another Peronist victory in the mid-term elections due to be held in March, 1967. In June, 1966 the government was overthrown without difficulty or bloodshed by the army led by General Juan Carlos Onganía. The coup was welcomed by the entrepreneurs, by Perón, and by the unions. The latter had been involved in the intrigues which had led up to the movement.[47]

[46] Presidencia de la Nación Argentina, Consejo Nacional de Desarrollo, *Plan Nacional de Desarrollo, 1965-1969*, Buenos Aires, 1965.

[47] See press reports June-July, 1966. Perón greeted the coup in the following way: 'I regard this movement with sympathy, because it has brought to an

By the time of Illía's fall it was apparent that the economic cycle, whose importance had first become apparent during the later stages of Peron's government, was the most important guiding factor on the institutional structure. Cyclical upswings in the economy, 1945-6, 1957-8, 1963-5, coincided with the restoration of elections and a civilian constitutional government. Periods of depression, accompanied by strong pressures towards changes in the distribution of income between profits and wages, were invariably resolved by changes in the political structure — the suspension of constitutional government, a freezing of political activities and open inter-class bargaining, and the assertion of a unitary system of military power.

The restoration of Peronism, 1966-73

The advent of the Onganía government marked an important political hiatus. For the first time a military government was in power rejecting the transitional and provisional role of its predecessors, and declaring its intention to rule for an indefinite period.[48] The responsibility for change, which had been previously left to the civilians, was now to be carried out by a military regime, if necessary by force and without the encumbrance of having to seek the support of public opinion. As soon as it took power the government moved quickly into an assault on the major institutions which had played an important part in politics in the immediate past. The political parties were abolished, and the universities purged of their left-wing and centrist elements. Of the major civilian institutions, which before had been overtly involved in political activities, only the C.G.T. escaped.

At first the government pursued a conciliatory line towards the unions reminiscent of that of General Lonardi in 1955. There was talk of a pact between them, and this suggested that the government, in spite of its strong right-wing direction, would eventually pursue a populist line. This was encouraged by the most powerful of the union leaders, the secretary of the Metallurgical Workers' Union (U.O.M.), Augusto Vandor. Between 1964 and 1966 Vandor had become a person of great importance in the Peronist union

end a situation which could not continue. Every Argentine felt this. Onganía has ended a period of complete corruption . . . If the new government acts well it will succeed. It is the last opportunity for Argentina to avoid a situation where civil war is the only way out' (quoted in *Primera Plana*, 30 June 1966). In the light of subsequent developments these were prescient words.

[48] For an analysis of the ideology of the 1966 revolutionaries see Darío Canton, *La política de los militares argentinos, 1900-1971*, Siglo XXI, Buenos Aires, 1971, Chapter 2, pp. 63-92.

movement. He had repeatedly snubbed Illía, had strongly supported the military coup against him, and his influence was such that he was able to some extent to disregard Perón himself. Indeed Vandor was regarded as the main advocate of the transition of Peronism into an arrangement where the former president would hold merely titular leadership of his party, and real power would rest with domestic figures like Vandor. By this time the prospect of Perón's return from exile seemed remote. He was ageing rapidly, and apparently happily esconced in Madrid. The deference of many union leaders, like Vandor, towards him was based less on affection or any real desire to see him return as President, than on the aspiration to inherit the leadership of the movement. The growing influence of Vandor emphasised further the power of the union cliques in Peronism, and this tended to move it even further away from its old coalitional identity between entrepreneurial and working-class groups.

If Vandor's importance grew during this period around 1966, Peronism itself began to look a little weaker than before. The prospect of Perón's death, and the hidden struggle for the succession, led to a number of partial splits in the movement. The chief of these was between Vandor and Jose Alonso, a garment workers' leader. It mainly revolved around relations with Perón, Alonso presenting himself as a more faithful and orthodox Peronist supporter.[49] This split, and others which developed later during the Onganía government, weakened the union movement. The Peronists, who save for minor excisions had remained strong and united since 1955, were now showing signs of atomisation and division along similar lines to the political parties in the early 1960s.

Signs of this became apparent in March, 1967. Vandor and other union leaders had spent some months in negotiations with the government in the hope of moving it in a direction favourable to union interests. As had happened so often in the past, the government's commitments elsewhere prevented its labour policy from evolving far beyond mere window-dressing. It wanted trade union support, but refused to make even minimal concessions on the wages issues which could serve to buttress the alliance. When the C.G.T. led by Vandor moved to a confrontation through a general strike, the government used its police powers liberally to quash union opposition.[50] This weakened the unions even further. Although Vandor continued to play an important role afterwards, the real power he had wielded in 1966 began to decline.

[49]   See Varas Durán, 'Porqué se dividen los peronistas' *op. cit.*
[50]   The various stages of the confrontation are summarised in *Primera Plana*, 14 March 1967.

In 1967 the Onganía government was in a stronger position than any of its predecessors. The last barrier to its authority, the C.G.T., was broken. It was now free, it seemed, from the need to bargain with any of the major groups, and could implement whatever policies it chose. It now appeared that the complex competing 'horizontal' and 'vertical' pressures from the past had been finally superseded by a united and purposeful military dictatorship. Simultaneously with the confrontation with the C.G.T., the government revealed its plans on the economic front. Onganía appointed as Minister of the Economy a leading member of the neo-liberal school, Adalbert Krieger Vasena. He announced a programme of diversifying and rationalising Argentine industry through another major attempt to quicken the flow of foreign investment. It was hoped to overcome the balance of payments bottleneck by encouraging the export of industrial products. To prepare for these objectives a new anti-inflation stabilisation programme was announced which included a strict incomes policy.[51]

The Krieger Vasena plan posed a threat to two vital political groups. It was opposed first by the smaller domestic entrepreneurs and their leading association, the General Economic Confederation (C.G.E.). There were fears that the stabilisation programme, as had happened under Frondizi, would trigger a major recession and widespread bankruptcy.[52] Once again there was talk of a 'takeover' of Argentine industry by 'foreign monopolies'.

The Krieger Vasena plan was also opposed by the unions, which saw it as a disguised attack on wages and an attempt to raise the level of domestic savings at the cost of working-class consumption. In 1968 another major division occurred in the ranks of the C.G.T. Vandor continued in the hope that he could eventually pressure the government into making concessions. He therefore maintained his contacts with members of the administration. He was opposed in this by a rebel C.G.T. group led by a printers' leader, Raimundo

[51] The Krieger Vasena plan aspired for the creation of a 'competitive society' free from the constraints of 'outmoded' economic and social structures. The State's role was perceived as clearing away 'the obstacles, interferences and rigidities' affecting 'productive efficiency'. There was to be a 'frontal attack on inflation to promote self-sustained growth' (cf. Krieger's speech, 10 July 1967).

[52] 'The C.G.E. regards as essential that the measures should not have a recessive effect . . . especially on the small and medium firms, creating drastic unemployment problems and imposing restrictions on the size of the market. This could have unforeseen economic and social consequences' (*Clarin*, March 12 1967). In these guarded terms the C.G.E. warned against the consequences of the Krieger Vasena plan.

Ongaro.[53] Although at first this group had little following, it rapidly evolved into the most vocal source of opposition to the government.

The Onganía government had thus brought about several very significant changes. Added together these threatened to disrupt and transform the essential pattern of politics, as it had evolved since 1955. In spite of its retention of certain superficial vertical features, the class-based horizontal structure, based on the conflict between Peronism and anti-Peronism, had been the central axis of politics since Perón's downfall. This was now threatened by the military regime which had put all the parties on an equal footing in the ranks of the opposition. In doing so it had abruptly cut the normal channels of communication through which sectional opinions were expressed and the horizontal pattern of politics maintained. For the first time ever Radicals and Peronists found themselves in the same camp. Secondly, the adoption of the Krieger Vasena plan, and its aggressive provisions for eliminating inflation and enhancing the flow of foreign capital, had a similar parallel effect on two key interest groups, the unions and the smaller employers. This not only meant the intensification of the gathering confrontation between 'nationalist' and neo-liberal groups, but also implied a new common interest between the former and the unions against the government. A third major factor was in part a by-product of the first. In suppressing conventional political activities, the Onganía government weakened the capacity of formal political vehicles like the parties and the C.G.T. to act as articulating agents for the major socio-economic groups. The protests of entrepreneurs tended less to be expressed through the parties, and those of the workers less through a C.G.T. dominated by Vandor. A further stage in the growing atomisation of formal political bodies before 1966 was the tendency afterwards for new vehicles of political articulation and mobilisation to emerge. Examples of this were the growing importance of the C.G.E., representing the entrepreneurs, and Ongaro's wing of the union movement representing dissident segments of the working class.

All this implied a potentially radical change in the system of political alliances which had prevailed since 1955. It threatened to supersede the established dichotomy between Peronism and anti-Peronism, and it left the way open for a new class alliance against the neo-liberals. It thus engendered, if in a complete reverse fashion, an analogous situation to that which had prevailed during the Second World War, as workers, smaller entrepreneurs and other groups moved into a major confrontation with the liberal establishment. The

[53] For the energence of Ongaro's group, the *C.G.T. del los argentinos*, see *Primera Plana*, 2 April 1968.

new alliance was not, as in the 1940s, sustained by a recognition of common positive interests. Rather it was brought together by the negative force of shared adversity. Although the rhetoric which would be adopted to give this movement a semblance of ideological coherence was largely nationalist and radical-left in inspiration, its underlying impulse was to a large degree defensive and reactive. Ultimately it was a reflection of the structural inertia of Argentine society, when confronted by the possibility of major changes in the traditional status and economic position of a number of key groups.

For a little over two years the Krieger Vasena plan seemed highly successful. By 1969 the rate of inflation had fallen to a comparatively negligible amount. Wages were falling, but gradually and without the traumatic shocks of the past. There was no apparent sign of any dangerous build-up of working-class opposition. Fears that the plan would provoke a major recession proved largely unfounded. Unlike Frondizi's stabilisation plan in 1959, Krieger's had the advantage of having been introduced during a period of depression. Cyclical forces encouraging economic recovery for a time proved stronger than the deflationary influences of government policy.[54]

However, the *pax onganiana,* and the determined effort it marked to escape from the mould of stagnation which had begun in 1949, eventually failed. Suddenly in May 1969 there was a spate of student unrest in the interior cities of Resistencia, Corrientes, Rosario and Córdoba. In Rosario and Córdoba these movements quickly and spontaneously evolved into major urban riots. The more significant was in Córdoba where the students were joined by large numbers of striking car-workers. Only when the army was brought in in strength was the outbreak quashed.

These events destroyed the Krieger Vasena programme and led directly to Onganía's downfall a year later. The army, which since 1966 had remained united behind the government, now divided between the adherents of repression like Ongania himself, and other groups led by the army Commander-in-Chief, General Alejandro Lanusse, which supported a more conciliatory policy in the hope of curbing unrest. The *cordobazo,* as the rebellion in Córdoba became known, remains the central event in contemporary Argentine history. It underlay the fundamental realignment of political forces which culminated in the restoration of Peronism in 1973.

Yet this and other less significant movements like it remain events which are very difficult to explain. They were closely related to the

[54] The best analysis of the economic dimensions of the Krieger Vasena plan is Oscar Braun, *El desarrollo de la capital monopolista en la Argentina,* Buenos Aires, 1970.

general disruptive processes set in motion by the Onganía government. But it is difficult to express the precise pattern of causation.
Most of the riots were middle-class movements; only in Córdoba did
sectors of the working class take a leading part in the action. The
government blamed Castroite agitators for what had occurred,
though this can be dismissed as it stands at complete variance with
the evidence. The most commonly held view on the Left, which
accords much more closely with the real pattern of events, was that the
cordobazo marked a spontaneous alliance of students and workers
against the Krieger Vasena plan and its 'general impoverishment of
groups outside the oligarchic bourgeoisie; the medium and small
bourgeoisie, the middle sectors, sections of the working class displaced
by the growth of monopoly capital'.[55]

Regional aspects have also been seen as important. The location of
unrest in the cities of the interior had been viewed as a reaction to
the centralisation of economic control in Buenos Aires and its
increasing appropriation of regional wealth and resources.[56] In this
respect it was significant that there was no major riot like the
cordobazo in Buenos Aires.

These hypotheses are a fair, if very preliminary, assessment of the
situation so far as the middle-class groups go. The revolts in the
universities were closely associated with pressures deriving from or
complementing the central orientation of the Krieger Vasena plan.
Since 1966 there had been an effort to 'functionalise' the universities
by emphasising technical and managerial training, and by restricting
their intake in accordance with estimates of demand for different
professional qualifications. The revolts of 1969 were triggered by
dramatic changes in the food prices charged in university refectories

[55] Quoted in Horacio González Trejo, *Argentina, tiempo de violencia*, Buenos
Aires, 1969, p. 72.

[56] Cf. Francisco J. Delich, 'Córdoba: la movilización permanente', *Los Libros*,
No. 21, August, 1971. Considering that the *cordobazo* came as such a
surprise, it is worth quoting the remarks of *Primera Plana's* correspondent on
25 March 1969: 'The increase in taxes, the closing of some factories,
redundancies in some of the province's industries, added to the failure of the
harvest, are conditions capable of creating a difficult situation in Córdoba
towards the middle of the year. Who can be sure that the liberal policies will
not sprout a popular insurrection?' The C.G.E.'s reaction to the *cordobazo*
was also significant. Having paid lip-service to the government's thesis that
'agitators' were responsible, it declared: 'It must be taken into account that
beyond the question of violence there is a state of disconformity among the
social sectors, workers, students and even businessmen, which is more
accentuated in the interior, and is motivated by a climate of insecurity and
disharmony. This results in the first instance from an economic policy which
has cut purchasing power: an effect fundamentally felt by the middle and
lower income sectors' (*Clarín*, 6 June 1969).

as part of a compaign to rationalise costs.[57] Reactions like this clearly relate to frustrated mobility aspirations among students, and were culturally based responses to sudden, violent changes in disposable incomes.[58] This illustrated the chronic political problems produced by twenty years of economic stagnation, combined with the government's praetorian zeal for efficiency.

Similar pressures were apparent among the Córdoba car workers. Throughout the 1960s the car industry had been subject to wide oscillations in output, and this made for great insecurity among the work-forces. The flashpoint for the strike in 1969 was the sudden waiving of traditional privileges concerning Saturday afternoon working.[59] But again this can be a preliminary basis for any general explanation. Any simple Marxist argument along the lines of progressive pauperisation cannot be applied literally in this context. As Krieger Vasena remarked soon after his resignation in June, 1969, the Córdoba car-workers were among the best-paid in the country. It was not that the car-workers were becoming any poorer in the literal sense. The source of their reaction is more explicable in terms of fluctuations in output and intensivity of labour.

Further facilitating the links which developed in Córdoba between the students and the car-workers was that many of the students were themselves shift-workers in the car plants. A second point relates to the divisions in the national C.G.T. between Vandor, Alonso and Ongaro. In Córdoba this had produced a chaotic situation among the groups in different plants claiming to represent the work-force. When the spark came, the different factions proved unable to exercise any form of effective leadership, and were simply carried along by

[57] González Trejo, *op. cit.*, p. 19.

[58] 'In a dependent society like ours . . . the students are economically oppressed. The system puts limits on the social mobility en masse of professional groups . . . The student enters the university with expectations of social ascent and with the hope of putting his knowledge at the disposal of the community. These hopes are brutally shattered in the course of his apprenticeship' (*ibid.*, p. 69). Many students in the universities of the interior were said to have working-class backgrounds. Restrictions in intake meant that they had little chance of professional careers. In Buenos Aires, where student rioting was much less marked during this period, most students were from middle-class families. Also, unlike many students elsewhere, they were resident with their families and less affected by university policies on food prices etc. The other factor most frequently mentioned is that in Córdoba and elsewhere the students lived in separate quarters of the city, and this facilitated united action among them. The Barrio Clínicas in Córdoba is the best known example. During the *cordobazo* this was one of the main centres of the riots and the main source of resistance to the army.

[59] *Primera Plana*, 20 May 1969. The working week was suddenly increased from 44 to 48 hours.

events.[60] These conditions of institutional fragmentation, which again relate to government policy and behaviour since 1966, seem to have played some part in the central pattern of events.

Although the *cordobazo,* and the other lesser movements, were largely spontaneous and leaderless, it was not long before attempts were being it to fashion their energies into a new popular opposition front against the government controlled by New Left groups. None of these was ever successful. At first it seemed that Ongaro's group would gain the upper hand. Within a short time a rough alliance had emerged between him and the most active of the Córdoba union leaders, Agustín Tosco of the Light and Power workers.[61] In 1970 a new radical union, Sitrac-Sitram, emerged among the Córdoba car-workers. It too began to call for the formation of a 'Popular Liberation Front'.[62]

1969 thus saw the emergence of the threatened new popular force. If it lacked a unified leadership and a coherent shared ideology, it had some of the vertical, cross-class features of the populist alliances of the past. Workers, students, and in some cases businessmen, had united in a violent protest against the government. In doing so they isolated the neo-liberal groups which had supported the Onganía government and the Krieger Vasena plan. Onganía's destruction and repression of traditional political institutions in 1966, and the weakening of the unions in 1967, underlay the violence of the reaction in 1969 and its tendency to spawn new organised groups like the radical Sitrac-Sitram.

This new movement was not Peronist. Neither Perón nor Vandor, who was murdered in mysterious circumstances a few weeks after the *cordobazo,* had played any significant part in its conception or execution. If the new movement sought inspiration in anyone, it was in the mythical figure of Ernesto Guevara. For the first time in twenty years the division between Peronist and anti-Peronists had been superseded. Instead of dividing society along class lines, the policies of the Onganía government had finally come to unite them.

In 1970 the dangers to the military government posed by the new alliance were increased with a sudden profusion of Marxist and Peronist guerrilla groups. This was a novel phenomenon, and it

---

[60] 'The alliance [between students and workers] emerged in the streets in a spontaneous fashion among the workers. I believe that neither the C.G.T. nor ourselves [the students] foresaw such large support . . .' (quoted in González Trejo, *op. cit.,* p. 48).

[61] Ongaro was a Catholic militant with connections with the Third-World Priests movement. Tosco's links were with the Marxist Left.

[62] For an important study of Sitrac-Sitram and its programme see Osvaldo Raíz, 'Los nuevos sindicatos', in *Los Libros,* August, 1971.

illustrated the point to which opposition to the military government had escalated. From the end of 1969 onwards the guerrilla groups made a series of spectacular raids on police stations, army outposts and banks. There was also a spate of kidnappings. The most important was the abduction and execution of former president Aramburu by the Peronist Montoneros group. This event was the signal for an army coup led by General Lanusse against Onganía in June, 1970, and his replacement by a former military attaché in Washington, General Roberto M. Levingston.[63]

The presence of the new popular opposition movement against the military government thus raised the vital question of who was finally to control it — the new moderates, Ongaro, Perón and the C.G.T., or Sitrac-Sitram, Tosco, or the guerrillas. Fear that it might finally be the latter evoked a ruthless reaction from the army. An 'anti-subversion' force and special courts were set up, and the torture and gross ill-treatment of suspects became widespread. These measures met with scant success. The activities of the guerrillas progressively increased, and their campaign to win popular support intensified.[64] It was apparent that if the army stayed in power it could expect little more than mounting popular and guerrilla opposition and the eventual possibility of an escalation of revolt to the point of a major popular rebellion in Buenos Aires. Such an event, by threatening to divide the army over how to deal with it, raised seriously the spectre of open civil war.

In 1970 and 1971 the economy again plunged into recession, and as in the past this gave a further impulse to unrest. There was a marked slowing of industrial production, coupled with a heavy deficit on the balance of payments. Soon after the abandonment of the Krieger Vasena plan inflation had again swiftly developed. Unemployment also increased, and by the middle of 1971 had reached the same level as in 1967 during the first phase of the Krieger Vasena plan.[65]

On the political front the most significant events occurred in March, 1971. Following the resignation of a popular provincial governor, Bernardo Bas, there was another major uprising in Córdoba

---

[63] It was suspected that the Onganía government was itself responsible for Aramburu's abduction and death, as the former president was involved in plots against the government and seemed Onganía's most likely successor.

[64] For accounts of the growth of the guerrilla groups see *Primera Plana*, 20 July 1971; James Petras, 'Building a popular army in Argentina', *New Left Review*, January-February, 1972; *La Nación* (International Edition), 11 June 1973.

[65] Oscar Braun and Ricardo Kesselman, 'Argentina 1971. Estancamiento estructural y crisis de coyuntura', mimeo. Buenos Aires, 1971.

again involving students, middle class groups and car-workers.[66] The difference between this and the movement of 1969 was that in 1971 there was much greater control and coordination over it, led in particular by groups like Sitrac-Sitram. It was also widely reported that sections of the leading Marxist guerrilla group, the E.R.P., were closely involved. The feared links between Marxist guerrillas and popular uprisings appeared to be in an advanced form of gestation. Although this may have been exaggerated, it proved to be the spur to a radical change of policy by the army. Within a week of the movement in Córdoba Levingston's short rule was brought to an end, and Lanusse himself personally took control. The principal aim of his government, constantly reiterated by himself and other members of the administration, was to drive a wedge between 'subversion' and the popular uprisings, to eliminate the former and to control the latter.[67]

Lanusse immediately announced presidential elections for March 1973 and called upon the traditional political parties to join with the government in a Great National Agreement to save the country from revolutionary anarchy. By restoring the privileges and full legal status of the parties, the Agreement marked the final abandonment of the practices followed by Onganía's 'Argentine Revolution' in 1966. The about-turn on the economic front which had begun with the downfall of Krieger Vasena in 1969 was now followed in 1971 by a change of equal scope at the political level. These efforts at conciliation did not include the New Left groups. Ongaro, Tosco and others were imprisoned. Militant unions like Sitrac-Sitram were dissolved by government decree. Under government promptings the official C.G.T. reacquired the privileges and bargaining power it had lost in 1967. Meanwhile the war against the guerrillas continued without quarter. In August, 1972, a number of imprisoned guerrillas,

---

[66] The new governor of Córdoba after Bas referred to the city as a 'nest of vipers'. The second uprising in Córdoba thus acquired the name of the *viborazo*.

[67] This is conveyed in the following remarks of General Tomás de Bustamente: 'The anti-Communist laws have not proved very efficient in practice. The ideological enemy has continued active ... and the development of its procedures with their paramilitary characteristics suggests clearly the need for a new tactic to combat it. This ought to be developed on the ideological plane, with social, economic and political measures with an emphasis on welfare' (*Primera Plana*, 15 June 1971). Most of the activities of this type carried out by the Lanusse government were entrusted to the Minister of Social Security, Francisco Manrique. Between 1970 and 1973 Manrique obtained a substantial popular following especially in some of the interior provinces. For a time in 1972 it seemed that Lanusse's plan was for Manrique to succeed him on the basis of a conservative populist programme.

who had been recaptured after an escape attempt, were summarily shot in the naval garrison of Trelew. These were the central guidelines of government policy — the revival of the traditional political bodies to fill the institutional vacuum left by Onganía, accompanied by a root and branch campaign against the New Left groups.

However, Lanusse's boldest stroke, achieved in the face of bitter opposition among certain groups in the army, was to include the Peronists in his project of reviving the traditional structures and using them as a buffer between the government and the forces of popular unrest. In a further energetic attempt to shift popular attention away from the Left, the government began a campaign to persuade the Peronists to join the Great National Agreement, and then to speculate publicly on the possibility of Perón's return from exile. It was evident that if the old grudges against Perón were far from dead, the government felt that the situation was sufficiently desperate to justify a major change of attitude. In this way the sixteen-year ostracism of Perón suddenly ended.

The government's gestures towards Perón did achieve their primary objective of focussing expectations on him and away from the Left. Support for Ongaro and Tosco quickly drained away, and Peronism quickly evolved once more into a major mass movement. By 1972 it had changed substantially for the second time in form and structure. In the 1940s it had subsisted as a coalition between segments of the army, the import-substituting entrepreneurs and the industrial working class.

In the mid-1950s under Aramburu it had become much more a working-class party. After 1971 it regained much of its middle-class support from the smaller entrepreneurs grouped in the C.G.E. and other associations. However, the major effect of Lanusse's policy was to win for it massive support among the groups which had been at the forefront of the revolts of 1969, the students and other lower-middle-class groups. After 1971 the latter evolved into a new left wing of the Peronist party, the Peronist Youth (*Juventud Peronista*). From henceforth the battle for popular support, which before had been fought by the students and the radical unions, now became transposed into an internal struggle within the Peronist party, between the *Juventud Peronista* (J.P.), some of the old middle-class remnants of Peronism from the past, and the C.G.T. bureaucracy. The paradox of this situation was that the C.G.T. adopted a moderate line, and the J.P., which was essentially middle-class, attempted to commit the party to a socialist position, or at least to a neo-populist position with a strong emphasis on nationalism and anti-imperialism.

Lanusse's strategy was thus only half successful over the short-term. He did manage to halt the growth of the independent Left and prevent a repetition of the second Córdoba uprising of March, 1971. But it was also apparent that the Left had merely changed its own tactics. Instead of struggling to supersede Peronism, it had switched its operations to within the movement in the hope of eventually taking it over.

At the same time in 1972 negotiations between Perón and Lanusse continued. Once Perón found himself the beneficiary of massive popular support, he was able to press for further concessions on the threat of refusing his participation in the 1973 elections. Lanusse's plan of restricting the Peronists to a secondary role through the Great National Agreement gradually foundered against Perón's creation of a separate alliance of parties, the Justicialist Liberation Front (*Frejuli*). On the other hand in 1972 Perón finally acceded to the government's prohibition of his own presidential candidature, and instead nominated one of his more pliant protegés, Dr Héctor J. Cámpora. In the elections of March, 1973, Cámpora won a clear majority, and in May he formally succeeded Lanusse.

By committing his party to these elections, and by accepting implicitly Lanusse's stipulations that the new government would have a transitional role under the Army's supervision, Perón vindicated the anti-Peronist Left's thesis that rather than wanting 'revolution' he was ultimately committed to preventing it.[68] In spite of the vivid contrasts at the ideological level between *peronista* nationalism and the neo-liberalism of the military governments, the changes implied by the restoration of Peronism were in method rather than in objective. They aimed to regenerate Argentina's capitalist structure by promoting political consensus, rather than by Onganía's technique of forcing it through by military dictatorship. This was illustrated on one level by the fate of the Cámpora government in 1973. Instead of pacifying the situation, Cámpora's radical programme and his gestures of support towards the Peronist

[68] The E.R.P. issued the following statement in 1971: 'The figure of Perón constitutes at present the last means of escape for the Argentine bourgeoisie, and in this sense it is counter-revolutionary' (*Primera Plana*, 6 July 1971). It is difficult to disagree with the Left's basic contention that Peronism was courted by the Lanusse government ultimately as a means to prop up the conservative order. This was also warned against by the more radical segments among the Peronists themselves: 'If Peronism accepts the political game imposed from outside and tailored according to the needs of the dominant neo-bourgoisie it will weaken forever its capacity to become the principal instrument of the National Revolution' (Gazzera and Ceresole, *op. cit.*, p. 313).

Youth merely served to accentuate the political crisis. Whether it emerged out of personal conviction, or whether it was forced by threat of military intervention against the government, Perón's opposition to this radical position became evident when he withdrew his support from Cámpora, and forced him into resignation only a few weeks after he had taken office.

In this fashion the wheel came full circle. The traditional opponents of Perón finally came to recognise in 1973 that only he had the political strength to bar the way forward to the leftist groups both within and outside the Peronist movement. Thus they came to support his candidature for the presidency. Perón, by finally accepting this, made himself a party to these objectives. After he successfully won the second presidential election held in 1973, and formally took office in October, the influence of the Peronist Youth began to decline markedly. At the same time the campaign against the Marxist guerrilla groups was revived with renewed intensity.

Perón's restoration was thus in many ways the obverse of the radical change it seemed to be at first sight. If it marked a revolution in institutional procedures, and the advent of a new reformist orientation on questions of social policy and relations with foreign capital, essentially it adhered to the same objectives as all the governments since 1955 — rapid growth and the creation of a modern capitalist economy. Perón's great advantage over his predecessors was his massive popular support. Yet there could be no final guarantee that this would persist indefinitely. There were still some potential dangers from the Left. In 1973 Perón had the advantage of having attained power once more during a period of economic expansion. This allowed for a new edition of the old pact between the C.G.T. and employers. The alliance was further assisted by the heavy overseas demand for Argentina's traditional beef exports, and the sudden increase in world commodity prices in general during 1973. If this brought an unaccustomed level of prosperity to Argentina's economy, again there was no final proof that the stop-go cycles of the past had been finally overcome. The economic programme of Perón's government, despite its ambitious housing provisions, was largely a repetition of past policies to curb inflation, to seek to promote agricultural exports by restrictions on domestic consumption, and to subsidise an increase in industrial exports. Its nationalist orientations revealed themselves as little more than an attempt to replace American by European or Japanese capital, or to seek aid from the socialist bloc.

Any renewed depression in Argentina would immediately revive the critical issue of incomes policy, and impose a new burden on the alliance between workers and employers created in 1969. In 1973

Perón took power under the close supervision of the army. He was compelled to operate without the complex instruments of political control he had used twenty years previously. Without these the task of maintaining popular support in depression conditions would be much more difficult. Thus by the time of Péron's death in 1974 there were few convincing signs that Argentina's political crisis had been overcome. If the old conflict between Peronism and anti-Peronism had finally ended, there was no firm evidence that the new populist coalition would be any more capable than its predecessors of shielding itself from the divisive effects of unfavourable economic forces, or freeing itself from the latent threat from the Left.

Perón's choice of his wife, Isabel, to serve as his running-mate in 1973 was a reflection of the accentuated divisions among different Peronist factions. It was conceivable that on his death she could continue on the same general lines as he. But Perón's main asset, his tremendous personal popularity, would be missing. Already by mid-1974 there were signs of acute economic problems in the offing. The balance of payments was threatened by European restrictions on beef imports from Argentina, and this lack of access to markets was compounded by increasing shortages in supply. On the domestic front the government's attempts at price control, added to measures favouring the trade unions in the distribution of income, appeared to have engendered shortages and a thriving black market. However, at this stage such problems had not found any full reflection at the political level. At the time of Peron's death there was no immediate alternative to an attempt to continue the incumbent administration. As a result there was a peaceable transfer of power to Isabel Perón. Nevertheless this did not bring any final guarantee of the durability of the new system. There was still extreme factional rivalry, and either fresh elections or a pre-emptive military coup were still strong possibilities.

Conclusion

This account of Argentina's political development since the 1940s has stressed the importance of general economic trends as a conditioning variable over the type of political structures adopted during different periods. The rapid growth period of the mid-1940s permitted the development of a populist structure in the form of a class alliance between import-substituting entrepreneurs and the urban working class. Economic stagnation, and the peculiarities of the economic cycle, eroded this system by dividing the classes on the question of income distribution and restoring a horizontal structure of politics. This undermined Peronism in the early 1950s and underlay the great instability of all the governments which followed. The final stage beginning in 1969 was brought about by the dissolvent effects on the established structure of the growth of a concentrated foreign-controlled new industrial sector. Eventually, after a shift of attitude in the army, this led to the restoration of a new vertical alliance dominated by the Peronists.

In many respects the train of events from the fall of Levingston onwards recalled events between 1912 and 1916. There were hopes that a system of representative democracy could, by promoting consensus, eliminate political tensions, and thus help to establish the preconditions for further economic growth. The success of this system would depend again on economic performance and on its ability to maintain a class alliance and the isolation of its radical opponents. The long-term possibilities for this would seem to have been not significantly greater in 1974 than in the past twenty-five years. The main hope would be that Perón and his successor would be much more successful than their predecessors in persuading the unions and the working class to forego improvements in their standards of living in return for the benefits of integration into the power structure of the State.

Index